LIGHT FOR OUR PATH
2009
Bible readings with short notes

Light for our path 2009

IBRA
International Bible Reading Association

Light for our Path aims to build understanding and respect for different Christian perspectives through the provision of a range of biblical interpretations. Views expressed by contributors should not, therefore, be taken to reflect the views or policies of the Editor or the International Bible Reading Association.

Cover photograph by Sarah Bruce
Editor – Kate Hughes

Published by:
The International Bible Reading Association
1020 Bristol Road
Selly Oak
Birmingham B29 6LB
United Kingdom

Charity number 211542

ISBN 978-1-905893-01-0
ISSN 0140-8267

Designed and typeset by Christian Education
Printed and bound in Slovenia by 1010 Printing

Contents

Foreword

Dear Friends

Welcome to this year's *Light for our Path*. Our new format has settled in; although some people have problems with the book's increased size and weight, most of our readers seem to appreciate the simpler format and clearer text. And we have more photos of our writers this year, so that you can connect the face of a real person with their contribution.

When I tell people in England that I lived in Africa for 14 years, some of them react as if I must be an intrepid traveller, constantly exploring remote places. I do point out that Johannesburg is not in the least remote, and even Lesotho and KwaZulu are hardly the Amazon jungle! Since I returned to England, I have hardly travelled abroad at all; I enjoy exploring the many places in my own country that I have never seen. This is a pity, really, because having now edited *Light for our Path* for several years, I feel that I have friends all over the world, as I exchange emails with our writers and edit their contributions. If I wanted to travel, I would have plenty of people to visit! Some of them have been writing for us for many years, others each year are new, but all have a unique contribution to make to this book, writing out of their own country and culture, their own church, their own life experience and, above all, their own experience of God. *Light for our Path* gives us the rich experience of worldwide travel without having to leave our own homes, the chance to meet and share with our fellow Christians. What they have in common is God: his presence, his love, his help, his expectations, and the joy we have in belonging to him and to his family. I hope you will enjoy and be strengthened by your travels through *Light for our Path* this year.

Kate

Kate Hughes (Editor)

Reading *Light for our Path*

- Before reading, be quiet and remember that God is with you. Ask for his Holy Spirit to guide your reading.
- If you do not have a Bible with you, you can work solely from *Light for our Path* by referring to the short Bible passage printed in bold type. (Only the editions printed in English have this.)
- You can begin by reading just the short extract from the daily Bible passage that appears in the notes. Or you may prefer to read the full text of the daily passage from your Bible. The weekly notes use a variety of Bible translations, which are named at the beginning of each week. You may like to see how the extract in bold type compares with the same passage in your own Bible. And if your Bible mentions parallel passages in other places, comparing these passages can widen your thinking.
- At the beginning of each week's notes there is a text for the week, which can be used as a focus for worship or reflection throughout the week.
- When you finish each day's reading, spend a little time reflecting on it. What does it say to you about God? About yourself? About others? About the world in which we live? Has it changed your thinking? Does it suggest something that you should do? Then use the final prayer (marked with a cross), or any prayer of your own you need to make.
- At the start of each week's notes, there are questions and suggestions for group discussion or personal thought. These are only suggestions – your own reading and prayer may have drawn your attention to other aspects which you would like to explore further. The important thing is that you should let God speak to you through his Word, so that as you read steadily through the year you will be able to look back and see that you have got to know him better and have grown spiritually.
- As there is only one reading provided for the weekend, you may like to spend a little time on Sunday looking at the Introduction page for the coming week, reflecting on the theme and the text for the week.

Abbreviations and acknowledgements

We are grateful for permission to quote from the following Bible versions:

GNB Scriptures quoted are from the *Good News Bible* ©1994 published by the Bible Societies/HarperCollins Publishers Ltd, *UK Good News Bible* ©American Bible Society 1966, 1971, 1976, 1992. Used with permission.

JB From *The Jerusalem Bible*, Popular Edition, published by Darton, Longman & Todd, ©Darton, Longman & Todd Ltd and Doubleday & Company, Inc., 1974.

NEB *New English Bible*, ©Oxford and Cambridge University Presses, 1970.

NIV Scripture taken from the *Holy Bible, New International Version*®. Copyright ©1973, 1978, 1984 International Bible Society. Used by permission of Zondervan. All rights reserved.

NLT Scripture quotations marked NLT are taken from the *Holy Bible, New Living Translation*, copyright 1996. Used by permission of Tyndale House Publishers, Inc., Wheaton, Illinois 60189. All rights reserved.

NJB *The New Jerusalem Bible*, published by Darton, Longman & Todd, ©Darton, Longman & Todd Ltd and Doubleday & Company, Inc., 1985.

NKJV Scripture taken from the *New King James Version*. Copyright ©1982 by Thomas Nelson, Inc. Used by permission. All rights reserved.

NRSV Bible selections are from the *New Revised Standard Version of the Bible*, copyright 1989 by the Division of Christian Education of the National Council of the Churches of Christ in the USA. Used by permission. All rights reserved.

REB *Revised English Bible*, ©Oxford and Cambridge University Presses, 1989.

RSV *The Holy Bible, Revised Standard Version*, published by Thomas Nelson & Sons, ©Division of Christian Education of the National Council of the Churches of Christ in the United States of America, 1952.

The Message: scripture taken from Eugene H Peterson, *The Message*. Copyright © 1993, 1994, 1995, 1996, 2000, 2001, 20002. Used by permission of the Nav Press Publishing Group.

* An asterisk beside the daily reading indicates that it appears in the Revised Common Lectionary during that week.

Who is Jesus?

1 Epiphanies of Jesus

Notes by John Birch
based on the New International Version

John Birch is a Methodist lay preacher and worship leader based in South Wales, who has written a book of Celtic-inspired prayers entitled *heart2heart* and hosts a website: www.faithandworship.com.

Introduction

Who is Jesus? Why did he come? Questions that have kept theologians busy for centuries, and yet even for ordinary Christians like us they have to be tackled – if we are unclear in our own hearts, then how can we answer those who ask us to share our faith? When we take our first steps as Christians we begin a journey of discovery that never really ends, as we learn more about, and draw closer to Jesus.

Text for the week: Luke 2:15

'Let us go to Bethlehem and see this thing that has happened.'

For group discussion and personal thought

- In your journey of discovery, do you travel alone or have you companions? What are the advantages of travelling as a group?
- When you look at Jesus, whom do you see?

Luke 2:8-18

A journey of discovery

Our whole life is in a very real sense a journey of discovery: experiencing and learning about the world we live in and our place within it; growing in knowledge and hopefully maturing in wisdom through the years. There is a spiritual parallel as well, as our Christian journey with God leads us to an increasing understanding of the wonderful outpouring of love that brought Jesus into the world.

> **'Let's go to Bethlehem and see this thing that has happened, which the Lord has told us about.'**
>
> *(part of verse 15)*

We start our journey as children, and grow in our faith into spiritual adulthood – and God is gentle in the way that he leads and teaches us. Sometimes, in quiet moments like the shepherds sitting in a field under the starry night sky, God reveals himself to us. This revelation may not involve angels and stars, or a journey to Bethlehem, but simply God drawing close to us, taking us by the hand and saying in that wonderful whisper that is impossible to resist, 'Come child, walk with me … I've so much that I want to share with you!'

> **'Do not be afraid, I bring you good news of great joy.'**
>
> *(part of verse 10)*

† *God of the journey, take my hand and lead me to greater knowledge of the love that came to earth as a baby called Jesus.*

Hebrews 1:1-14

Removing the veil

But in these last days [God] has spoken to us by his Son, whom he appointed heir of all things, and through whom he made the universe.

(verse 2)

Throughout the pages of the Old Testament we read about the Prophets revealing the Word of God to an often critical and unfaithful people. It's the story of the failure of a nation to realise how great a blessing had been bestowed upon them. When times were good the people followed their God and were greatly blessed; but when times got hard they turned their backs on him and worshipped idols.

In the New Testament, says the writer to the Hebrews, God has revealed himself through and in his son Jesus. 'Revelation' in the Greek means removing a veil, in order that the face of God might be known – and in Jesus we find the perfect revelation of God because in him we see the image of his heavenly Father. The people of the Old Testament were afraid to look at the face of God in case they were struck down dead, but Jesus invites us to look at him, see God and have life in all its fullness!

The Son is the radiance of God's glory and the exact representation of his being . . .

(part of verse 3)

† *Open our eyes, Lord. Remove the veil that prevents us from knowing you through the life, death and resurrection of your Son, Jesus*

Colossians 1:13-23

The image revealed

> **[Jesus] is the image of the invisible God, the firstborn over all creation. For by him all things were created: things in heaven and on earth, visible and invisible . . .**
>
> *(verse 15, and part of verse 16)*

In his book *Reaching for the Invisible God* the author Philip Yancey is not afraid to tackle head-on the question 'How can I have a personal relationship with a being when I'm never quite sure he's there?' This is probably a question that many Christians have posed inwardly at times of doubt. We're not all spiritual superstars and it's perfectly acceptable to say 'I don't know!' or be honest enough with ourselves and God to admit that there are areas of our faith that we're unsure about.

The apostle Paul's message to the Colossian church was simple. 'If you're struggling to comprehend an invisible God, then look at Jesus because they are one and the same. God emptied himself into the human form of Jesus in order that humankind might be drawn back into a relationship with its creator.'

> **For God was pleased to have all his fullness dwell in him, and through him to reconcile to himself all things . . .**
>
> *(verse 19, and part of verse 20)*

If you struggle to imagine a relationship with the creator of all things, then picture Jesus holding out his hand for you. As Charles Wesley so eloquently put it in one of his hymns, 'Our God contracted to a span, incomprehensibly made man.'

† *In our journey of faith, help us to see you through the life and love of Jesus.*

Matthew 1:18-25

God with us

> **'Joseph son of David, do not be afraid to take Mary home as your wife . . . She will give birth to a son, and you are to give him the name Jesus, because he will save his people from their sins.'**
>
> *(verse 5, and part of verse 7)*

That the Creator of the universe should choose to enter our world at a particular time and place is beyond our understanding. That he should do this out of love and in order to bring humankind back into his family, welcoming home the prodigals and forgiving them for their rejection of him, only adds to the wonder of the birth of Jesus.

> **'[T]hey will call him Immanuel' – which means, 'God with us'.**
>
> *(part of verse 23)*

For Mary and Joseph, their closeness to God was truly intimate. 'God with us' was the baby in their arms, flesh and blood that they could feel and cuddle! For us, two thousand years later, it's not so easy. We have to rely on their experience and the evidence we have in the Bible concerning the life of Jesus. If God seems too vast and awesome for you to feel a closeness with him, then think about that baby who would grow up into the adult Jesus, walk this earth among us and literally love us to death – and beyond! 'God with us' means accepting that baby into our lives, whose name means 'The Lord saves'.

† *Help us to know real closeness and intimacy in our relationship with Jesus.*

Epiphany

Matthew 2:1-12*

For richer and poorer

> **[Jesus] is the image of the invisible God, the firstborn over all creation. For by him all things were created: things in heaven and on earth, visible and invisible . . .**
>
> *(part of verses 1 and 2)*

Introduced in the fourth century, today is celebrated in the Western Church as Epiphany, a word which means 'to reveal' or 'make known'. We remember the coming of the wise men bringing gifts to visit the Christ child, and in so doing they 'revealed' Jesus to the whole world as Lord and King of all people and all nations.

All Christians walk a journey of faith. Often it starts with a similar question to that posed by the Magi, 'How do I find Jesus?' and if the questioner is to find what they're looking for, then they need an honest and open answer to their query. The journey might be long and hard, as it was with the Magi, but the joy at reaching the destination makes the journeying worthwhile.

> **Then they opened their treasures and presented him with gifts of gold and of incense and of myrrh.**
>
> *(part of verse 11)*

When we come into the presence of God, what do we bring with us? He doesn't actually need gold as an offering, though I'm sure the gift was accepted in the spirit it was given. God would much prefer that we give our lives as an offering. He would like us to be his love in the world. That's a response more valuable even than gold!

† Father, I thank you for revealing yourself in the person of Jesus Christ.

Philippians 2:5-11

The Servant King

And being found in appearance as a man,
he humbled himself
and became obedient to death – even death on a cross!

(verse 8)

In a small chapel in Maaloula, Syria, I saw a remarkable icon depicting the Last Supper. We are used to seeing Jesus in the centre, with disciples either side, but in this picture Jesus is at the left hand side, at the head of the table, a position from which it is much easier to serve his disciples at this special meal. There seems to be something wrong with the concept of God as servant: the Creator of the universe washing his disciples' feet, being the obedient carpenter's apprentice who later allowed himself to be nailed upon a piece of crudely cut wood. But that was the life that Jesus chose, and it's the one that he told his followers to copy if they wanted to be his disciples.

[A]nd every tongue confess
that Jesus Christ is Lord,
to the glory of God the Father.

(verse 11)

God is the God of the unexpected, and it was only by becoming one of us that Jesus could take our place on that cross – our sins crucified in his body that we might know forgiveness and life in all its fullness, be reconciled to God and acknowledge him as Lord and Saviour.

† *Father, I offer my life as servant to you and my neighbour, whoever that may be.*

John 5:19-29

Life giver

Even for Christians it can sometimes be a struggle to connect the person of Jesus who walked this earth with the Creator of the universe, and yet we have to make that connection in order to understand the God whom we serve: the God who saves, the God who gives life in all its fullness.

> **'I tell you the truth, whoever hears my word and believes him who sent me has eternal life . . . I tell you the truth, a time is coming and has now come when the dead will hear the voice of the Son of God and those who hear will live.'**
>
> *(part of verse 24, and verse 25)*

For many, life can be summed up by the words 'If only . . . ' and missed opportunities, which is sad because none of us can go back in time and undo mistakes or bad decisions, take a different path, try a different door. All we have is today and tomorrow. Jesus came to bring life, both for the present and for eternity. Through faith, he allows us to look forward, not back, and with joy and certainty, because of that wonderful promise that he gives for 'whoever hears and believes'.

† Life-giving God, enlarge our vision and increase our faith.

1 Corinthians 15:20-28

Death defying

Our journey of faith is an adventure which does not stop when we leave this life – the hope of Christianity is eternal life, and the death and resurrection of Jesus is God's proof, if it were needed, that he is Lord of All, of life and death.

> **But Christ has indeed been raised from the dead, the first fruits of those who have fallen asleep. For since death came through a man, the resurrection of the dead comes also through a man. For as in Adam all die, so in Christ all will be made alive.**
>
> *(verses 20-22)*

The 'first fruits' refer to the first sheaves of the harvest given to the Lord as a token that all the harvest belongs to him. There's comfort and hope in the field of corn ripening in the summer sun until ready for the harvest gathering – a picture of Jesus, whose resurrection draws all God's people together in this world and the next.

Fear of death is a burden that afflicts so many in this world. Hope of eternal life is the promise open to all people who believe and trust in Jesus Christ.

† *Risen Christ, the destination of our journeying, be our hope for this world and the next.*

Luke 9:18-22

Who do you say I am?

> **Once when Jesus was praying in private and his disciples were with him, he asked them, 'Who do the crowds say I am?'**
>
> *(part of verse 2)*

Now, there's a question! What would be the first thought that came out from your mouth? 'Jesus, you're someone special.' 'A prophet sent by God.' 'Miracle worker.' 'Healer.' 'Teacher.' And of course Jesus was all these but so much more. It is important that we are sure in our own minds on such an important question, because someone may ask us 'How do I find Jesus?' The honesty and certainty of our reply could be the catalyst that brings another soul into the kingdom of God, and what could be more of an honour than that? To be the hand that guides another into the presence of Jesus.

> **'But what about you?' [Jesus] asked. 'Who do you say I am?'**
> **Peter answered, 'The Christ of God.'**
>
> *(verse 20)*

This was one of Peter's more confident moments. For once he was sure, no dithering or uncertainty, he'd thought this one through and now he knew he was in the presence of Christ, the Anointed One, Messiah. That's where we need to be – sure of whom it is we follow, who he is and what he has done for us!

† *Jesus, Teacher, Healer, Creator, King and Servant: you are beyond our understanding and yet we worship you as our Saviour.*

Who is Jesus?

2 A window to God

Notes by Su Blanch
based on the New Revised Standard Version

Su Blanch is a single mum with two young daughters: as well as looking after her family, she works as a business consultant and is active in planning and implementing Outreach projects for her church in Hertfordshire, UK.

Introduction

Who is Jesus? The Bible provides us with a very rich and multi-faceted answer. We are not told the peripheral and trivial, for example, what Jesus looks like, as this would not answer the vital question. Instead, we have a body of meditations and stories to draw on. Our understanding of Jesus increases in part by our personal, developing relationship with him over time, in part by an increasing comprehension of the revelations of the Bible, and in part by the witness of Jesus-led actions in the communities around us.

Text for the week: John 6:51

'I am the living bread that came down from heaven. Whoever eats of this bread will live forever; and the bread that I give for the life of the world is my flesh.'

For group discussion and personal thought

- Why isn't the answer to 'Who is Jesus' more obvious?
- Could love exist without God?
- How does the symbol of Jesus as light help me in my understanding of him?
- What is the Transfiguration? How did Jesus appear to the disciples? What did he physically look like?

1 John 4:9-16

Jesus is love

This passage reverberates with love: God is love, God's actions are love, God requires our love – and the best evidence for this love is Jesus, the Son he sent to bring us life. There is great simplicity in this: God and love are synonymous. Reading the passage over and over is a joyful and rewarding experience: the word 'love' or its derivatives is mentioned twelve times! Yet as I close my Bible and cast my eye over the newspaper to see the terrors of the world, or try and make sense of the competing pressures of my daily life, God's love can seem very far away: a faint bell in the distance, rather than a tumultuous pealing joining heaven and earth.

How do we reconcile this? It is a useful exercise to start looking for God's love within the world. It may be easier to see evidence of the bad things, but look out instead for God's love. It may come in a quiet way: neighbours looking after each other; a supportive hand from a friend at a difficult moment; peace deals being brokered. These aren't big things: but the individuals have bothered to make a difference.

> **[S]ince God loved us so much, we also ought to love one another . . . if we love one another, God lives in us . . .**
>
> *(part of verses 11 and 12)*

God's love is ringing in us and around us: we get very easily distracted from our awareness of this. We need to open our ears and eyes to what is going on. In doing so, we will see more facets of love played out, and consequently our understanding and awareness of God will deepen.

† Lord, let me be open to feel and know your love.

1 John 5:1-12

Jesus is active love

Our love for God is not to be a passive love: his love for us is unquestionably active and sacrificial. Whereas yesterday we learnt about the constancy of God's love, this passage makes clear that it is also an active experience.

> **For the love of God is this, that we obey his commandments.**
>
> *(part of verse 3)*

God's love is inspirational, inspiring us to action. The passage goes on to say that his commandments are not 'burdensome' or, in another translation, 'not too hard for us'. I have to remind myself of this when I am doing my least favourite job for church, collecting gift envelopes door-to-door. I find it embarrassing to ask for money, I find people's negative responses frustrating, and I can think of many more pleasurable ways to spend an afternoon. I have to admit to making this job 'burdensome' by my reluctance to do it, but it is certainly not 'too hard' for me. However, this is an example of a task to be performed out of love: firstly, it develops and challenges me; secondly, it is an outreach opportunity: introducing local people to the work of the church and the possibility of giving money; and thirdly there is a clear benefit to the individuals who are in receipt of the money, whether here in the UK or overseas.

God's love is active, and demands an active response.

† *Lord, let me receive your love revealed in Jesus, and actively display it to the world around me.*

John 6:35-51

Jesus is the bread of life

'I am the bread of life. Whoever comes to me will never be hungry, and whoever believes in me will never be thirsty.'

(part of verse 35)

I was at the communion rail with my four-year-old daughter, when the enormity of the words 'the body of Christ' suddenly hit her. 'Don't eat that!' she shouted. The notion of drinking the blood of Christ was too much for her to bear and she left the communion rail in disgust.

The idea of Jesus being able to satisfy our appetites was a problem for the Jews too. A disturbing notion, certainly, defining Jesus in this way. In this passage the Jews were struggling to comprehend that Jesus was from God, as well as the concept of a living, human sacrifice that all believers could partake in. Nothing else is necessary in order to have eternal life – no requirement to appease gods with burning incense, the slaughter of sacred animals or the hierarchy of the priesthood.

There are many rich layers of symbolism in the concept of Jesus being the bread of life: we can understand how God and his people can become physically linked; God tends to our most basic requirements for life; God gave up his precious son to save us. For me, the link between taking the bread and the wine and Jesus' affirming words reminds me of the personal nature of my relationship with our loving God.

† *Lord, thank you for providing us with the sustaining bread of life.*

Matthew 17:1-13

Jesus is the Son of God

'This is my Son, the Beloved; with him I am well pleased; listen to him!'

(part of verse 5)

What an incredible spectacle Peter, James and John witnessed that day: firstly, Jesus' amazing Transfiguration; secondly, Moses and Elijah appearing before them; and finally, God directly addressing them from a cloud. Not only was this profound and remarkable in itself, but it was profoundly and remarkably symbolic. Nothing could have made it clearer to the disciples: Jesus is the Son of God and the accomplishment of God's plan.

How could the disciples recover from this? I can imagine them bursting with amazement, and fear, and joy, stumbling over themselves as they ran down the mountain in their desire to let everyone know what they had seen. How wonderful, to pass this news on to all the people they had talked with about Jesus: their like-minded families and their patronising friends and their cynical work-colleagues.

But Jesus said no: they were not to tell anyone until after he had been raised.

Jesus was resurrected and it is now our duty to take the passion and fear and excitement of those first disciples and to tell our families and friends and colleagues, as they had desperately wanted to. Jesus is the Son of God, promised by the prophets to come and set us free. Alleluia!

† *Lord, fill us with the joy of knowing that you have come to set us free.*

John 1:1-18

Jesus is Light

The light shines in the darkness, and the darkness did not overcome it.

(verse 5)

The descriptions of Jesus that we read in the Bible are wonderfully compelling as we learn more about what is expected of us. The image of light is particularly useful, I find, and has many layers to investigate. As you read this, Christmas will still be in our minds. I particularly enjoy my church's candlelit carol service: at the beginning of the service, as the congregation gather with their unlit candles, the church is in darkness. Helpers then take tapers to random parts of the church, and the light is passed along from person to person, pew to pew, until the whole church is dotted with candle lights. Each light represents one person, and each light adds to the wonder of the whole. This activity is not cloaked in ceremony: in fact it is quite matter-of-fact, with people chatting and laughing as they speak to their neighbours.

As we go about our regular daily business, whatever that may be, we have the opportunity to continue the advancement of Jesus' light. What a joy, to have the responsibility of passing on the light of Christ to our friends and neighbours. And as well as the implicit mystery and wonder, it is as practical and necessary as sharing candle lights to illuminate the church.

† *Lord, let me shine in the world, reflecting your love and glory to people around me.*

John 1:24-34

Jesus is the Lamb of God

'Here is the Lamb of God who takes away the sin of the world!'

(part of verse 29)

In Western culture, a lamb is a symbol of purity and peaceful innocence: lambs gambolling happily in the spring sunshine promise sunny days and better things ahead. The Lamb of God also stimulates us to consider hope and promise, but that hope and promise can only be achieved as a result of Jesus being sacrificed.

Lambs were, of course, used as sacrifices to the gods in many religions: something of real worth that would be a fitting offering. So right at the start of Jesus' ministry, in John's gospel, John the Baptist is already prophesying that Jesus will be sacrificed to atone for the sin of the world. Jesus is the sacrificial Lamb of God, whose blood must be spilt in order to free the world from sin.

How ready are we to sacrifice our chosen lives and paths for the good of the world around us? In some countries around the world, following Jesus is a path beset by danger and fear, and demands real faith and courage. But even in a privileged society, making the step to be outwardly different to the world around does demand sacrifice, it means turning away from tempting comforts and security. It's a tough and difficult journey ahead, but one with wonderful hope and promise along the way.

† *Lord, help me to sacrifice my selfish desires and focus instead on your greater goal.*

Widows, Orphans and Aliens

1 The sacred duty to care for the alien, the orphan and the widow

Notes by Gillian Kingston
based on the New International Version

Gillian Kingston is a Methodist local preacher, living in Shinrone, Co. Offaly, Ireland. For many years, she has been involved in inter-church activity in Ireland and further afield. She is the Director of the Glenstal Ecumenical Conference, based at Glenstal Abbey, Co. Limerick, and a former President of the Irish Council of Churches. She and Tom have three sons and a daughter.

Introduction

The poor we have always with us – and there are many ways of being poor. Think of the horror of feeling unwanted, the frustration of being trapped in a situation where you cannot realise your potential, the despair at being deprived of everything which gives life meaning – home, loved ones, country, culture, identity. The Bible highlights the imperative of care to those so deprived. As God has loved us, so we must love and care for the vulnerable among us. We are one in Jesus Christ and we are called to live that unity in word and deed.

Text for the week: Zechariah 7:9

'This is what the LORD Almighty says: "Administer true justice; show mercy and compassion to one another."'

For group discussion and personal thought

- Have you ever felt utterly alien and excluded? What helped you?
- Who are the people in your community who feel they are on the margins? What could you do to make things better for them?

Exodus 22:21-24

Don't forget!

As a young man, Jack left his own country and went where he could make a better living for himself. It hadn't been easy, mind you. People weren't friendly, work was hard to get, and it had been a bit of a struggle, but he'd made it and now he was well-off, married with children. But he had a big problem with all these 'foreigners' coming in: his taxes were paying for their upkeep, they were taking jobs his children might be needing, and they wanted houses and facilities.

> **'Do not ill-treat an alien or oppress him, for you were aliens in Egypt.'**
>
> *(verse 21)*

When things go well, it is all too easy to forget how it was in difficult times. Perhaps we just don't want to remember that there were days, even years, when we needed help from someone, when we felt on the margins, alienated, forgotten. And seeing someone in that place is a painful reminder. But this is not what God says – we *must* remember what it was like and have compassion on those who are as we were. We must put ourselves in their moccasins, as the American proverb says, and help them overcome their difficulties, just as we may have been helped ourselves. 'No man is an island', wrote the English poet John Donne. Today you need me; tomorrow, I may need you.

† *Caring God, teach us to care for others as we ourselves have been cared for – by you and by others.*

Deuteronomy 24:17-22

Plenty and to spare...

A Dublin supermarket ran a rota to enable a variety of groups in turn – churches, charities and the like – to pick up bags and baskets of bread and even cakes after closing hour on a Saturday evening and distribute them to people in need. Why not give folk a treat at the weekend – why put it all in the dump?

> **'When you are harvesting in your field and you overlook a sheaf, do not go back to get it. Leave it for the alien, the fatherless and the widow . . .**
>
> *(part of verse 19)*

And it's not just the sheaves, what about the olives and the grapes? There *is* plenty and to spare. Aid and development agencies have been saying for years that there is plenty of food in the world for everyone – the issue is distribution and the problem is greed. Now, clearly, it's not as simple as it sounds: there are transportation difficulties and there are dietary considerations – can we get it there and will they be able to eat it if we do? But there's no such excuse for not sharing with those around us. What have you got that you don't need? Can you open your home and offer hospitality? There are all sorts of need: food and cash, but what about love, friendship, encouragement, a smile? The song asks, 'When I needed a neighbour, were you there?' Were you? Was I?

† *Providing God, open our hearts and hands to share with others what you have given us.*

Fair is fair – isn't it?

Of course we all pay lip-service to the notion of equality – equality of opportunity, equality before the law, equal rights. But, as the novelist George Orwell once observed, 'All are equal, but some are more equal than others!' And if people don't like you, resent you, wish you weren't around, can you expect them to be fair in their dealings with you? Probably not.

> **Do not oppress the widow or the fatherless, the alien or the poor. In your hearts do not think evil of each other.**
>
> *(verse 10)*

Zechariah is clear about where he sees the problem. It is a matter of attitude – 'do not think badly of each other', or, as one translation (NRSV) puts it, 'do not devise evil in your hearts against one another'. And look at how he goes on – even the law is not enough if people are determined to discriminate against the vulnerable (verses 11-12). How we think about each other is of fundamental importance, because our thinking almost invariably has an effect on our words and our actions. God reminds his people that they too have been aliens, they too have suffered. Now they must empathise with the vulnerable among them and ensure that they are treated with equity. And the interesting thing is that being fair, showing justice, is in our own long-term interest – Zechariah could see this (verse 14) and history teaches it.

† *Loving God, teach us to love with our hearts and minds – and with our hands.*

Acts 6:1-6

How these Christians love one another . . .

Or do they? Someone needs to take this in hand, you know. I'm not getting anything like as much as *she* is getting. They always seem to run out of food and clothes just before they get to me. If they didn't give so much to *some* people there'd be enough for *all* of us – we're *all* hungry!

> **Brothers, choose seven men from among you who are known to be full of the Spirit and wisdom. We will turn this responsibility over to them.**
>
> *(verse 3)*

It is a thankless task taking responsibility for everything – delegation has to be the name of the game! It would be a mistake to interpret these verses as indicating that the Apostles thought the ministry of the word, one way or another, was the only thing needed in the community. No, this is about the importance of the right people doing the right things: the Apostles attend to that for which they were called – prayer and ministry of the word – and those identified by the community for administration of resources attend to that task. The seven are not only Spirit-filled, they are wise, people of discernment and faith. One will be a martyr, one is a convert, one will be an articulate missionary – and who knows how the lives of the others developed? These are the right people for hands-on service.

† *Serving God, teach me to serve you in whatever way you choose to call me.*

Practise what you preach!

Peg was a 'regular' at the prayer meeting; any Bible study group any night of the week, you could be sure she would turn up and she never missed a Sunday service, morning and evening. But ask her to do a car run for the Seniors' Club or to pick up a few groceries for old Mrs Smith, she just never had time!

> **Do not merely listen to the word, and so deceive yourselves. Do what it says.**
>
> *(verse 22)*

This is direct stuff from James. Words are no good on their own, in fact they can be dangerous, he says. The important thing is to get out and get on with it! We all know people who are so heavenly minded that they are no earthly use – and perhaps we are guilty of this ourselves on occasions. Prayer can be the easy option – we need to get our hands dirty too. The Lord who healed, provided food, touched the so-called untouchable and lifted the oppressed, calls on us to get off our knees and do the same. We *do* need to listen to the word – it is the fundamental guide for how we act; what James makes clear is that, hearing it, we then practise what it is teaching (verse 25). Little wonder we are not taken seriously if we pay lip-service to compassion, but do nothing to make it real; we love one another – do we really?!

† *God of action, make me in your image.*

Psalm 146

All together now!

'How wonderful it is', says the psalmist somewhere else (Psalm 133), 'when brothers live together in unity', and I think we would be justified in including sisters in there too! These are the last days of Christian Unity Week and not a bad time to think of *all* the ways we can be one with each other. Real unity is about affirming the truths of justice and love along with those of worship and belief. It is about affirming, as the psalmist does here (verse 6) and in yet another psalm, that 'the earth is the Lord's and everything in it, the world, and all who live in it' (Psalm 24).

Blessed is he...
whose hope is in the LORD his God,
the Maker of heaven and earth,
the sea and everything in them –
the LORD, who remains faithful for ever.

(part of verse 5, and verse 6)

The psalmist rejoices because he is able to affirm the justice and care of God for all God's children. Look at the categories: those who are oppressed, hungry, prisoners, blind, bowed down (in whatever way), righteous, foreigner, fatherless and widowed. No wonder he rejoices: consider the inclusivity of the God he praises! And this isn't just for today; it is for always. Notice the different ways the psalmist expresses God's utter dependability – 'all my life', 'as long as I live', 'forever', 'for all generations'. Those who treat the vulnerable unjustly and without feeling are challenged.

† Uniting God, make us one with each other in you.

Widows, Orphans and Aliens

2 Sojourners and aliens

Notes by Philip G O'B Robinson
based on the New Revised Standard Version

Philip Robinson is a former President of the Jamaica District of The Methodist Church in the Caribbean and the Americas (MCCA) and of the Jamaica Council of Churches. He is a Director of National Religious Media Commission and Methodist Chaplain to the University of the West Indies (Mona Campus) and to the Excelsior Education Centre, where he also teaches.

Introduction

The subject of migrants – their plans, plights and pluses – is a constant item on the agenda of governments, civil societies and international groups, especially in the light of an increasingly globalised world. This week's readings consider the experience of the patriarchs as aliens and some exemplary foreigners used by God in Israel's salvation history; they then go on to look at Isaiah's vision of foreigners being drawn into the promise of Israel; and end with Jesus' famous parable lauding the compassion of the outsider.

Text for the week: Isaiah 56:6-7

[T]he foreigners who join themselves to the LORD *. . . these I will bring to my holy mountain, and make them joyful in my house of prayer; their burnt offerings and their sacrifices will be accepted on my altar.*

For group discussion and personal thought

- What impact have aliens or sojourners (either individuals or groups) had on your community? In what ways has God used these circumstances for good?
- Religious bigotry is still rife in today's world. Explore the evidence of this in your local community or the wider society.

Genesis 20:1-18

A resident alien

While residing in Gerar as an alien, Abraham said of his wife Sarah, 'She is my sister.' And King Abimelech of Gerar sent and took Sarah.

(part of verse 1, and verse 2)

Every day, people migrate from one country to become aliens and sojourners in another, in order to escape the effects of severe social, political, religious or economic circumstances that threaten their very existence. Citizens of a country have rights by virtue of being born citizens, but aliens have none except what have been granted to them. Since earliest times, aliens have been at a great disadvantage. Their possessions, wives and livelihood could be taken away, they could be killed and they would have no recourse to justice in the land. Abraham resorted to telling only so much of the truth as he believed would ensure his safety. However, what he revealed gave Abimelech an excuse to take Sarah to be his wife, since he innocently thought she was only Abraham's sister.

But, as he had done before (see Genesis12: 10-20 and 26: 6-11), God intervened on Abraham's behalf without doing injustice to Abimelech's innocence.

Those who engage in right living will know justice, because God's protection of those who are his – by virtue of their commitment to him and his promise to them – will never fail.

† *O God of justice and mercy, help the millions who have left home by force of circumstances. May they acknowledge you in all their ways and experience the freedom of divine intervention.*

Genesis 47:1-12

Help from an unexpected quarter

'We have come to reside as aliens in the land . . . because the famine is severe in the land of Canaan. Now, we ask you, let your servants settle in the land of Goshen.

(part of verse 4)

When Joseph's family arrived in Egypt as aliens they encountered what could have been a major problem: they were shepherds and the Egyptians despised shepherds (see Genesis 45:34). Through Joseph's intervention, however, Pharaoh allowed them to settle in the land of Goshen.

Today is Holocaust Memorial Day, when the world remembers the murder of six million Jews during the Second World War. One of the effects of this event was the mass migration of Jews to other countries. Escaping was not easy but help often came from unexpected quarters: from people in all walks of life, professional people who went beyond their professional obligation, and those whose sense of justice, morality and decency could not let them stand by as mere witnesses. They saved the day by allowing the new aliens to settle in their homelands and in their homes. It was like Goshen revisited.

Although, both for Jacob and his sons and the holocaust survivors, help came from unexpected quarters, it was not itself entirely unexpected. Joseph knew that his horrific experience was part of God's plan to save the lives of his family (see Genesis 45:4-8). And the rescue of many from the Holocaust can only be explained as divine intervention through unexpected people and means. To the faithful, there is no mystery: God continued to work his purpose out as he had promised (compare Genesis 12:2 and 45:7).

† *God, thank you that your hand is still strong to save. May the memory of the faithfulness of your people in the midst of trials and tribulations keep us faithful and confident that you are with us as we face the difficulties of each day.*

Isaiah 56:1-8

I have other sheep

> **Thus says the Lord GOD . . .**
> **I will gather others to them**
> **besides those already gathered.**

(part of verse 8)

God declares through the prophet Isaiah that his blessings are available to all people who faithfully offer their lives in worship and service to him. He leaves no place for doubt about the privileged status of the faithful. They will have access to Jerusalem and to the joyous worship of the temple; what they offer in worship will be accepted – a sign of their own acceptance by God – and the temple will be redesignated 'a house of prayer for all peoples' (verse 7).

It is a sober reminder to churches today that we have no monopoly on the blessings of God and that everyone who truly desires to serve God should be recognised and welcomed as equal before God. Jesus echoed this sentiment when he said 'I have other sheep that do not belong to this fold. I must bring them also . . . So there will be one flock, one shepherd' (John 10:16). God will exercise his prerogative to add to the community of faith everyone who truly serves him.

† *Lord and God, your love is truly immeasurable, your mercy extends to all, and you give your blessings to all who are faithful in worship and service. May the Church that bears your name embrace all who come seeking your kingdom and your righteousness so that our Lord's purpose of having one flock under one shepherd may be fulfilled.*

Ruth 1:22 – 2:23

God works out his purpose through an alien

So Naomi returned together with Ruth the Moabite, her daughter-in-law, who came back with her from the country of Moab. They came to Bethlehem . . .

(part of verse 22)

When Neil Armstrong stepped on the moon in 1969, he said: 'That's one small step for man, one giant leap for mankind.' In history God works out his purpose, stamping his authority on the direction and outcome of human affairs through people – even aliens and sojourners.

'They came to Bethlehem'. The story could have ended here but Ruth eventually married Boaz. Many years after Ruth and Naomi came to Bethlehem, a man and his fiancée came to Bethlehem and something phenomenal happened there – Christ the Saviour was born. That journey was a small step but in that birth was a gigantic leap for humanity. Ruth and Boaz are mentioned in the genealogy of the Jesus the Messiah (Matthew 1:1-16). Ruth could not have guessed that her choice would link her so directly with the Messiah. Her uneventful journey to Bethlehem was a small step that led, eventually, to the gigantic leap in saving hope for humanity. The fact is, God was working his purpose out through this alien, and it was not just matter of a human choice.

† *God, help us to realise that we are part of your purpose and that we can only fulfil that purpose when our lives and our will are consecrated to your service and your plan.*

Isaiah 45:1-7

The anointed Gentile

Thus says the LORD to his anointed, to Cyrus,
whose right hand I have grasped
to subdue nations before him
and strip kings of their robes,
to open doors before him –
and the gates shall not be closed.

(verse 1)

God often does wonders through the small, the weak, the insignificant and the despised, but here he is about to do a great work of deliverance and renewal for his chosen people through a powerful Gentile and a foreigner. To the Jewish mind, an 'anointed Gentile' was a contradiction, but that was how Cyrus is designated in Isaiah's prophecy. This Persian, though not a worshipper of Yahweh, was going to be used by Yahweh to overthrow Babylon, where the exiled Jews were being held captive. He was going to allow them to return to their homeland, help them to resettle, allow them to rebuild the temple that the Babylonians had destroyed, and give back the temple articles stolen by Nebuchadnezzar.

In Old Testament times God raised up leaders not only among the Israelites, but also among foreigners. Israel's position as the chosen people was a privilege that assumed certain ongoing responsibilities with eternal implications; it was not meant to put them on a pedestal of personal pride, to the exclusion of other peoples. God's appointment of Cyrus, an unlikely candidate for Israel's deliverance from exile, underscores this point. There are times when an alien or sojourner becomes the anointed one, the chosen one, the one consecrated to God's service and for God's purpose.

† Lord, you equip for the task and you are with those whom you anoint; continue to raise up leaders who will do your bidding from among all peoples.

An exemplary alien

> **'Which of these three, do you think, was neighbour to the man who fell into the hands of the robbers?' He said, 'The one who showed him mercy.'**
>
> *(verse 36 and part of verse 37)*

The Samaritans were aliens – their Jewish ancestors intermarried with other peoples after Israel's exile, and the Jews despised them. The parable was told in response to an expert in religious law asking 'Who is my neighbour?' The conversation began with the expert's question, 'What must I do to inherit eternal life?' (verse 25). The criteria for receiving eternal life involve love for God and neighbour (verses 26, 27). In keeping with Mosaic Law, the priest and the Levite were wary of touching the body (Numbers 19:11-13) and seemed to be so concerned about the ceremonial requirements of the law that they failed to observe the fundamental requirements of God. It was the despised Samaritan who responded most appropriately and Jesus pointed to his example and advised the lawyer to follow suit (verse 37). It is the practical out-working of our faith that reaps eternal rewards, and Jesus used the example of a Samaritan to make the point. In the final analysis, this tells us that God is no respecter of persons and shows no partiality, 'but in every nation anyone who fears him and does what is right is acceptable to him' (Acts 10: 35).

† *Lord, help us to bring loving service to those in need. May our faith find expression through our living and bring honour to you.*

3 Widows and orphans

Notes by Joan Stott
based on the New Living Translation (NLT) and The Message.

Joan Stott is a lay preacher in the Uniting Church in Australia, and has served the church and community in a variety of roles.

Introduction

Computers have a profound influence on our daily life, not only on the way we live, work and do business, but also on how we use language. 'Widows and orphans' is a term used with computers. If a new paragraph begins with one line at the bottom of a page (an orphan), the computer automatically moves the whole paragraph onto the next page; and if the last few words of a paragraph appear at the top of a page (a widow), the computer automatically moves a line from the previous page to join them. Even computers are programmed not to ignore 'widows and orphans', and to justify Jesus' commission on behalf of vulnerable people!

Jesus said: 'God's Spirit is on me; he's chosen me to preach the Message of good news to the poor, sent me to announce pardon to prisoners and recovery of sight to the blind, to set the burdened and battered free' (Luke 4:18, *The Message*).

Text for the week: Luke 2:38 (*The Message*)

[S]he spoke . . . to all who were waiting expectantly . . .

For group discussion and personal thought

- Why does God have a preferential love for widows and orphans?
- Within your culture, are widows considered a burden or an asset?
- How are orphaned children cared for within your community?

Contrasting responses

> **[Anna] came along, ... and began praising God. She talked about Jesus to everyone . . .**
>
> *(part of verse 38, NLT)*

Cataracts in the eyes are normally considered a condition of ageing, and Anna probably had cataracts. But Anna the prophet had an inner sight that was something very different to normal sight; as a result of her commitment to a life of worship, prayer and fasting, she 'saw' with her heart and mind.

I recently had cataracts removed from my eyes, and it made a miraculous change to how I saw the world, people, and even myself in the mirror. Everything was brighter, colours were more vivid, and both distant horizons and tiny insects were much clearer and easier to see.

The contrast in the physical appearance between an aged person and a new baby is stark, but the greater contrast is in their experience and understanding of life. Anna was widowed after only seven years of marriage, and she was now aged 84. Although Jesus was the Word Incarnate when he was brought as a young baby for presentation in the temple, at that age he could not articulate that knowledge. Anna, with the perception of years of committed faith in God, had the spiritual perception to identify God at work in the world, and especially in the reality of this special baby, and she spent the rest of her life in praise and thanksgiving to God.

† *God, help me to see you at work in the world.*

1 Kings 17

Contrasting emotions

Then Elijah said to her, 'Do not be afraid.'

(verse 13, NLT)

Some people intimidate others by their appearance, voice and manner, and can cause fear, panic and anxiety as they manipulate their victims. When I was a child, it was planned that Queen Elizabeth would visit my home town. There was great excitement, but then, unexpectedly, there were several cases of polio diagnosed within our township. Powerful-looking men with loud voices, and intimidating manners decreed that the Queen could not step out of the royal train at my town, because of the risk of infection. Instead, all the town's children were lined up at the train station, and the Queen slowly passed by in the royal train.

If the Queen of England and her entourage were intimidating, how much more intimidating would be God's own messenger! Elijah, the Old Testament prophet, a strange and frightening man, suddenly appeared out of the wilderness. Guided by God, Elijah visited a widow and asked her to feed him. The prophet was confident and sure of his instructions, whilst the widow was frightened, hungry and rationing her supplies for one last meal before she and her son died of starvation. Elijah calmed her fears and gently explained why her fears were groundless: God would provide well for her and her son until the drought ended. The widow's courage enabled her to be hospitable to the man of God.

† God, help me to deal with my fears – real or imagined.

Contrasting attitudes

> **'A widow in that city kept after him: "My rights are violated – protect me."'**
> *(part of verse 3,* The Message*)*

There are many statues that symbolise 'Lady Justice'. The more famous statues depict 'justice' as a blindfolded woman holding a set of scales in her left hand, and a two-edged sword in her right hand. The blindfold symbolises the impartiality of justice, and the two-edged sword symbolises the power of reason and justice.

Understanding God's preferential treatment of powerless widows and orphans, Jesus told a story about the importance of persistence and belief in the power of prayer, and the need for faithfulness in prayer in the face of harsh injustices. In Jesus' story, a powerless widow whose rights had been violated was persistently seeking justice from a corrupt judge. The woman believed in and trusted the justice system and was quite convinced of her rights, and therefore expected to have them upheld. The judge was corrupt and self-serving, but he eventually gave in to her because he was tired of her.

As far as the justice system is concerned, this 'case' is a complete denial of all that 'Lady Justice' stands for, but the motive for Jesus' story is encouragement for believers to have an active and sincere prayer life. Jesus challenged us all to have the same belief, commitment and perseverance in our prayer life as this widow who was seeking confirmation of her innocence.

† *God, help me to believe in the power of prayer.*

Numbers 27:1-11

Contrasting influences

God ruled: 'Zelophehad's daughters are right, give them land as an inheritance . . . '

(part of verse 7, The Message*)*

When I travelled the world visiting groups of Christians on behalf of the World Federation of Methodist and Uniting Church Women, I had many experiences of flying in very small aeroplanes. These normally short flights were necessary because the journeys were either over inaccessible mountains, or were from island to island. Sometimes the time taken in preparation for take-off was longer than the actual flights, as each passenger and every piece of luggage was weighed. Then the crew decided who sat in which seat, and where each piece of luggage was placed, to help maintain the balance within the plane, and so that safety issues were not compromised. Whether you were included on the flight depended on who the passengers were, and how important they were considered to be, which meant that often the local women were left behind until the next flight.

This story in the Old Testament is about five courageous young women who challenged their tradition and culture to demand their rights to an inheritance, as they had no brothers. The authority of Moses, the priest, tribal leaders and the entire community outweighed the status of these five women, yet they still petitioned their leaders, requesting their unusual rights. The God-influenced decision in their favour overturned the traditions of centuries, and marked a new beginning for women and orphans.

† God, may I worship you each day with courage and integrity.

Contrasting motives

Joash and his nurse remained hidden in the Temple of the Lord for six years.

(*part of verse 3, NLT*)

A family feud!
Murder! Revenge! Plotting!
Ruthlessness! Manipulation!
Judah's darkest history!
King David's royal line almost obliterated!
A vindictive and evil woman!
A trusted and courageous servant!
The infant heir to King David's throne safely smuggled into hiding!

These words have the hallmarks of a popular film or book, with plots and counter-plots as various people murderously struggled for power. The nation of Judah experienced its darkest days as its future was determined through secretive and murderous plotting. God's rule and purposes were forgotten in that rush for power.

This was the reality in which vulnerable little Joash now lived. As the infant and orphaned heir to the throne in Judah, following the murder of his father, he was helpless as his grandmother schemed to seize power in the kingdom. All the other living descendants of King David were now under threat of murder, so that no one could challenge his grandmother's power! Joash's aunt formed a pact with a trusted and courageous servant, and together they smuggled little baby Joash into their secret care and protection within God's temple, with his nurse looking after him.

In this story, the contrast between evil and innocence is profound. God's presence and blessing were with the innocent, and God's mercy with the vulnerable.

† *God, may my motives and ambitions be in accordance with your will for my life.*

Esther 2:5-18

Contrasting challenges

After her parents died, Mordecai adopted her.

(part of verse 7, The Message)

An adopted child is often called a 'chosen' child. Some years ago, my children and I were asked to officially 'adopt' an orphaned kangaroo whose mother had been shot. Very small and unable to survive on her own, 'Snoopy' soon became a 'chosen' member of our family.

As the kangaroo was far too young to have left her mother's pouch, she was totally dependent on us. Her substitute pouch was a hessian bag. She needed company, constant warmth, endless numbers of 'bottle' feedings, and she also needed many baths, as she always spilled her 'milk'. She and our pet rabbit 'Bugs' often shared her hessian bag, and on sunny days they chased each other around the garden. Snoopy developed a loving and secure relationship within our family. Despite living in a foreign environment, this beautiful Eastern Grey kangaroo stayed true to her nature as a kangaroo and exhibited all the behaviour of her species, but with a trusting and rare relationship with some human beings. When Snoopy was fully grown, the time came for her move to live in a wildlife research sanctuary. We visited her regularly until her kangaroo mates became more important to her than we were.

Despite living in a foreign environment, Esther remained true to her faith, beliefs, tradition and culture, and brought blessings to her people.

† *God, may I have the faith to live out my calling as your beloved child.*

1 Rebuilding the walls of Jerusalem

Notes by Marcel Valentin Măcelaru
based on the New Revised Standard Version

Dr M V Măcelaru is a Romanian theologian, living in Osijek, Croatia, where he teaches the Old Testament at the Evangelical Theological Seminary. He is also a visiting lecturer at Elim Theological Seminary in Timişoara, Romania.

Introduction

The book of Nehemiah narrates events in Judaea during the fifth century BC, after the descendants of the Israelites deported to Babylon were allowed to return to their homeland. Such a return was a common Persian strategy, probably aimed at the political and economic consolidation of subject territories as provinces of the empire. However, the biblical account sees this homecoming as Yahweh's renewed activity on behalf of his people. As the returnees rebuild the walls of Jerusalem, the Lord supports their effort with miraculous provision and protection. This is a lesson in perseverance and a message of encouragement that God is faithful to intervene in our lives in similar ways.

Text for the week: Nehemiah 1:8-9

'If you return to me and keep my commandments and do them, though your outcasts are under the farthest skies, I will gather them from there and bring them to the place at which I have chosen to establish my name.'

For group discussion and personal thought

- Do I trust God to work in my life? How do I ask for his intervention? Have I done my part?
- Is there any pride manifested in my life?
- What is my attitude towards material possessions? What are my priorities in life?

Nehemiah 1:1-11

The secret of a powerful prayer

Remember the word that you commanded your servant Moses, 'If you are unfaithful, I will scatter you among the peoples; but if you return to me and keep my commandments and do them, though your outcasts are under the farthest skies, I will gather them from there and bring them to the place at which I have chosen to establish my name.'

(verses 8-9)

Like the disciples two millennia ago (e.g. Luke 11:1), many of us have also wondered about the 'secret' that makes Jesus' prayers recorded in the gospels powerful and effective. Interestingly, Bible commentators have long noted that the prayer which Jesus teaches his disciples to pray in Luke 11 follows an 'outline' similar to that of Nehemiah's prayer given in the reading for today. I believe, however, that praying successfully takes more than following a given pattern. The first chapter of Nehemiah discloses two great principles that are characteristic of successful prayers throughout the Bible. First, prayer must be based on God's promises. In order to ask according to God's will, when praying one should rely on God's recorded words – the Bible. Second, prayer should never cease. When praying one must persevere until God's answer comes.

† *Lord Jesus, as you have taught your disciples, teach me also today to pray a prayer according to your will. And help me to never give up, but to persevere on the path of righteousness.*

God's timing is good timing

'The God of heaven is the one who will give us success, and we his servants are going to start building.'

(*part of verse 20*)

The reading for today shows Nehemiah four months after he first heard the news concerning Jerusalem. Surprisingly, he is still in Babylon, performing his daily duties for the king. At this point in the narrative we might be tempted to accuse Nehemiah of procrastination. Why is he not in Jerusalem? Has the concern shown earlier run out already? That, however, would be missing the point, for Nehemiah does not show lack of enthusiasm here. Rather, he is patiently waiting for the right time, that is, the time when God begins to move. Many a time we sense needs and seek to do something about them but our impulsiveness and haste come in the way of accomplishing the best results. I have found that the wise thing to do in most situations in life when we feel under pressure to make a move or take a quick decision, is in fact to wait patiently on God. It is when things happen in God's perfect timing that we experience the peace and joy that come when one is walking in God's perfect will.

† *Heavenly Father, may my spiritual clock be adjusted to yours so that in all matters I will act according to your timing and not my own.*

Nehemiah 3:1-14

How will you be remembered?

[B]ut their nobles would not put their shoulders to the work of their Lord.

(*part of verse 5*)

To the inattentive reader, Nehemiah 3 may appear as a simple, boring list of duties performed by various Israelites as they rebuild the walls of Jerusalem. Nevertheless, the author of this text does more than just make a simple inventory. He intends to help us 'remember'. And he is candid enough to mention even the nobles of Tekoa, who stand out negatively as people who out of pride did not join in the national effort of reconstruction. The word translated 'shoulders' is a reference to an unbending neck, a standard description of pride in the Hebrew Bible. Now we all know that pride is a dangerous sin and we work hard to suppress its obvious manifestations, such as arrogance and self-praise. However, have we identified the more subtle ways in which pride works? In the nobles of Tekoa it produced disunity (or maybe 'constructive opposition'!). What are its manifestations in our lives? False pity, dishonest concern, insincere humility, gossip, exaggeration, sarcasm – all these, and others like them, are but symptoms of the same sin. Let us not deceive ourselves into believing that we have attained a pride-free state! The text is asking each one of us today: How will you be remembered?

† *Lord Jesus, please enable me to recognise how pride is being manifested in my life. I want to take your humbleness as example. Help me reject pride in all its facets and symptoms.*

Trust God and focus on doing your part

So we prayed to our God, and set a guard as a protection against them day and night.

(*verse 9*)

The resourcefulness and wisdom with which Nehemiah leads the reconstruction of the wall described in today's reading has always impressed me. The steps he takes to ensure the success of the work reveals a fundamental principle, one that underlies any thriving enterprise, be it spiritual, material or intellectual. He focuses the attention of the people on what they can do, on what they can manage, and teaches them not to worry about things beyond their control. Specifically, he focuses their attention on the work that needs to be done and teaches them to trust God for provision and protection. What a simple, yet powerful model! It has been said that over 90 per cent of the things we worry about never happen. Yet, paradoxically, their destructive power is real; for when we focus on what 'might be', the fear of, and worry about, things that lie beyond our control grow to nullify the creative energy God has placed in us. There is, however, an alternative. 'Cast all your anxiety on him', urges the apostle, 'because he cares for you' (1 Peter 5:7).

† *Lord Jesus, I cast my fears, my worries and my anxiety on you. I trust that you will take care of tomorrow as I focus on the task for today.*

Nehemiah 5:1-19

The danger from within

'The thing that you are doing is not good. Should you not walk in the fear of our God, to prevent the taunts of the nations our enemies?'

(*part of verse 9*)

Of all the divisions within society, the separation into rich and poor, into affluent and underprivileged, is the most common and at the same time most difficult problem we face. This kind of discrepancy has plagued and continues to plague our communities, and there seems to be little that can be done to resolve it. Even in today's reading we see that, after successfully facing the threats coming from the outside, the Israelite community is almost destroyed from within because a 'Babylonian' model of society, one based on 'haves' and 'have-nots', is being perpetuated. The new possibility affirmed by Nehemiah is to 'walk in the fear of Yahweh' (verse 9). This includes respecting regulations given to ensure the wellbeing of all the members of the community (e.g. Deuteronomy 1). In practical terms, Nehemiah's alternative model calls all of us to a wise management of what we own, a redistribution of what we have so that the emptiness of the have-nots is properly addressed within our communities.

† *Thank you, Lord, for all your blessings, for all the things which you have given me. I understand now that it is my duty to meet the needs of my neighbour, to bless others as you have blessed me.*

Let us set our priorities straight!

'I am doing a great work and I cannot come down. Why should the work stop while I leave it to come down to you?'

(*part of verse 3*)

There are occasions in life when each one of us has to decide on the priorities. This, it seems to me, is the fundamental truth we can draw out of today's reading. Nehemiah chooses wisely. He puts the work God called him to do for the benefit of the community above any other concerns. What do we choose to do? When we are tempted to give up the work God has assigned to us, what becomes the priority of our life? Are we able to spot the temptation for what it is or are we subtly tricked into deserting our call? The temptation in Nehemiah's case begins with a 'noble' invitation to the negotiation table and progressively deteriorates into lies, threats and blackmail. In our case it may begin with what may seem the more desirable option, or the more profitable thing to do. But let us not deceive ourselves – if the option we choose causes godly work to come to a halt, then we have been deceived into selecting wrongly. Today we are urged to set our priorities straight.

† *Lord God, we are faced with options every day. Help us to recognise and reject temptations and give us the wisdom to set our priorities straight.*

Nehemiah

1 The religious life of the city

Notes by Yordan Kalev Zhekov
based on the New International Version

Yordan Kalev Zhekov is an Evangelical Christian born in Bulgaria. He holds a Doctor of Science degree in theology from the Catholic Faculty of Theology of the University of Ljubljana, Slovenia. He is a lecturer at South London Christian College in London and a project worker in a rehabilitation hostel for the homeless people in Watford.

Introduction

Twenty-first century societies have been torn apart by violence, vandalism, fanaticism, corruption and abuse, despite human scientific and technological advances. What impact could bring positive change? It was the impact of God's Law and God's covenant promises that resurrected the society of God's people after their return from exile. The heart of this society was a community committed to God's Law, led by faithful and devoted leaders who embraced God's commandments without compromise. This week's readings present important dimensions of the life of this community.

Text for the week: Nehemiah 12:43

And on that day they offered great sacrifices, rejoicing because God had given them great joy. The women and children also rejoiced. The sound of rejoicing in Jerusalem could be heard far away.

For group discussion and personal thought

- Why was the reaction of sadness considered an inappropriate response to understanding of the Law (8:9)?
- Was Nehemiah's attitude towards mixed marriages justifiable and on what grounds (13:23-29)?
- How can success that brings deep joy and satisfaction be defined from a Christian point of view?

The city and its people

The pressure from the enemy continued after the wall of Jerusalem was completed and its gates installed. The physical barrier was not enough to secure the life of the city. Nehemiah understood the need for safety as an important task related to management of the city's population and its administrative structures. The administration was strengthened with the appointment of gatekeepers, singers and Levites. The appointment of a city governor was essential and the choice fell on a trustworthy and God-fearing individual. Through God's guidance and the support of community leaders, Nehemiah organised the population of the city, registering them according to the record of those who had returned first from exile. God's leading role in the matter was demonstrated by the emphasis on deliverance, guidance and settlement in the Promised Land. The city's structures and its population were further secured through voluntary financial support from all levels of the community.

> **The total given by the rest of the people was 20,000 drachmas of gold, 2,000 minas of silver and 67 garments for priests.**
>
> (*verse 72*)

The turbulence of life in our societies defines people's efforts to find security in having somewhere to live, being part of society, and having enough money to live on. The constant struggle for a better existence can only be truly productive under God's guidance, leading to personal experience of his deliverance from sin, salvation in Jesus Christ, and daily dependence on his mercy and grace.

† *Please Lord, help us to follow your guidance in every aspect of our life.*

Nehemiah 8:1-18

The Law of God and the people

The time had come when the people were ready to hear the Law of God. They enthusiastically welcomed the organised event, and the chosen location was open and accessible to everyone, including women and children. The comprehensive reading was accompanied by interpretation to bring God's message home. The initial response of sadness had been replaced with joy when the Law had been presented in its entirety. The understanding of God's Law should bring joy to those who submit to it because God's intentions and purposes are for the salvation and protection of his covenant people and his grace and mercy overcome human unfaithfulness.

> **Then all the people went away to eat and drink, to send portions of food and to celebrate with great joy, because they now understood the words that had been made known to them.**
>
> (*verse 12*)

The people re-enacted God's salvation, which had become real for them since the return from the exile, through the celebration of the Feast of Tabernacles. They renewed their covenant commitment to God. Today's constant manipulation of information has made an impact on the holistic understanding of the Word of God. The message of God's grace and mercy should produce joy and satisfaction in the life of those who believe in Jesus.

† *Please help us, Lord, to perceive your Word in its entirety and live according to it.*

The people and God's promise

The whole community gathered voluntarily, eager to confess their sins and look for God's deliverance. They expressed their feelings of mourning and repentance through fasting and penitential clothing. They defined their standing with God as a covenant community through their separation from all foreigners. The prayers, guided by the Law, began by underlining two aspects of the people's faith. The first was the recognition of God's power and authority as creator and ruler over the whole of creation and all the powers and authorities in the universe. The second expressed their understanding of the covenant made with Abraham for the Promised Land, which extended to all of them and was maintained through God's faithfulness and righteousness. These two aspects defined the people's hope for the complete and final fulfilment of God's promise for absolute freedom in the Promised Land in spite of the sins and unfaithfulness of their ancestors and themselves.

> **'O our God, the great, mighty and awesome God, who keeps his covenant of love, do not let all this hardship seem trifling in your eyes'**
>
> (*part of verse 32*)

Our faith in Christ should inspire us to formulate our daily life as a service to God who is over all the rulers and authorities. And in spite of the difficulties of life our hope should never cease that God who is faithful and righteous will complete his promises with the second coming of Jesus in the renewal of this world.

† *Lord, strengthen our hope!*

Nehemiah 10:28-39

The people's dedication to fulfilling God's law

The entire community of God's covenant people entered into a binding agreement to fulfil the requirements of God's Law.

> **'[A]ll these now join their brothers the nobles, and bind themselves with a curse and an oath to follow the Law of God given through Moses the servant of God and to obey carefully all the commands, regulations and decrees of the LORD our God.'**

(*verse 29*)

The seriousness of the people's commitment was summed up in the oath and the curse components of the agreement. The oath formulated the people's decision to devote themselves to the thorough fulfilment of God's Law. The curse provided grounds for judgement in the case of failure in dedicated observance of the Law. The nature of the Law's stipulations and the need for the people's active response in fulfilling them focused on important spheres of community life: preservation of the covenant purity based on marital distinctiveness; observance of the designated seasons and their nature; above all, the importance of support for God's temple, its ceremonial system and personnel, the priests and the Levites, with the necessary financial and material help. The embodiment of one's faith in deeds and actions reveals the depth of one's spiritual growth. Our Christian faith should lead us to a life of commitment to Christ based on actions prompted, formed and guided by faith.

† Please Lord, help us to live our faith daily.

The time of joy

The culmination of the events narrated in the books of Ezra and Nehemiah is found in this passage. The return from exile, the rebuilding of the temple and the wall, the organisation of the city's population and its administrative structures, and the renewal of the people's commitment to the Law lead to this climactic point. The dedication of the wall was well organised and executed, with the involvement of the entire worship squad, singers, priests and Levites. Two processions performed the ritual, moving around the wall and meeting at the temple. For all the participants, the route brought back memories of hard work brought to great success through God's help.

> **And on that day they offered great sacrifices, rejoicing because God had given them great joy. The women and children also rejoiced. The sound of rejoicing in Jerusalem could be heard far away.**
>
> (verse 43)

The stress on feelings of great joy underlines the overwhelming experience of all the people. The source of this joy is God, who has brought his covenant people to such a time of success. Times of success which bring joyful fulfilment are the product of hard work and dedication to the desired goal. The very nature of the success determines the depth of the experience of joy. The success which brings joy and satisfaction in Christian life is based on hard work and commitment, but is defined entirely by God's purpose and involvement.

† *Lord, formulate our success!*

Nehemiah 13:15-31

The time for endurance

The sound of great celebration and joy for renewed devotion to God still echoed in the streets of Jerusalem. However, it was not long before the desires of the sinful human heart led some members of the community to break the Law. Some defiled the Sabbath by engaging in unlawful activities, and the nobles tolerated this. Others, part of cross-cultural marriages outside the covenant community, failed to raise their children properly as effective members of that community. Lack of language skills created significant obstacles to the understanding and keeping of the Law. Such cases of anti-religious upbringing could not be tolerated within a community that defined itself entirely by its religion. And even more extreme measures needed to be taken against those who had entered such marriages in spite of their religiously elevated status and responsibilities. Nehemiah intervened with measures that underlined observance of the Law and preservation of the community's sanctity. His prayers to God for remembrance contained no requests for personal benefits; they were a stand against unrighteousness which appealed for God's support.

> **Remember me for this also, O my God, and show mercy to me according to your great love.**
>
> (*part of verse 22*)

To stand by our Christian beliefs and convictions without compromise in this world of sin, which constantly bombards us with temptations, is a lifelong endeavour accomplishable only through the strength of the Holy Spirit.

† Strengthen us, Lord, to be faithful!

1 Source of light, life and love

Notes by Catherine Williams
based on the New Revised Standard Version

Catherine Williams is an Anglican priest working as Vocations Officer for the Diocese of Gloucester, England. Her role is to help individuals and churches discern God's call on their lives. Catherine is married to the Vicar of Tewkesbury Abbey and they have two teenage daughters.

Introduction

In our readings this week we are exploring God as the source of light, life and love, as depicted in both the Old Testament and the Gospel of John. From the huge expanse of God's creation of the world to the intimate meetings of Jesus with needy people, we see a continual process of God as Creator, Redeemer and Sustainer. God's light, life and love order, cleanse, heal, restore and transform the world. As disciples of Christ we are equipped by the Holy Spirit to witness to God's renewing and restoring action.

Text for the week: Psalm 36:9

With you is the fountain of life; in your light we see light.

For group discussion and personal thought

- Which part of the creation story in Genesis 1 and 2 affects you most powerfully and why?
- In which area of your life do you most need to receive God's cleansing power? Strive to do something about it this Lent.
- Record and share with others the astonishing things that God is doing in your part of the world.

Genesis 1:1-5

Order from chaos

The creation narrative in Genesis 1 gives us a picture of God calling everything into being. From the very beginning of creation God works to bring order from chaos, substance from nothingness, light out of darkness. God, as creator, word and breath commands the elemental forces, calling, separating and naming until everything knows its place, pattern and purpose. The darkness is not banished, but is subject to God's authority and has a new and important role to play as 'night-time'.

> **God separated the light from the darkness. God called the light Day, and the darkness he called Night. And there was evening and there was morning, the first day.**
>
> (*part of verse 4, and verse 5*)

God, whose creative power formed the universe, continues to work in us through his word Jesus, and his breath, the Holy Spirit. We are brought to life, we grow and become fully ourselves through God's grace and power, demonstrated most completely in Jesus Christ, God with us. God is not merely the source of all creation but remains active through his love. He renews and transforms everything so that we may enjoy life in all its fullness. Where lives and communities are in chaos, God's word in Jesus can bring order, purpose and new life. We share in God's work of creation wherever we enable others to grow and develop, serve, love or express faith.

† *Lord God, thank you for your gift of creation. Continue to bring order from chaos.*

Fat Tuesday

Today is celebrated across the world as a time of carnival, or Mardi Gras (Fat Tuesday). It's a time of festivity before the church moves into a period of austerity and preparation for Easter through the season of Lent. In my culture in the UK, this day is known as Shrove Tuesday or Pancake Day. It's the day when traditionally all the fat, cream and eggs are used up and made into pancakes. Pancakes are eaten, tossed and even raced. It's a time for feasting, games and parties.

The people of Israel used the image of feasting with God as an expression of God's goodness and unfailing love towards them. Belief in Yahweh inspired a sense of security and plenty in difficult and dangerous times:

> **All people may take refuge in the shadow of your wings.**
> **They feast on the abundance of your house,**
> **and you give them drink from the river of your delight.**
>
> (*part of verse 7, and verse 8*)

Images of feasting should also remind us of the heavenly banquet which awaits all God's faithful people in eternity and of which we get a foretaste at each celebration of the Eucharist. Take time today to feast on God's goodness in whichever way is appropriate. Celebrate God as our fountain of light, life and love.

† *Thank you, Lord, for your goodness towards all. May we feast on you and celebrate your great love for creation.*

Psalm 51:6-12

Wash me!

There are times in our lives when we know beyond doubt our need of God's cleansing power to wash us and save us from ourselves. For King David the events leading up to the writing of this psalm were just such a time. Following his adultery with Bathsheba, David entered a period of remorse and shame where he called upon the Lord to give him a fresh start:

> **Purge me with hyssop and I shall be clean;**
> **wash me, and I shall be whiter than snow . . .**
> **Hide your face from my sins,**
> **and blot out all my iniquities.**
>
> (*verses 7 and 9*)

This psalm speaks deeply to our human condition and is used more than any other in our liturgies of confession and repentance. God, the source of light, love and life, longs to redeem his people – to turn us around so that we walk in the light of Christ and bear witness to his healing and renewing spirit working within us.

David longed to be restored to a place of joy and gladness, and asked God to forgive him and sustain him on his journey of faith. Today, on this Ash Wednesday, as we embark on Lent, let's take time to confess our sins, receive God's forgiveness and endeavour to walk afresh in Christ's light.

† *Forgive me, Lord, fill me with your Spirit, and lead me in the way of Christ.*

John 4:7-14

Living water

A Samaritan woman going about her daily business is about to have the shock of her life. A young Jewish man speaks to her. Not only does he speak, but he asks her for a favour and engages her in conversation. She, who is despised and ostracised because of her race, gender and lifestyle choices, finds herself accepted and treated as an equal. Then she is offered the gift of a lifetime – the water of life, from the Lord of life.

> **[T]hose who drink of the water that I will give them will never be thirsty. The water that I will give will become in them a spring of water gushing up to eternal life.**
>
> (*verse 14*)

Jesus may engage with us when we least expect it: on an ordinary day amidst life's everyday pattern. The way we respond to his gentle and compassionate invitation offered to all, no matter who they are or what they've done, can be life-changing for ever. As disciples of Jesus we too can offer living water to others. The Samaritan woman rushed home to tell everyone what she had discovered. We too can share the message of God's gift of new life with those around us. And like Jesus, we need to engage with compassion and openness – never prejudging and always opening doors for the Spirit to work.

† *Lord, fill me afresh with your living water. May it overflow to all around.*

John 9:1-7

Seeing the light

So often we look for someone to blame for the things that hinder us in life. We are anxious to know 'why' things go wrong, and whose fault it is. At the time of Jesus it was thought that disability was caused by sin. The disciples approached Jesus with a puzzle. If someone had been blind from birth, was it the parents who committed some grave error or the child who sinned whilst still in the womb? As so often happens in the gospels, Jesus sheds fresh light on the situation:

> **'Neither this man nor his parents sinned; he was born blind so that God's works might be revealed in him . . . As long as I am in the world, I am the light of the world.'**
>
> (*part of verse 3, and verse 5*)

God's glory is revealed in this situation through a miraculous healing. Jesus recreates the man, giving him sight and a new life. He does it by using the dust of the earth, from which the first man, Adam, was made. So this man, born blind, is made new through the power of God at work in Jesus. Let's not get stuck questioning why things go wrong, but let's look for God's creative solutions, those ways in which light is shed to transform and recreate broken lives.

† Lord, let me believe that nothing is impossible for you.

An astonishing thing!

The man born blind is astonished. He is astonished because not only can he now see clearly, he soon realises that his spiritual sight is much better and more finely attuned than those who are supposed to be the spiritual experts. The Pharisees have missed the point in a spectacular fashion. They cannot believe that Jesus could have healed the man, because they see Jesus as a sinner and do not recognise his pedigree. The man challenges them:

> **Here is an astonishing thing! You do not know where he comes from, and yet he opened my eyes . . . Never since the world began has it been heard that anyone opened the eyes of a person born blind.**
>
> (*part of verse 30, and verse 32*)

The man cannot believe that the Pharisees are so short-sighted. They simply can't see that Jesus has fulfilled Isaiah's prophecy that when the Messiah comes he will open the eyes of the blind (Isaiah 29:18). The Pharisees are so immersed in the Law that they cannot recognise the reality of what has happened. They have missed the Spirit at work amongst them. This does not deter the man from praising God and witnessing to Jesus. It's vital that we open our eyes and witness to the astonishing ways that God is at work in his world every day.

† *Lord, keep my eyes open to the astonishing things you are doing.*

March

2 The Good Shepherd

Notes by John Holder
based on the New Revised Standard Version

John Holder was born in Barbados and for several years was Deputy Principal of Codrington College, the Anglican theological college for the province of the West Indies. He is now Anglican Bishop of Barbados, and is married with one son.

Introduction

The shepherd is a great Hebrew image of just, compassionate leadership, used both of God and of human leaders. The shepherd is the one who leads by anticipating the needs of the flock, providing for them, guiding them and protecting them. The shepherd knows the sheep and is dedicated to their welfare. The true disciple recognises the voice of the shepherd, whose words are life-giving for the sheep. Shepherding requires devotion and courage: the shepherd hazards his own life to guard the flock from savage predators.

Text for the week: John 10:11

'I am the good shepherd. The good shepherd lays down his life for the sheep.'

For group discussion and personal thought

- For whom do you need to be a good shepherd? What shepherding qualities do you need in order to care for that person or group?
- Many people now live in an urban environment and have never seen a shepherd at work. Do you think the picture of the Good Shepherd still has meaning for them – or is there an image from the city streets that could convey the same meaning of care and protection and be part of their experience?

The Lord is my shepherd

One of the most powerful images used in the Bible to describe, and indeed to explain, God's relationship with us is that of the shepherd. Psalm 23, known and loved by millions of Christians and Jews, captures this image better than most other biblical passages; it speaks of God's care, guidance and support in a way we can readily embrace. God here is like the shepherd who looks after the needs of his sheep. The psalm begins with a statement of sufficiency: 'The Lord is my shepherd, I shall not want' (verse 1). Not that every physical need is met, but the comprehensive and all-embracing love of God leaves no areas of our life exposed and uncovered. The shepherd never becomes detached from his sheep. This conviction about God produces great assurance:

> **Even though I walk through the darkest valley,**
> **I fear no evil;**
> **for you are with me;**
> **your rod and your staff –**
> **they comfort me.**
>
> (*verse 4*)

For the psalmist, nothing in life can prevent him experiencing the love and care of God. The trials and tribulations of life are not evidence that God no longer cares. Indeed, God's care is experienced even in the face of the enemy (verse 5). We can therefore be assured of God's love not only in the present but also as hope for the future. There will be no time when God is not in touch and in tune; his 'goodness and mercy shall follow me all the days of my life' (verse 6).

Take another look at Psalm 23; pray it today. For you too it can be a source of great assurance and hope.

† *O God, give us the hope and assurance of the psalmist.*

John 10:1-6

The shepherd's voice

[T]he sheep follow him because they know his voice.

(part of verse 4)

As the writer of Psalm 23 uses the image of the shepherd to describe his relationship with God, so John's gospel uses the same powerful elements to describe the relationship between Jesus and the Christian: care, support, hope, love, assurance, guidance and protection. The shepherd is a caring and trusted leader. He does not engage in short cuts in his work, but follows the correct path. He enters by the gate, not by the illegitimate way. As seen in the shepherd, leadership involves a large measure of trust, reflected in the sheep's response to his voice. The voice of the shepherd is the voice of assurance and safety. It separates the genuine leader from the imposters (verse 5). The voice is not just a sound: it indicates the way of safety and salvation. Both voice and gate are symbols of salvation:

> **I am the gate. Whoever enters by me will be saved, and will come in and go out and find pasture.**

(*verse 9*)

Jesus as our shepherd is *the* Good Shepherd. Jesus does not simply give us a purely 'spiritual' understanding of leadership; he gives us the best model of a godly life that others will want to follow. Such a life embraces all the essential and critical elements that help us to experience and understand the goodness, care and love of God. Each of us, in our own way, should be the good shepherd for someone. Be the best model of godly living for someone who may need this guidance and support in their life at this time.

† *Help me O Lord, to be the best example, to be more like the Good Shepherd each day.*

The attentive disciple

This section of the book of Isaiah is one of the collection of poems in Isaiah 40-55 that we call the 'Servant Songs'. They tell of a special servant of God who has been sent on a mission but is subjected to inhuman treatment and eventually killed. The servant is the model of discipleship. He is a great listener and so is also a great teacher. He is portrayed as one who is always ready to listen and learn:

> **The Lord GOD has opened my ear**
> **and I was not rebellious,**
> **I did not turn backward.**
>
> (*verse 5*)

This devotion to learning and to duty enables the servant to withstand the assaults inflicted upon him (verse 6). He shows that discipleship can include suffering and rejection. Like a shepherd, he has a leadership role, to provide the best example of commitment to a given task and acceptance of the consequences. The servant displays a strong message of hope, not unlike that of the psalmist. He is sure that God will help him in the face of his adversaries (verse 7). God is still with his servant in spite of all his negative experiences. Holding on to God is the midst of pain and rejection is never easy. We all find it easier to relate to God through good and pleasant experiences. The challenge that we all face is to be like the servant and never let go of our faith in God, even when our experience makes him seem absent. Like the servant, we can believe that God never forsakes us whatever our experience in this life.

† *O God, give us the grace to see you at work in our lives even when everything seems to suggest that you are absent.*

John 6:58-69

Words of eternal life

The Bible tells us that words – especially spoken words – have power. God speaks and creation comes into being; the prophets speak words from God that can bring salvation or judgement. This understanding of the word of God is also present in the ministry of Jesus. His words have power. They heal, they bring life where there is death, they transform rejection into affirmation. The words of Jesus are words of life.

They are also words of eternal life. They have power to support us in this world, and indeed transform the world, but also power to lead us to eternal life. This is a major concern of St John's Gospel. In 6:66-69 there had been a negative reaction to the words of Jesus. The words of salvation had been rejected. There had been a walk out and a walk away. Would the disciples follow them and leave? Jesus asks them directly (verse 67) and Peter replies on their behalf:

> **'Lord, to whom can we go? You have the words of eternal life.'**
>
> (*part of verse 68*)

In the teaching of Jesus, eternal life means far more than life beyond death. It is an experience of God that guides and sustains us in this life and gives us hope for the life to come. As followers of Jesus, we have to share this great experience of eternal life with other people, not simply by word but also by deed. When is the last time you were such an experience for someone? Be an experience of eternal life for someone today.

† O God, in Jesus our Lord you have shown us what it means to live belief in eternal life. Give us the grace to do so each day.

1 Samuel 17:31-40

The shepherd's courage

The Old Testament has some very endearing images of David. In today's reading he is the brave young shepherd who is prepared to risk his life in order to save his people, although he has no training in this area. He is only a shepherd. But God had protected him as a shepherd, and will protect him now:

> **'The LORD, who saved me from the paw of the lion and from the paw of the bear, will save me from the hand of this Philistine.'**
>
> (*part of verse 37*)

It is an act of faith. But journeying with God demands taking many steps in faith. Sometimes it can demand moving out of our comfort zone and doing something courageous. The shepherd is the one who stands between the sheep and the wolves. We encounter many Goliath-type experiences in life. Some challenges are outside our control, but many others we can address if only we can find the courage. David saw the challenge of Goliath as the latter type and his faith enabled him to tackle it with courage. Are you facing that kind of challenge? Could you tackle it if only you had the courage? Why not ask God for the faith you need? Many of your challenges may seem like Goliath, but with the grace of God we can, like David the shepherd, conquer many of the things that seem impossible. God's grace is always sufficient for us.

† *Lord, give us the courage to face the many challenges of life.*

John 10:10-15

Laying down his life for the sheep

In our thinking this week about the Good Shepherd we have seen that he is someone who cares, whose voice can be trusted as a call to salvation. He is not only a leader but a learner, and he is full of courage, prepared to protect his sheep from the destructive experiences symbolised by the wolf.

Today's reading adds another great quality: the shepherd is prepared to sacrifice his life for his sheep, an idea that makes most of us feel very uncomfortable. But the Christian faith is founded on one who did exactly this: Jesus was prepared to sacrifice his life to help us to understand the depth of God's love and compassion.

> **'I am the good shepherd. The good shepherd lays down his life for the sheep.'**
>
> (*verse 11*)

Death is a sacrifice made in order to make life better for the sheep, the culmination of a costly commitment. We all long for this type of commitment, but it may include sacrifice, and today sacrifice is not a popular word. It is, however, a word that the Christian must not allow to disappear. Without the element of sacrifice, with its emphasis on giving rather than receiving, life can be no more than a struggle for money and position; compassion and love disappear. Jesus the Good Shepherd challenges his followers never to forget that we are called to give, and give without counting the cost.

† *O God, strengthen in us the spirit of sacrifice and your grace to give without counting the cost.*

3 The Way

Notes by Sister Christopher Godden OSB
based on the New International Version

Having decided not to become a teacher, Sr Christopher worked for 13 years in the supply industry, during the advent of computers. In 1982 she sold her house, bicycle, canoe and cat and entered the Benedictine Monastery at Talacre in North Wales. Shortly after her Final Profession she moved with the Community to Chester where she does her best to live according to the Rule of St Benedict and grow nearer to God.

Introduction

The Bible is a book of journeys. In Lent we travel from the desert to Golgotha and beyond. This week's readings cover Jesus' deliberate journey from a place beyond the Jordan (John 10:40) to Jerusalem and the upper room. Jesus faces the fact that he is walking into a volatile and difficult situation. By his choices, actions and words Jesus shows his disciples and us not only the Way but also how to face and live it.

Text for the week: Psalm 84:12

O Lord Almighty, blessed is the man who trusts in you.

For group discussion and personal thought

- Why do you think the Bible is called a book of journeys? What sort of journeys are included within it?
- Is it best to wait for guidance or plunge in, trusting when the way ahead is not clear?
- How do the 'I AM' sayings in St John's Gospel compare with the Synoptic parables?
- On bad days, how do you find a way to live both the spiritual and physical journey of life?

John 14:4-7

Back to the future

'You know the way . . . ' Thomas said to him . . . '[H]ow can we know the way?' Jesus answered, 'I am the way.'

(*part of verses 4, 5 and 6*)

The Ancient Greeks saw the future as something that came upon them from behind their backs, with the past receding before their eyes. Jesus' reply to Thomas' question, however, points him straight back to his Jewish roots: to Moses and the Exodus, the Covenant and the Decalogue and, most of all, to God who revealed himself to Moses as 'I AM WHO I AM'. This is an odd thing to say – like saying that God is the way to God. And yet that is *just* what it is. Outside ourselves we have the Decalogue (Exodus 20:1-17) and the Golden Rule (John 13:34-35) to live by. Meanwhile, within each of us there is, if only we listen, 'a voice behind you, saying "This is the way; walk in it"' (Isaiah 30:21). By telling Thomas (and the Apostles) to look back to their Jewish heritage, Jesus shows them that they do know the way ahead even if they do not know the destination. It is a question of living out those roots. In times of difficulty we may look back and get comfort and confidence from our Christian roots to walk the situations and circumstances we face. As Mahatma Gandhi observed, 'Jesus called human beings not to a new religion but to a new way of living.'

† *Lord, instruct us and teach us in the way we should go; and counsel and watch over us.* (Based on Psalm 32:8)

Psalm 84

Lift up your voice

'Blessed are those whose strength is in you, who have set their hearts on pilgrimage.

(*verse 5*)

Looking up the word 'pilgrimage', I was fascinated to discover its roots are in the Latin *peregrinus*, meaning 'stranger', from *peregre*, 'abroad'; literally *per* = 'through' and *ager* = 'field/ land'. What a lovely biblical picture this evokes of Jesus and his disciples as they moved throughout the Holy Land. Traditionally Jews were expected to travel to Jerusalem to offer sacrifice in the temple three times a year for the festivals of Passover, Shavuot and Sukkot, bringing produce and offerings from their fields. But with no tarmac roads or motorised transport, just danger from bandits and blistered and sore feet from dusty roads walked in sandals with no socks, it can't always have been a pleasant or easy journey, burdened with their produce as they were. Those who could afford it might have had slaves to do the carrying and a donkey to ride on; for the rest . . . well, look ahead to your glorious destination, look around at the beauty of creation, maybe sing as you walk, and what has been a trudge can suddenly take on a new meaning.

Not all are able, or want, to go on a pilgrimage. But all are pilgrims on the journey of life from the cradle to the grave and beyond. We believe our God, Emmanuel, walks with us through the events of our lives. Do we walk with him?

† *Lord, make known to us the path of life; and fill us with joy in your presence.* (Based on Psalm 16:11)

John 12:27-36

Now

Today's reading contains hints of both the past (verse 34) and the future (verses 27, 31 and 32) but the real emphasis is on the present. Three times Jesus says 'Now' (verses 27 and 31). People are told to live in the present moment:

> **'Walk while you have the light . . . Put your trust in the light while you have it.'**
>
> (*part of verses 35-36*)

They should concentrate on present events so that later they will be able to understand and cope better when things change. Living in the present is easy to write about but not always easy to do. No doubt we all know someone who has a 'chip on the shoulder', who seems to be bogged down by some event in the past they cannot forget. And then there are those who seem to spend much of their time planning for a future that may not even happen. Living with present reality may not always be easy. It can be rather like driving a car or riding a bicycle when there's a need to concentrate on more than one thing at once: the road ahead, vehicles coming up behind, the vehicle itself. But at that moment it is the only place we actually are. Concentrating on Christ, what he said and did when he was with them, would prepare the disciples for difficult times ahead.

† *Lord, we pray today for those living in darkness and in the shadow of death. Guide their feet into the path of peace.* (Based on The Benedictus, Luke 1:79)

If

The LORD will keep you from all harm –
he will watch over your life . . .
both now and for evermore.

(verse 7 and part of verse 8)

Throughout the Old Testament there are instances of the people's unfaithfulness to Yahweh their God. They built altars to other gods and erected pillars and sacrificial poles on the 'high places', the hilltops. The author of today's psalm looks at the hills and recognises his help comes not from foreign or false gods but from Yahweh the true and only God, he who made the hills and all there is, who watches over all, and is protector of all who love him. This psalm reminds me of a Celtic blessing in the way it weaves in and throughout all the events of a day or a life. Here in the monastery we use it as an itinerary prayer. When one of us must be away overnight we recite it together in chapel before they depart so that our absent sister may be protected whilst out of the house and return home safely.

Many years ago I discovered the New English Bible translation of this psalm. It begins, '*If* I lift up my eyes . . . '. So much is contained and implied in that 'If': *If* I stop trying to be my own God, *If* I look beyond myself to God, *If* I deliberately choose God, then 'The Lord will watch over [my] going and coming' (verse 8) – always and all ways.

† *Lord, may your word be a lamp to our feet and a light for our path.* (Based on Psalm 119:105)

John 11:7-16

Light into darkness

'A man who walks by day will not stumble . . . It is when he walks by night that he stumbles.'

(*part of verses 9-10*)

There's a marked contrast in today's passage between Jesus' positive and focused attitude and the bewilderment and confusion of the disciples. It's easy to understand why the disciples are so puzzled: having narrowly escaped from danger Jesus now appears to want to walk straight back into it. We know the end of the story and that Jesus is the Light. The disciples have been with him for at least two years, listening to his words and teaching, witnessing to cures and miracles, yet they still do not really understand who he is. To walk back to where you have been threatened with death in order to 'wake up' someone who is dead (why did Jesus say to begin with Lazarus was only asleep?) seems patently absurd by anyone's standards.

Too often when things go well and smoothly we can assume we are walking by the Light, but that's not really the test. It's when things go wrong, when difficulties dissolve into chaos and we can neither think straight or even think at all, that we need somehow to remember to turn to God in trust that he does, can and will bring light into and out of darkness. He did it for Thomas – so why not for us?

† *Teach us your way, 0 Lord, and we will walk in your truth; give us an undivided heart so we may fear your name.* (Based on Psalm 86:11)

A rash promise

Peter asked, 'Lord, why can't I follow you now ? I will lay down my life for you.'

(*verse 37*)

'Think' and 'Don't make rash promises' are a couple of phrases I remember being told often when I was young. (Half a century later and I am still working at achieving them both.) The portrait of Jesus painted in St John's Gospel is of a man completely in control of himself (cf. James 3:2-12) and his life. This mastery of self and tongue does not come easily to anyone, so we can sympathise with Peter when, in a moment of incautious enthusiasm, he makes his declaration to lay down his life for Jesus. After all, isn't that what Jesus means when he says 'Love one another' (verse 34)?

In fact it is not. The disciples are charged with providing an example by their love for each other for all to witness, but as individuals they are to look at Jesus and try and model themselves and their lives on his. To become a disciple of Jesus needs thought and commitment, as Matthew 10:37-38, Luke 14:25-35, Matthew 8:19-22 and Luke 9:57-62 teach us. 'Be prepared' as Baden-Powell, the founder of the Scout movement, put it. No one knows what the future holds.

Poor Peter, he still had lessons to learn. But he did not lose heart and later, as tradition has it, his wish was fulfilled.

† *Teach us your way, O Lord; and lead us in a straight path.* (Based on Psalm 27:11)

4 Life that is stronger than death

Notes by Kate Hughes
based on the New Revised Standard Version

Kate worked for the church in Southern Africa for 14 years. Returning to England in 1990, she is now a freelance book editor, and is also active in her local church and community. She is currently editor of *Light for our Path.*

Introduction

Last week we looked at Jesus as 'The Way'. The 'Way' of Jesus leads through life and death to a life beyond our imagination. He gives us access to the life, love, grace and truth of God, a power beyond our comprehension. We trust in this power for our ultimate safety. Lazarus is raised as a sign that we can all be raised. Nevertheless, there is no 'short cut' to this life. Jesus goes before us on a narrowing way. Just as the seed 'dies' in the earth and a woman risks death in the pain and danger of childbirth, so the disciple must face death in various forms – in self-denial, adversity, persecution, even martyrdom – before reaching the place of light and peace prepared for us.

Text for the week: John 11:25

'I am the resurrection and the life. Those who believe in me, even though they die, will live.'

For group discussion and personal thought

- The pattern of salvation, death followed by resurrection, darkness followed by light, is also a pattern in human life. The power and life which God in Christ makes available to us enables us to live in hope through the times of death and darkness. Can you discern this pattern in your own life? And how can you share this understanding with others, so that they too can have hope?

Life beyond our understanding

The God figure in C S Lewis's Narnia stories is represented by a lion, Aslan. At one point it is said of Aslan that he 'is not a tame lion'. God reminds Job of this fact in today's reading. We may be able to talk to God as to a friend, to question and grumble at him like Job, to ask him for gifts, expect him to share our human joys and sorrows, and repeatedly forgive us when we are disobedient. But there is far, far more to God than that. Far more than our human minds can grasp, understand or even imagine. We cannot tame him and keep him in a cage. And death is getting closer to the unimaginable vastness that is God.

> **'Where were you when I laid the foundation of the earth?. . .**
> **who laid its cornerstone**
> **when the morning stars sang together**
> **and all the heavenly beings shouted for joy?**
>
> (*part of verses 4 and 6, and verse 7*)

The way that Jesus leads us in this world ends up at death. But death is not entry into a small, dark coffin, or destruction in a fire. It is a door that opens out into the vastness of God, the light and space and glory of God as he is, that is beyond our imagining.

† *Lord, help me to follow your way so that at the last you may bring me into the glory that is God.*

John 6:15-23

Power beyond comprehension

Our human relationship with the natural world is very much in the news these days. The relationship seems, in many respects, to have broken down beyond repair. It sometimes seems almost as if the natural world is taking revenge for centuries of neglect, ill treatment and exploitation by inflicting earthquakes, hurricanes, floods, drought and other disasters on its human tormentors. But this is not how it was meant to be. The picture of creation given in the opening chapters of Genesis is very different. There, God is the Creator, and his creation is 'very good'. Human beings are given their place in the world, to benefit from it but not to misuse it; to act as God's deputies in his creation. The partnership of God, the created world and human beings is how it was in the beginning, and part of God's redemption of the world is the restoration of this original relationship: 'the creation itself will be set free from its bondage to decay and will obtain the freedom of the glory of the children of God' (Romans 8:21). In today's reading Jesus shows us what this relationship should be like, and the power that human beings can have when they work *with* God and creation. Human beings and creation alike need this resurrection life.

The sea became rough because a strong wind was blowing . . . they saw Jesus walking on the sea and coming near the boat.

(*verse 18 and part of verse 19*)

† *O Lord, the life you bring us in abundance springs from a power that we can only guess at, but which you long to share with us. Work with this power in our lives.*

John 11:17-27

Resurrection life

Jewish thinking on the Resurrection at the period in which Jesus lived had been greatly influenced by the experience of the occupation of Palestine, first under the Greeks and then under the Romans. Resurrection was seen as something happening at the end of history, when the suffering and persecuted would get their revenge. Those who had ill-treated them would be punished, the kingdom of Israel would be restored, and the Jews would come out on top. When Jesus speaks about the resurrection, he is not referring to something that will happen in the distant future. 'I *am* the resurrection', not 'I *will be* the resurrection.' The writer of John's gospel stresses that what happens between human beings and God takes place *now*, as well as at the end of time. We are judged *now* by how we respond to God and how we act as his disciples. If we commit ourselves to God revealed in Jesus, we experience resurrection now, we begin to live a risen life which is unshaken by the almost irrelevant experience of physical death.

'I am the resurrection and the life. Those who believe in me, even though they die, will live.'

(*part of verse 25*)

† *Help me to experience your life, that I may also know your resurrection.*

John 12:20-26

The 'death' of the seed

If we experience life and resurrection already, we also experience death already. But not the finality of physical death. Since Good Friday and Easter Day, death is inextricably linked to resurrection. We die over and over again in our earthly life, but we also experience resurrection over and over again. Death can take many forms: suffering, bereavement, loss of every kind (of home, of work, of mental ability, of security), wickedness done to us, and wickedness done by us that diminishes us as human beings. But as Christians we know that death is followed by resurrection. We shall emerge from the dark tomb into the light, changed, renewed, strengthened. Like the seed, we need those periods of darkness in order to emerge into the light of Christ. Like the seed, we need to learn to wait patiently in the dark, expecting resurrection. And this pattern of death followed by resurrection is one of the most valuable things that as Christians we can share with other people; the fruit of our death is strength and hope for others.

> **'Very truly, I tell you, unless a grain of wheat falls into the earth and dies, it remains just a single grain; but if it dies, it bears much fruit.'**
>
> (*verse 24*)

† *Grant, Lord, that through the grave and gate of death we may pass to our joyful resurrection.* (Part of the Collect for Easter Eve).

The 'death' of childbirth

The death and resurrection of Jesus, the pattern of death and resurrection in the lives of his followers, the seed waiting in the ground, and now the pain that accompanies the birth of human life – and the transformation of that pain into joy. Modern Western society does not 'do' pain. We seem to regard a pain-free life as our right, and if we don't get it, someone must be to blame. Perhaps this is the result of making science, instead of God, the driving force in society – a movement which began in Europe in the eighteenth century. Science should be able to solve our problems, do away with them. So at the slightest twinge of a headache we reach for the painkillers. When life seems too daunting, we seek refuge in the temporary oblivion of drugs or alcohol. When we mess up relationships, we seek answers from a psychiatrist. Science can do wonderful things, and medicine has transformed many lives. But so many of life's pains have simply to be undergone, not overcome. And when we are finally through them, their memory is buried in joy that they have gone.

In spite of science, childbirth is still a painful and, for very many women, a dangerous process. It has to be endured. But when the new baby finally makes its appearance, the overwhelming feeling is of joy and relief. The power of the risen Christ can transform our pain into joy.

> **'You have pain now, but I will see you again, and your hearts will rejoice, and no one will take your joy from you.'**
>
> (*verse 22*)

† *Thank you, Lord, that the power of your risen life can transform our pain into the joy of new birth.*

John 14:1-3

Welcome home!

What makes a home a home? For some, home is a particular house or a much-loved landscape. For others, it is the local community, the extended family, a place where you are accepted and loved. Homes can be destroyed by violence or broken up when relationships break down. Some people move around so much that they never have a chance to make a permanent home for themselves. My parents were divorced when I was young and have now both died. My sisters have their own families and homes. I have lived in many different places and my present home is a small bungalow. But my most profound sense of being at home comes when I am with God. It took me a long time to find him (or allow him to find me) and to get to know him as a loving friend; yet, like the father of the prodigal son, God reached out to me, met me on the way and brought me home with joy. I still find it hard to believe my luck!

But so many people are still wandering, homeless and feeling far from God. If our home with God, which begins in this life and continues into eternity, means anything, we must long – and work – for everyone else to share it with us. This is God's salvation, made possible by the death of Jesus: to come home to him for ever.

'[W]here I am, there you may be also.'

(*part of verse 3*)

† *Father of all, we give you thanks and praise, that when we were still far off you met us in your Son and brought us home.* (From the Church of England's *Common Worship*)

5 The beloved

Notes by Paula Fairlie OSB
based on the New Jerusalem Bible and Grail Psalter

Paula is a Benedictine nun and lives in Chester, England.

Introduction

Each one of us is the Beloved of God. The weekly texts indicate how we learn to know the mind of God the Lover. Israel was given a practical demonstration of sheltering love: they abused it and lost it. Jesus taught that true love needs to be pruned. The Song of Songs revealed the awakening desire for the Lover. The crucifixion scene demonstrated total self-giving. The Lover desires that we have the same mind as Christ – but this requires training.

Text for the week: Isaiah 5:7 and 1 Corinthians 2:14

The people of Judah [is] the plant he cherished . . . The natural person has no room for the gifts of God's Spirit.

For group discussion and personal thought

- Do we only learn love through relationships?
- Why do we tend to think that we initiate our relationship with God?
- Would you say that the inequality of love between God and human beings is also true in human love?
- Why are patience and example so important in love?

Isaiah 5:1-7

Love's reversal

[T]he vineyard of Yahweh Sabaoth
is the House of Israel,
the people of Judah
the plant he cherished.
He expected fair judgement,
but found injustice,
uprightness, but found cries of distress.

(*verse 7*)

God loves gardens, vineyards, sheepfolds and cities. Each is carefully walled or hedged or fenced in to keep that which is inside sheltered and safe. The enclosure is a safe area in an unsafe world, a place where God and human beings can meet in friendship. A constant theme in the scriptures is the rejection or abuse of God's sheltering love by his creatures. The parable may speak of the vineyard, or sheep, or a sown field, but it is always human beings who are not fully responding.

My first reaction to these verses was that the poem is not even remotely a 'love song': it is an account of disappointment, judgement and desolation. It is God's desolation, which Christ personified on the cross. God has given us everything: the created world, life, the hope of salvation, relationships and love. Every single thing has been selfishly misused. Throughout the ages he stayed his hand from total destruction, leaving a remnant. He hears cries of distress – even the cries of his only Son. This love only God can give.

† *Dear Lord, help us not to abuse and neglect your gifts, devastating life and love around us.*

Enabling love

I am the true vine,
and my Father is the vinedresser.
Every branch in me that bears no fruit
he cuts away,
and every branch that does bear fruit he prunes
to make it bear even more.

(*verses 1-2*)

Pruning and cleansing share the same root in Hebrew. This simple image of a vine gradually reveals the loving purpose of discipleship. Its 'fruit' is a life of obedience to the commandments of God. Thus God's expectations of 'fair judgement' and 'uprightness' will be fulfilled.

The 'cleansing' word can remind us of baptism and absolution from sin. We are urged to 'remain' in Christ: this is our free choice. How often we pray with the psalmist: 'I am lost like a sheep; seek your servant for I remember your commands' (Psalm 118: 176).

Jesus pleads: 'Remain in me, as I in you' (verse 4); he knows our fickle hearts. It is only the 'sap' of the life and love that flow from him that keep us united with God. We can block this flow. Not acting with mercy, love and justice means that we will either be pruned or cut off: neither is a pleasant prospect.

The most difficult part of the discourse for me used to be the promise: 'You may ask whatever you please and you will get it' (verse 7). Then I understood that the true disciple only wants the glory of God: 'Thy Kingdom come . . .'.

† *'Happy are they who know that discipleship simply means the life which springs from grace'* (Dietrich Bonhoeffer).

Song of Songs 1:1-8

Love longing

This collection of romantic poetry is usually interpreted as an allegory – the loving relationship between God and his people, Christ and the Church – or it is accepted as love poetry.

We do not all experience enduring romantic love in this life, so it is acceptable to regard these songs as the mutual longing between God and the soul for mystical union. In most love songs it is not the consummation which is of interest but the love-longing, the search, the daydreams, and the occasional introspection, the desolation and the desire to be together. Lovers often speak of their passion to others, who give them support and encouragement.

> **Let him kiss me with the kisses of his mouth,**
> **for your love-making is sweeter than wine;**
> **delicate is the fragrance of your perfume,**
> **your name is an oil poured out,**
> **and that is why girls love you.**

(*verse 18 and part of verse 19*)

The sensuousness of these lines refers not only to the kiss of love but also to the wine, perfume and oil of the male lover. Christians will almost inevitably think of Christ when his feet were kissed, and nard (perfumed oil) poured over them by a loving, sinful woman prior to his passion, death and resurrection. The beloved has been exposed to the elements, spurned by her brethren, and yet loves: God's love will perfect us. He is the Lover waiting for his Beloved – you and me.

† Let us respond to Christ, who longs for our love.

John 19:23-27

Love all

Throughout his life Jesus revealed a love that surpasses our understanding. He came not only to share his life with us but to connect us to its source. No single image or event could convey the fullness of his love. During the Last Discourse he revealed the possibility of mutual indwelling between God and us: he promised us the Paraclete, to enlighten our minds. He had indicated sacramental means of communion. The divine gifts had been given. All that remained now was his final stripping of clothing, relationships and life.

For those who pray the Stations of the Cross, the naked vulnerability of Christ is poignant:

> **When the soldiers had finished crucifying Jesus they took his clothing . . .**
>
> (*part of verse 25*)

The soldiers were poor, the clothing a perk. How much more so the seamless undergarment, usually worn by the high priest. The 'casting of lots' could have many nuances: at its best, it was leaving the decision to God.

It is usually women who attend to both birth and death.

> **Seeing his mother and the disciple whom he loved standing near her . . .**
>
> (*part of verse 26*)

They must have been at some distance from the cross for Jesus to see them. Instead of self-pity, he felt sorrow about the coming severing of relationships. Mary and John were bonded. Mary is now the spiritual mother of all the faithful. Jesus cared for the soldiers, cared for his disciples, for the faithful and the false. For us.

† *Make our hearts a home for others.*

John 12:1-8

Empty enough to fill

Lazarus' tomb was emptied: the house was filled with guests. Hearts were filled with gratitude. Some other token of love was called for, beyond cooking and serving.

> **Mary brought in a pound of very costly ointment . . . and with it anointed the feet of Jesus . . . the house was filled with the scent.**
>
> (*parts of verse 3*)

In a demeaning description of Judas Iscariot, we are told that he was filled with greed for money. Had this emptied his soul of love? He resented 'waste', heedless prodigality, and to disguise his true desire mentioned 'the poor'.

What has happened to prevent us recognising the divine gifts lavished upon us? Are we tainted by materialism, too, so that only material gifts will convey the scent of intangible love?

> **'You have the poor with you always, you will not always have me.'**
>
> (*verse 8*)

These are not easy verses to comment on. We know, in faith, that the whole earth is filled with the 'fullness of God'. Yet our hearts are often empty, and poverty abounds – both materially and spiritually. Love abounds, yet we are dissatisfied (*satis*: to have enough). God laments, 'What more could I have done for you?' It is now our task to deal justly and listen to the cries of the poor. But none of this has value without love.

† *Where love and loving-kindness are, the God of love will always be . . . Please God, may we give and receive in love.*

The pearl of great price

The Emperor Theodosius said that he found his wife 'like a pearl in the gutter'. The prophet Hosea wrote that God found Israel like an abandoned newborn child in the wilderness. How did God find us? He found us as 'natural persons . . . who cannot recognise the gifts of God's Spirit' (see verse 14). So God, in Paul, could not speak to his people as spiritual persons:

> **I had to talk to you as people still living by your natural inclinations, still infants in Christ.'**
>
> (*part of chapter 3, verse 1*)

We were not discovered like 'a pearl of great price': we have to become people who have the mind of Christ. Only the Spirit can assess our value, nobody else can. I find this incomprehensible. Does it tie in with not judging anyone? Does it mean simply living in the loving presence of God, as Christ did?

While we are living according to our own 'natural inclinations . . . among jealousy and rivalry', we are 'still infants' (see 3:1, 3). Our spiritual development very rarely coincides with our intellectual development; neither does our emotional development. The skilled spiritual teacher requires great patience. We need the experience of pruning and of loss. We need to experience the grace of relationships – of acceptance *and* rejection. Love may be 'unconditional' but certain standards need to be maintained. We can learn from the outside in (showing courtesy and respect) as well as from the inside out (feeling compassion and love) before the integration of maturity.

† *Lord, I do not understand. Please teach me.*

Holy Fools

Notes by Kevin Ellis
based on the New International Version

Kevin Ellis is a priest in the Anglican Diocese of Carlisle. He lives in Maryport, on the west coast of Cumbria, with his wife, Jennifer, and son Shaun, as well as two dogs and a cat.

Introduction

At first glance this would seem a strange topic for a week's Bible reading notes. Whilst fools, as well as clowns of all varieties from the whiteface to the auguste, make us smile, we may struggle to see them as holy. This ignores the fact that the role of the fool is not only to make us laugh, but often to point to a deeper reality. Biblical characters and saints alike have often been seen as foolish, when in fact they have just been demonstrating a wisdom that others cannot comprehend. Foolishness from God's perspective is often wise, and the world's wisdom often foolish.

Text for the week: 1 Corinthians 1:21

God was pleased through the foolishness of what was preached to save those who believe.

For group discussion and personal thought

- Have you ever been stopped in your tracks by a holy fool? How did it make you feel? At the time, did you recognise that person as both holy and a fool?
- The old English words holy and fool come from the same root word. What do you think are the common characteristics of holiness and foolishness?

The folly of rejoicing

This is a wonderful passage with which to begin a week of study exploring the theme of 'holy fools'. The ark of God is brought to Jerusalem, and David rejoices in worship before the Lord in what seems to be complete ecstasy. However, it is in this heartfelt worship so freely offered that David finds himself despised (and rejected) by Michal, his wife and the daughter of Saul.

David's response to Michal's criticism of his conduct illuminates both our theme and our understanding of worship:

> **'It was before the LORD, who chose me rather than your father or anyone from his house when he appointed me ruler over the LORD's people Israel – I will celebrate before the LORD. I will become even more undignified than this, and I will be humiliated in my own eyes. But by these slave girls you spoke of, I will be held in honour.'**
>
> (*verses 21-22*)

Fools, even holy ones, are indeed held from time to time to be contemptible. They do not fit in with the order of things. Indeed, you might say that they are slightly chaotic. A fool is not a clown who might poke fun without purpose: rather the holy fool stops us in our tracks and asks us questions that we might prefer not to answer. In the case of this passage, the question is: what part of yourself would you not offer to God in worship? For many, the offering of our whole selves seems to be complete folly.

† *Holy God, help us to worship you in spirit and truth, regardless of what it might cost us in terms of resources and reputation. Amen.*

Hosea 3

The folly of faithfulness

Jesters in the courts of kings have rightly been described as having a rather similar function to the prophets of Israel. Both prophets and jesters were allowed to say and do things that others would not dream of doing. They are called to behave in such a way because they are pointing beyond their words and actions to a deeper truth. The prophet always calls people – faithful and unfaithful – back to God's perspective.

At the beginning of Hosea, the prophet had been commanded to take a faithless woman as his wife. If this act of folly was not enough, the prophet is told again:

> **Go, show your love to your wife again, though she is loved by another and is an adulteress. Love her as the LORD loves the Israelites, though they turn to other gods and love the sacred raisin-cakes.**

(*verse 1*)

We can imagine what the reaction of those around Hosea would have been to his actions. I myself think they would not have been kind. However, the prophet's action points to the fact that God is faithful to each one of us. I wonder whether God's faithfulness to us is sometimes foolish. As I look back on my own journey, it occasionally seems as if it is.

† *Holy God, remind us again of your faithfulness even when we are unfaithful. Help me to be faithful today, even if it does appear foolish. Amen.*

Jeremiah 32:6-15

The folly of hope

Picking up on the theme of jesters and prophets having things in common, I am reminded of the story of an English jester who was banished by the King of England and told not to set foot on English soil again. Three months later, the jester reappeared in the court. When the king reminded him of his command that he not set foot on English soil again, the jester simply smiled and took off his shoes, which contained soil – French soil – for him to walk on. An amusing tale which points to the truth that fools can often get away with saying and doing things that others cannot.

You would not usually compare the prophet Jeremiah to a jester or a fool – he seems far too serious for that; and yet in today's passage he purchases a field and places the deeds of sale in a clay jar. It is not the field or the jar that is important, but rather what the action points to.

> **Take these documents, both the sealed and unsealed copies of the deed of purchase, and put them in a clay jar so they will last a long time.**
>
> (*part of verse 14*)

Jeremiah's actions were to be a sign of hope to Israel that the owning of property would be worthwhile once again, even with the impending threat of exile. The prophet's actions are the same as those of the holy fool, who often takes the ordinary and make it beautiful. For the fool, treasure is always found in earthen vessels – or clay jars.

† *Holy God, grant me the ability to hope beyond all expectations today, and to see beauty in the ordinary and mundane. Amen.*

Luke 20:9-17

The folly of trust

In this story, who is demonstrating folly by trusting? Jesus told this parable in the last week of his earthly life, in the midst of heightened tension between himself and his opponents. In the parable the one who trusts is the owner of the vineyard, and by implication God is the one who trusts the most.

> **Then the owner of the vineyard said, 'What shall I do? I will send my son, whom I love; perhaps they will respect him.'**
>
> (*verse 13*)

It seems impossible to think of God demonstrating folly, because we would not easily want to compare God with foolishness. Yet God's boundless love for humankind can appear just that.

We have already discovered, however, that one thing we need to know about holy fools is that what appears foolish often deserves a second look, and when glanced at again can suddenly appear totally different. Treasure, for example, can be found in earthen vessels and crosses can be seen as thrones. For just as the fool's ways do not seem to fit with those who claim to be wise, neither are God's ways quite like ours – especially when it comes to showering love on those who walk away from it.

† *Holy God, give us the opportunity to demonstrate your boundless, and seemingly foolish, love to someone today. Amen.*

1 Corinthians 1:17-25

The folly of God

Myskin is a character in Dostoevsky's novel, *The Idiot*. He is an outsider, a fool, who also happens to be a royal prince. At one point in the novel, it is observed that Myskin sees and appreciates things that others do not. Someone – Myskin - who seems foolish in the context of the novel is anything but. In a sense it makes him slightly less comfortable: the fool cannot be shut up in a box.

The Christian gospel also cannot be boxed. It is both rational (wise) and irrational (foolish). It makes the sweetest of sense, and yet appears totally absurd.

> **For since in the wisdom of God the world through its wisdom did not know him, God was pleased through the foolishness of what was preached to save those who believe . . . For the foolishness of God is wiser than man's wisdom, and the weakness of God is stronger than man's strength.**
>
> (*verses 21 and 25*)

God cannot be boxed either. It is this that makes God uncomfortable for many. God cannot be fully understood. For this reason, some consider faith to be foolish. But just as the holy fool works on a different level to most other people in order to demonstrate truth in surprising situations, God also works on a different level in order to give us a different way of being and living.

† *Holy God, reveal yourself in us to others today, even if it means we might appear foolish. Amen.*

1 Corinthians 1:26-31

The fruits of God's foolishness

The events of Palm Sunday might be described as clown-like. Think of the images that spring to mind. The king of all creation rides into the holy city on a donkey. At the end of Holy Week, God-made-human makes a cross his throne. Fools are dismissed at our peril, for what seems foolish can sometimes be the wisest thing in the world. Isn't this true of donkeys and crosses in this instance?

Paul, in this section of his letter to the Corinthians, reminds his hearers that they were not special by the world's standards. Indeed, for them as for us, the most significant thing about us is the calling of God on our lives.

> **But God chose the foolish things of the world to shame the wise; God chose the weak things of the world to shame the strong . . . It is because of him that you are in Christ Jesus.**
>
> (*verse 27, and part of verse 30*)

That God's foolishness is in fact holy should not surprise us. The old English word for foolish comes from the same root as the old English word for holy. Those who were in Christ before us understood more than we do that the holy fool is not a misnomer; rather, she or he is someone dependent on God. Indeed, the laughter of the fool masks a seriousness that takes us into the presence of God; a God who loves us so much that he became human for us. Isn't that a very foolishly wise idea?

† *Holy God, help your Church to be filled as we approach Holy Week with such foolishness that others get a glimpse of the wisdom of God. Amen.*

1 To the cross and beyond

Notes by Pedro Vieira Veiga
based on the New International Version

Pedro Vieira Veiga is a young pastor who lives with his family in Rio de Janeiro. He works at an independent Christian church in the neighbourhood of Ipanema, though his main responsibility lies with a small group from the nearby town of Petrópolis. He is also a psychology and theology student.

Introduction

During Holy Week, the Church recalls the most important events in its history. As the years go by, however, these events may seem to be less and less important to us. Yet if we pay even slight attention to them, their impact can shatter our routine religion. The Last Supper, the vigil at Gethsemane, Peter's denials, the choice of Pilate, the Crucifixion, the Resurrection – how meaningful these events are! May we meditate on them this week in the hope that we too may be completely transformed by them.

Text for the week: Mark 16:6

'Don't be alarmed,' he said. 'You are looking for Jesus the Nazarene, who was crucified. He has risen! He is not here. See the place where they laid him.'

For group discussion and personal thought

- How did Jesus feel in those days that led up to his death? What made him go on? What gave him strength?
- Christ's death can only be understood through his life, as his life can only be understood through his death. What are the risks of valuing one of them, while neglecting the other?

Mark 14:10-25

True communion

Holy Week begins for us as it did for Jesus: with a meal. Just as they are today, back in his time meals were moments of great importance, symbols of festivity and communion. Sharing a meal with someone meant that you had a close relationship with each other. But how could he remain so close to someone he expected to betray him?

> **'It is one of the Twelve,' he replied, 'one who dips bread into the bowl with me.'**
>
> (*verse 20*)

It's really difficult to understand why a friend might deceive or betray us. None of us, however, is safe from the breaking of bonds. But what Jesus shows us in this passage is that the most important thing is not betraying *yourself* – after all, he could have used that supper to prevent Judas from betraying him. But in doing so he would have given up what was most essential to him: his unconditional and forgiving love.

It may be really difficult for us to overcome resentment and forgive, but this is the essence of true communion. It is only because Jesus shared everything with those who loved him and those who did not, that his sacrifice was unlike any other. It is only because of his attitude of absolute indiscrimination that today we are still called to share his bread and his wine.

† *Dear Father, we ask for your help in learning to love and respect others as we want to be loved and respected. May this change begin in each one of us, so that many others may come to learn of your love. Amen.*

Steadfastness

Choosing to go your own way, no matter what everyone around you says, is really hard to do. Even for the disciples, who had been with Jesus for three whole years, it was a heavy task.

> **'Watch and pray so that you will not fall into temptation. The spirit is willing, but the body is weak.'**
>
> (*verse 38*)

Judas did not betray Christ because he wanted money, but because he gave up resisting the pull of the world. Jesus told him that the kingdom would come in peace and completely transform the world, but Judas could only think in terms of war and conquest. And so he betrayed him.

Jesus himself faced this same challenge, and even for him it wasn't easy. But how did he manage to succeed? Why didn't he give himself away, or flee like the others? Jesus managed to hold on to his beliefs because he realised he was not alone. These were not merely *his* beliefs, but the path God had chosen for him – and because of that, he knew he would not be alone. This is indeed a strong reminder to us all. Remaining steadfast is a much easier task when we too give room to 'what he will'.

† *God, this day I make Jesus' prayer my own: 'Everything is possible for you. Take this cup from me. Yet not what I will, but what you will.' I need you by my side. Amen.*

Mark 14:53-72

Repentence

Peter had a strong character. He had sworn he would never betray his master or leave his side, but Jesus knew better than that, and loved him all the same.

> **Immediately the cock crowed the second time. Then Peter remembered the word Jesus had spoken to him: 'Before the cock crows twice you will disown me three times.' And he broke down and wept.**
>
> (*verse 72*)

How many times have we sworn not to do something, or promised to be or do some other thing, only to break our own word in the end? Countless times we have believed ourselves strong enough to keep from falling, and have suffered later on. All of us are familiar with that kind of feeling, and in such moments we can feel as if we will never get back on our feet.

Peter may have thought that he had lost Jesus' love for good, but the scriptures show us that if he did, he was completely wrong. This event may have been a very important and positive turning point in Peter's life. The feeling that overcame him then caused a change of attitude that transformed him into one of the greatest preachers in history. God has the power to turn wrong into right, evil into an even greater good. Our part is to repent and to go back to his ways.

† *Lord, I know I have gone astray but I want your forgiveness and love. Make me anew. And may I always come to you for strength. Amen.*

Mark 15:1-24

Decisions

The decisions we make define who we are. Whether we recognise it or not, we often find ourselves wanting to avoid paying the price for a particular choice. Yet there are many occasions in which this is not an option.

> **'What shall I do, then, with the one you call the king of the Jews?' Pilate asked them. 'Crucify him!' they shouted. 'Why? What crime has he committed?' asked Pilate. But they shouted all the louder, 'Crucify him!' Wanting to satisfy the crowd, Pilate released Barabbas to them.**
>
> (*verses 12-14 and part of verse 15*)

The gospel of Mark presents Pilate not as an evil man, but as one troubled by a decision he does not want to make. He knew that Jesus was not a menace to him – he had no political aspirations. But he realised that the chief priests and elders of Jerusalem did not feel the same way: they wanted to use him to get rid of Jesus. What Pilate did then was simple: he assessed the situation and made a decision based not on what he judged right, but on what favoured him more.

When we are in the position of having to decide about something, we usually make sure we can favour both our consciences and our particular interests – which means we normally only walk into *easy* decisions. It is when we are forced to make up our minds that we really learn what we are made of. And when that happens, more often than not we face the need to grow.

† *Lord, help us face the challenges you present us with, knowing that through them we will come closer to you.*

Mark 15:25-47

Silence

There are moments in our lives when we cannot help feeling utterly alone. While he was being nailed to the cross, Jesus certainly felt that way – and even the Father began to seem far away.

> **At the sixth hour darkness came over the whole land until the ninth hour. And at the ninth hour Jesus cried out in a loud voice. . . 'My God, my God, why have you forsaken me?'**
>
> (*verse 33 and part of verse 34*)

Suffering is part of life. No matter how well we shield ourselves from it, in some unexpected way it always manages to reach us. That is why living a good and joyful life does not imply that we remain untouched by suffering. Living life fully means being able to mourn, to feel pain when necessary – but never to lose hope.

Most of us will never have to endure the physical or emotional pain that Jesus had to go through that afternoon. But our pain troubles us nevertheless, making us feel – at times – completely alone. Yet even in our darkest moments, if we can hold on to hope, all is not lost.

How aware was Jesus of his coming resurrection? Scripture is not clear on this point. To me, it seems that, just as we do, he had to struggle to keep on hoping – and his success brought hope to the whole world! Every time we face the silence and manage to hold on, we do the same.

† *Dear Father, I thank you for the courage and selflessness of your Son. May I always remember that suffering and joy are both important parts of life. Thank you for your love. Amen.*

April

Freedom

Can you imagine what those women felt that morning? The sun was rising . . . The stone was moved . . The body was gone . . . He is alive! He has risen!

> **But when they looked up, they saw that the stone, which was very large, had been rolled away. As they entered the tomb, they saw a young man . . . 'Don't be alarmed,' he said. 'You are looking for Jesus the Nazarene, who was crucified. He has risen!'**
>
> (*verse 4 and part of verses 5 and 6*)

To receive good news is always a pleasure. But to receive excellent news when all hope is lost, when it is absolutely unexpected, is an incredible experience. Today, across the globe, the church of Christ recalls the experience of those women, and listens to its echoes that reach out through time. And so we are reminded that death is not the end, but a new beginning. Just as Christ did before us, we shall all one day rise to a new life and a transformed world, a world with no pain or injustice, a world of love and joy.

On the other hand, Easter Sunday must also remind us that while this world lasts, we are not to sit and wait for its transformation, but must, like Jesus, work towards change – no matter the cost.

† *Dear God, we thank you for the Good News that came to us through Christ. May I never forget that just as his Resurrection announces my own, so must his determination not to let things remain as they are. May your name for ever be praised. Amen.*

2 The good news of Jesus Christ

Notes by Robert Draycott
based on the New Revised Standard Version

Robert Draycott is a Baptist minister who has had a varied ministry over thirty years, firstly as minister of a church in Northamptonshire, England, then as a lecturer in Theological Education in Brazil, before returning to Britain to be Chaplain of Eltham College in London.

Introduction

Mark is generally agreed to be the first to write a gospel. He was a trail-blazer, followed by the other three gospel writers. As a pioneer he faced a challenge: simply put, how to tell the story of Jesus when those who would hear this gospel read aloud to them already knew the ending. In other words, he was writing for those who already knew Jesus through faith, those who believed he was the Risen Lord. Thus Mark begins his gospel very boldly, with a clear declaration of who Jesus is and this is our text for the week.

Text for the week: Mark 1:1

The beginning of the good news of Jesus Christ, the Son of God.

For group discussion and personal thought

- Does the call of Jesus still come to us with force and challenge?
- Are we the sort of people through whom Jesus can exert his attraction today?
- Is there anything paralysing you?

Follow me

The Christians for whom Mark was writing faced the same problems that Christians face today. On the one hand they have faith in Jesus Christ as Saviour and Lord, yet there is also the puzzling challenge of why he was not recognised as such, why Jesus died on a cross. Non-Christians could say to us, 'You say that Jesus was the Son of God, but you also say he was crucified. That doesn't make sense, surely you wouldn't end up being crucified if you were God's Son?' Mark's answer is to tell the story of Jesus. He does it dramatically, urgently, and in a way that captures our imagination. The next episode after his baptism and time in the wilderness shows this clearly:

> **As Jesus passed along the Sea of Galilee, he saw Simon and his brother Andrew casting a net into the lake – for they were fishermen. And Jesus said to them, 'Follow me and I will make you fish for people.' And immediately they left their nets and followed him.**
>
> (*verses 16-18*)

In these few words our imagination is captured, we can picture ourselves there, and we feel the sense of urgency conveyed by one of Mark's favourite words, 'immediately'. The call of Jesus is personal in two senses. Firstly, it is to each one of us as unique individuals. Secondly, it is a call to follow Jesus, wherever he leads us in life.

† *Jesus, help me to hear your call and obey it.*

Mark 1:21-39

Authority to teach and heal

Mark has told us who Jesus is, yet there is also a hiddenness about Jesus who lived his earthly life 2000 years ago. Mark's narrative is vivid and compelling in the way we are introduced to Jesus as he was during his ministry. Having told us that Jesus calls people to follow him, Mark next establishes the authority of Jesus. The setting is the synagogue in Capernaum.

> **'They were astounded at his teaching, for he taught them as one having authority . . . They were all amazed, and they kept on asking one another, 'What is this? A new teaching – with authority! He commands even the unclean spirits, and they obey him.'**
>
> (*part of verse 22, and verse 27*)

One of the secrets of this gospel's attraction is its appeal to the imagination. We can imagine we were there in that synagogue, hearing the shrieks of the man with the unclean spirit, followed by quiet as the man came to himself. Then we can picture the scene as Jesus heals Simon Peter's mother-in-law. The focus is on Jesus, on who he is and his authority to teach and heal, But as we hear or read we find that we are being drawn into discipleship, into following Jesus ourselves.

Think of a magnet with its compelling attraction to metal, and we can begin to understand something of the attraction of this gospel story. Here is one to whom people in need can turn. Here is one who can heal.

† Jesus, draw us to yourself, that we may be your true disciples.

Faith and forgiveness

Two things emerge from today's reading: faith and forgiveness. Faith looks to Jesus and he has the authority to forgive sins. The leper clearly knew his physical need to be made well (verse 40). He trusts Jesus and is made clean. His needs were met and he could not stop talking about what had happened. He told his story. Few of us will have such a dramatic story to tell, but we still have our unique story of what faith means to us. All of us can point away from ourselves to Jesus, the one who met our needs. It is not a question of how much faith we have, but whether the object of our faith is dependable.

When it comes to the story of the paralysed man, we can once more picture ourselves there, listening to Jesus – but then he pauses because something is happening to the roof!

> **Then some people came, bringing to him a paralysed man, carried by four of them . . . When Jesus saw their faith, he said to the paralytic, 'Son, your sins are forgiven'.**
>
> (*verses 3 and 5*)

Notice the tiny detail, 'When Jesus saw *their* faith'. This may or may not include the paralysed man, but there are times in life when we need to be 'carried along' by the faith, care and love of our friends. The leper needed a healthy body; the paralysed man needed forgiveness first. Once that was granted, he got up and walked out. The inner healing worked its way outwards, as it still does for people today. Faith and forgiveness are a basic recipe for healthy living, inwardly and outwardly.

† *Lord, heal me both inwardly and outwardly, as you know I need.*

Mark 2:13-28

Feasting and fasting

> **[T]he scribes of the Pharisees . . . said to his disciples, 'Why does he eat with tax-collectors and sinners?' When Jesus heard this, he said to them, 'Those who are well have no need of a physician, but those who are sick; I have come to call not the righteous but sinners.'**
>
> (*part of verse 16, and verse 17*)

Fasting is a time-honoured religious discipline. Unlike Muslims with their fast in the month of Ramadan, most Christians do not fast as a regular discipline, though they may undertake some form of self-denial during Lent. Fasting is obviously a religious practice to be admired and emulated. Feasting, on the other hand, seems to involve excess and waste as people eat and drink more than they need. It can seem scandalous and frivolous in a world where so many are hungry. Yet celebrating with our friends is a time-honoured practice found in all human cultures.

Jesus is accused of being shallow, frivolous, 'out for a good time' as we might say. No one can take him seriously as a religious leader when he sets such a bad example. Worse still, he mixes with the wrong sort of people, with sinners. He is not to be trusted. His judgement and example are both faulty.

What would people have heard as they listened to the gospel being read aloud soon after it was written? Some of them might have identified with the sinners and recalled how they had been welcomed into the household of faith. Others might have heard and understood that while fasting has its place, so does feasting and celebrating.

† *Thank you, Lord, for welcoming sinners and feasting with them.*

(Note that the next paragraph – and the next reading – begins in the middle of verse 19)

Curing and calling

One main thread runs through Mark's gospel: who is Jesus? The gospel continually points to Jesus. One smaller thread is how people should respond to Jesus. That is the thread of discipleship, of following Jesus. In chapter 3 these threads emerge clearly, beginning with Jesus seeing the man with the withered hand. He cures him but only after confronting those who wanted to accuse him of breaking the Sabbath. As listeners or readers we know that Jesus is 'lord even of the sabbath' – but his enemies do not and they make plans 'to destroy him'. Christians have always been puzzled by the reason for Jesus's crucifixion. Mark gives a little clue here: it was because of who Jesus was and the threat his authority posed in his own day. We live in an age which questions authority and one reason why people reject faith in Jesus is because they understand correctly that he has authority, but do not understand that it is a positive and healthy authority which sets Christians free to find fulfilment as his disciples. Mark tells us how Jesus 'called and appointed twelve'.

> **He went up the mountain and called to him those whom he wanted and they came to him. And he appointed twelve . . . to be with him, and to be sent out to proclaim the message, and to have authority to cast out demons.**
>
> (verse 13, part of verse 14, and verse 15)

They are all named, from Simon to Judas Iscariot 'who betrayed him' (verse 19). Even at this point we see the shadow of the cross.

† *Help me to recognise the authority of Jesus in all my work, rest and play.*

April

Mark 3:19b-35

The stronger man

It has been a great privilege to write these notes. Mark was the first gospel I was introduced to as a child studying for a scripture exam. The memory passage came from chapter 8 and I can still repeat it word for word. It came shortly after the central question in Mark's gospel, when Jesus asks 'And who do you say that I am?' That question still remains a challenge. A series of lectures on Mark was also the highlight of my later theological studies, especially my lecturer's explanation of who the strong man is, and whose house is being plundered. Many years later I met her again and thanked her for opening up the gospel in such an inspiring way. The next day I received the invitation to write about these first three chapters.

> **And the scribes who came down from Jerusalem said, 'He has Beelzebul, and by the ruler of the demons he casts out demons.' And he called them to him and spoke in parables, 'How can Satan cast out Satan? . . . But no-one can enter a strong man's house and plunder his property without first tying the strong man; then indeed the house can be plundered.'**

(*verses 22-23 and 27*)

Because we know that plundering property is wrong, we assume that this refers to the activity of Satan. But it is Jesus who is the Stronger Man who plunders Satan's goods by setting men and women free from Satan's power. This parable points us forward to the crucifixion, but it also describes what the teaching and healing ministry of Jesus was achieving.

† Thank you for all that Jesus was and is as the 'stronger man'.

1 Justice, power and the state

Notes by Tim Brooke
based on the New Revised Standard Version

Tim Brooke has recently retired as an Anglican vicar, having previously been a teacher in Tanzania and a social worker in London. At different times he has been a member of pressure groups working with and on behalf of homeless people, refugees and people with mental health problems. He is acutely aware of how important the state is in improving the lives of its vulnerable citizens but also how easy it is for the state to do just the opposite.

Introduction

The former French President Charles de Gaulle said: 'Politics are too serious a matter to be left to the politicians.' There is much in the Bible to support his view. In particular many parts of the Bible give examples of just and unjust societies. They also give strong indications how we are to behave, whatever type of society we belong to. In other words, our actions are to be focused on God and his will for the world.

Text for the week: Micah 6:8

What does the LORD require of you but to do justice, and to love kindness, and to walk humbly with your God?

For group discussion and personal thought

- Where can we see God at work in the political life of our country?
- Can the Bible show us how to vote in an election?
- Bishop Richard Holloway has said: 'I do not think God has any politics, but it is his light that illuminates all politics.' Is that true?

Isaiah 45:1-7

God acts through unbelievers: Cyrus

God is a God of surprises not least when he gets involved in politics. God does not limit himself to using only Christians to carry on his work in the world.

Over 500 years before Christ, Cyrus the Great was King of Persia (now Iran). The Jewish people had been forced to leave their own country and live in Babylon (now Iraq). Cyrus conquered Babylon, freed the Jews from captivity and allowed them to go back to Judah. In this passage God calls him his 'anointed', his Messiah, the divinely chosen king, the title later given to Jesus.

Thus says the LORD to his anointed, to Cyrus,
whose right hand I have grasped
to subdue nations before him . . .
For the sake of my servant Jacob,
and Israel, my chosen,
I call you by your name,
I surname you, though you do not know me.

(*part of verses 1 and 4*)

If God chooses politicians like Cyrus to do his will, who might he be choosing in our world? Christians should rejoice when they see non-Christians working for justice and peace, combating the adverse effects of global warming, or giving hope to people who have no hope. We could even be glad that he does not always pick on us! Resentment towards others has no part in God's kingdom.

† *Lord God, help those who govern our country to be open to the promptings of your Holy Spirit. May they always work for the common good, not just for the good of one group.*

Micah 6:6-16

The call for us to act with justice

> **[W]hat does the LORD require of you**
> **but to do justice, and to love kindness,**
> **and to walk humbly with your God?**

(*verse 8*)

Children are always saying 'It's not fair!' They have a keen sense of justice. So too do many adults. Where does this special sense come from? Perhaps it is because we are made in the image of God who is, the Bible tells us, a God of justice. He lays down laws and gives us the grace to try to keep them. In particular he expects governments to administer justice and to do so with mercy. These are not two opposites. Justice is corporate love, the way that the state can show love and respect to its citizens.

But God has done more than give us laws to live by. He has given us Jesus who reminds us, like Micah, that we are to 'walk humbly'. 'Among the Gentiles those whom they recognise as their rulers lord it over them, and their great ones are tyrants over them. But it is not so among you, but whoever wishes to become great among you must be your servant. For the Son of Man came not to be served but to serve, and give his life a ransom for many' (Mark 10:42-44).

† *Lord God, help me to do justice, love kindness and walk humbly in your company all my days.*

2 Samuel 11:1-27

Abuse of power in the Old Testament: David and Uriah

Someone has said that there is nothing in the popular newspapers that you cannot read about in the Old Testament. That is why it has so much to say to our world today. Here is just such a story. A man in a powerful position is attracted to a beautiful married woman. He commits adultery with her and makes her pregnant. He schemes to get rid of her husband and succeeds in getting him killed in battle.

> **It happened, late one afternoon, when David rose from his couch and was walking about on the roof of the king's house, that he saw from the roof a woman bathing; the woman was very beautiful.**
>
> (*verse 2*)

How do we react when we see or hear of an abuse of power? It may be that we are in a position to stand up for what is right and challenge that person. This can take a lot of courage. But it is what the prophet Nathan does with David (see the next chapter).

More likely we feel that we can do nothing – but that is the moment for prayer. We need to pray that we and others may not be tempted to compromise our own standards because of what we see our leaders doing. And we need to pray too that the person concerned may come to their senses and recognise that what they have done was wrong. David does just that.

† *Lord God, grant that we may not be conformed to this world but transformed by your Holy Spirit and enabled to discern what is your will.* (Romans 12:2)

Abuse of power in the New Testament: Caiaphas

'You do not understand that it is better for you to have one man die for the people than to have the whole nation destroyed.'

(*verse 50*)

Jesus has just raised Lazarus from the dead and as a result the number of his followers is increasing dramatically. From the point of view of the politicians, led by the High Priest Caiaphas, the situation is becoming unstable. It makes good sense to stop Jesus in his tracks. It does not matter whether Jesus is right or wrong. What matters is keeping the colonial rulers, the Romans, happy and his own group in power. Caiaphas is a control freak and, in an unconscious prophecy, sees no problem about sacrificing Jesus for the good of the people.

How then does Jesus respond to this gross injustice? Not by whipping up the crowds to protect him, not by summoning legions of angels, not by letting his friends use violence to defend him. His way is the way of love, allowing himself to be tortured and humiliated but not getting into political slanging matches, not engaging in self-pity and not cursing his enemies.

The Indian independence leader, Gandhi, understood this. He said: 'To recognise evil and not to oppose it is to surrender your humanity. To recognise evil and to oppose it with the weapons of the evil-doer is to enter into your humanity. To recognise evil and to oppose it with the weapons of God is to enter into your divinity.'

† *Lord, help us to understand what the words of Gandhi and the actions of Jesus mean for us.*

Romans 13:1-7

The Christian duty to support the state

Whether you like it or not, Paul says, you really do have to pay your taxes! Why? Because the state needs the money to administer justice and to keep the peace. Justice and peace are what God wants for the world, and so the authorities – the powers that be – receive their power and authority from God. Like Cyrus the Great, our governments, whether they know it or not, can be agents of God.

This seems to have been quite obvious to Paul. He based himself in big trading centres like Ephesus and Corinth with all their comings and goings. Christianity could never have spread so quickly round the Mediterranean Sea and beyond if the Roman Empire had not kept the roads and seaways open and safe. Here was God at work.

Paul does not deal with what we should do if the state abuses its power and does not minister justice fairly. But that does not take away from his basic message – to be a good Christian we have to be good citizens.

> **Let every person be subject to the governing authorities; for there is no authority except from God, and those authorities which exist have been instituted by God.**
>
> (*verse 1*)

† *Lord God, guide us to see where you are at work in and through those who govern us and help us to be better citizens.*

The Christian duty to challenge the state

In South Africa, during the apartheid era, many Christians used yesterday's passage from Romans 13 to justify the most appalling abuses of power by the state. Other Christians felt helpless to oppose their government in the face of what the Bible said. Then, reading the Book of Revelation, they realised that Paul did not have the last word. The writer of Revelation, John, using picture-language to avoid arrest, wrote his book to encourage fellow Christians who were being persecuted by the Roman Empire. By this time, probably thirty years after Paul was writing, the Roman Emperor (John calls him the 'beast') had demanded that his subjects address him as God and worship his image (Revelation 13). Many Christians refused. They were therefore not allowed to receive the 'mark of the beast' on their hand or forehead; this excluded them from buying and selling and any life in society. Some were put to death.

The message of Revelation was that, despite the worst that the Roman Empire – or any other cruel regime – could do, God reigns supreme, and Christ, alive after his resurrection, has the power to overcome evil.

> **I also saw the souls of those who had been beheaded for their testimony to Jesus and for the word of God. They had not worshipped the beast or its image and had not received its mark on their foreheads or hands. They came to life and reigned with Christ a thousand years.**
>
> (*part of verse 4*)

† *O God, give us the courage to change what should be changed, serenity to accept what cannot be changed, and the wisdom to know the difference. (*Reinhold Niebuhr*)*

April

2 Marks of God's Kingdom

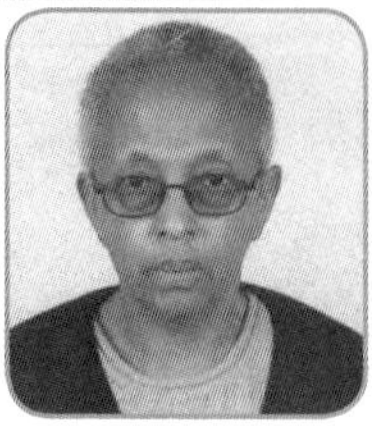

Notes by Jember Teferra
based on the New International Version

Jember Teferra is an Ethiopian who has worked for 27 years in the poorest slums in Addis Ababa, promoting the philosophy of the Integrated Holistic Approach which endeavours to address the root causes of poverty both through practical programmes and through advocacy on issues related to poverty.

Introduction

Those who have experienced living under different kinds of political systems know that there is no perfect ruler on earth. The Lord whose triumphant resurrection we have just celebrated was also unjustly judged by sinners. He appealed for social justice, he prayed for his followers to be protected, he dealt wisely with those who wanted him to be a political rebel. All of this helps us to realise why Our Lord taught us to pray 'Your kingdom come, your will be done on earth as it is in heaven.' We can try to lessen the burden of unjustly treated and neglected human beings by bringing heaven's values on earth.

Text for the week: Acts 4:34-35

There were no needy persons among them . . . those who owned lands or houses sold them, brought the money from the sales and put it at the apostles' feet, and it was distributed to anyone as he had need.

For group discussion and personal thought

- Why do you think our Lord prayed so earnestly for his followers?
- Why is it that the politicians with the largest support are those who compromise, while those who fight as Christians for justice, peace and stability do not get as many followers?

The sharing believers

No-one claimed that any of his possessions was his own, but they shared everything they had.

(*part of verse 32*)

During the Marxist military rule in Ethiopia, from the middle of the 1970s to the early 1990s, I observed something which at the time surprised me: when the currency notes were changed, people who did not trust the bank hoarded their money in boxes, in the back yard or in cupboards. Years later, when they brought this money out to change at the bank into the present currency notes, they found it ruined, totally destroyed and chewed into pieces by various creepy crawlies. The majority of people did use the bank, but when there was a mass round of imprisonments the money in the bank was confiscated and the owner dispossessed. Even those who had joint accounts with their husbands or wives were not allowed access to their bank if one of them became a prisoner.

It seems that human beings just cannot get it right. So why don't we share what we have with those who have not? Hoarding does not always pay – some even die before using their money. Too much hoarded money can also lead to inheritance disputes. Today's reading teaches us a very important lesson.

† *Heavenly Father, you are the most generous giver in the universe. May we learn from you to give generously and share what we have with those who have nothing or very little.*

John 17:6-19

Praying for protection

When do we ever hear of a brave leader appealing for the safety of his followers when he (or she) is facing arrest and ultimate death? Our selfless Lord could foresee persecution awaiting his followers:

> **'I am coming to you. Holy Father, protect them by the power of your name . . . While I was with them I protected them and kept them safe by that name you gave me.'**
>
> (*part of verses 11 and 12*)

This is definitely one of the marks of God's kingdom, where no one will be in danger and where there will be no more tears, suffering, persecution, arrest or death. What a perfect existence!

The very prolonged prayer of our Lord before his death just confirms that he does not call us to follow him without giving us his protection and ensuring that, come what may, he is going to stand by us and act to make us instruments for promoting his kingdom values. Without this support, his followers, as we see in the New Testament, would not have gone as far as they did. Even Peter, who denied him three times when he was cornered, changed into a leader who in the end shared his master's death. And look at Paul, who became the most outstanding follower after being the greatest persecutor of Christians!

† *Our loving and caring Lord, in this cruel and unjust world teach us to be selfless like you so that we pray for, support and stand by those who need your protection. And may we remember, for ourselves, that you continue to pray for us.*

A wise reply

Before being arrested and becoming a political prisoner I was interrogated half a dozen times. One of my interrogators accused me of plotting to overthrow the military Marxist government. Since on such occasions I always prayed for wisdom, I was given the right answer: 'My husband, with God's help, has not been executed like some of his colleagues, and I have four children all under eight years old. If I was so irresponsible as even to consider such action, you should take me to the mental hospital – not bring me here to interrogate me for the wrong reason.'

Nowhere in the gospels are we told to step outside the law, but we are taught to be law abiding for whatever reason and whomever we deal with, and to accept the ruler as the head of state (whether good or bad):

> **'[G]ive to Caesar what is Caesar's, and to God what is God's.'**

(*part of verse 25*)

Our Lord accepted Caesar's authority, but made clear his allegiance to God. His enemies were trying to provoke him to step out of line and criticise the powers that be, so that they would have a good excuse to catch him and arrest him. He did not give them that opportunity – he was wise in his response (even though they hunted him later with false accusations and arrested and killed him).

† *As you have taught us to respect the rules and rulers of the land, Lord, help us to accept what cannot be changed and to follow your example as law-abiding citizens.*

John 18:28-40

Jesus' kingdom

'My kingdom is not of this world. If it were, my servants would fight to prevent my arrest by the Jews. But now my kingdom is from another place.'

(*verse 36*)

Another example of why the Jews found it difficult to understand what Jesus said at his trial – he simply did not act like the criminal they wanted him to be! When I came out of five years of political imprisonment, I started to work in one of the worst slums. A military man, who had high position in the local authority, walked into the hall where I was interviewing more than 200 very poor mothers – a simple fact-finding session to find out their varied needs. He tried to talk to me but I had lost my voice from talking with so many women. So he asked one of my colleagues on the other side of the hall, 'Does this woman from the oppressing class think that the poor will thank her? Or does she think her husband will be released as a reward because she is working for the poorest of the poor?' My colleague replied, 'Major, you do not understand her values – she works for another king and another kingdom, not for yours or anybody's gratitude or thanks.' The little that human beings do to address social justice is not understood for what it is – and much less when our Lord tried to live by his kingdom values on earth and be an example. If he was misjudged during his life, why do we expect our good intentions to be correctly understood?

† *Lord, help me to accept that social justice, a better quality of life, will only fully come to earth when your kingdom comes. Meanwhile, help us to play our role, however insignificant, and thank you for being an example to us.*

Duty bound to pray for those in authority

> **I urge, then, first of all, that requests, prayers, intercession and thanksgiving be made for everyone – for kings and all those in authority that we may live peaceful and quiet lives in all godliness and holiness.**
>
> (*verses 1-2*)

What heaven on earth it would be if all Christians prayed for those in authority to have a social conscience and rule their nations justly, fairly, and with godliness! Wouldn't we have a better quality of life and, generally, a better world to live in, a world as God intended it to be, if we prayed as we are commanded?

We human beings just have not got it right! When Jesus said 'Your kingdom come, your will be done on earth as it is in heaven', he really was talking about equality, inclusiveness, social justice, sharing and selflessness – the qualities he himself embodied. He wants us to be trend setters as well as actors in bringing about changes for a better world, wherever we are and using whatever gifts he has given us – including being part of the praying community for those who rule over us.

† *Heavenly Father, please change the hard-hearted rulers in authority. Help us to pray for them so that poverty and human degradation, war and bloodshed, and many other injustices may vanish. Let your kingdom come.*

Matthew 5:1-12

The blessed: the unrecognised majority

Since our team works with one of the poorest communities in the world, I feel so comforted that our Lord has primarily blessed the poor, the hungry and those who thirst, because their hunger is for righteousness (I am sure he includes those who are hungry for food also). It comforts me too to see how God keeps them going, whether they are poor in spirit or flesh, whether they need the basic necessities spiritually or physically.

According to the United Nation Convention on Human Rights, the five basic necessities are shelter, food, health care, employment and education. According to our Lord's description of our spiritual rights, those who want to follow him will be poor in spirit, hungry and thirsty for righteousness, peacemakers, and so on, and will struggle with the best intentions – and be assured of his support through the Holy Spirit. This includes all of us – poor spiritually or materially.

> **'Blessed are the poor in spirit . . . Blessed are those who hunger and thirst for righteousness . . . Blessed are the peacemakers.'**
>
> *(part of verses 3, 6 and 9)*

Even though our Lord is praying here for the poor in spirit and those who hunger and thirst spiritually for righteousness, if physical poverty was alleviated and all poverty of spirit redeemed what a world it would be! Jesus' sermon on the mountain is so wholesome and an encouragement to all who follow him – especially to those of us working in areas of dual deprivation, material and spiritual.

† *Come down, Lord, and rule the world with justice, peace and godliness. We so look forward to seeing your kingdom come and the perfect world order established.*

1 One human family

Notes by Helen Van Koevering
based on the New Revised Standard Version

Helen has now worked for several years with the Diocese of Niassa in northern Mozambique, part of the province of the Anglican Church of Southern Africa. More recently, she has been involved as an ordained priest in training clergy and lay women for ministry.

Introduction

Love, expressed in the lived reality of human oneness, is still a crying need around the world, perhaps more than ever. God's desire for oneness is an underlying theme throughout the Bible, beginning within the heart of God at the creation of the world, and reaffirmed in the days after the Flood. Human history is about conflict, wars, unequal development, segregation, apartheid – the glaring reality of human disunity. But God, through Jesus Christ, continues to call us to a new oneness, empowered by God's Spirit, which transcends all boundaries and separations and unites us in our relationship to one another before and with God. Each of us needs to re-hear the profound message of reconciliation and justification that is the Good News.

Text for the week: Romans 3:22-24

[T]he righteousness of God through faith in Jesus Christ for all who believe. For there is no distinction, since all have sinned and fall short of the glory of God; they are now justified by his grace as a gift, through the redemption that is in Christ Jesus.

For group discussion and personal thought

- What does 'oneness of humanity' mean to you? Does your life reflect this desire of God's heart – is there anything you need to change?
- How is our lack of oneness reflected in a current local or global issue?

Genesis 1:26-31

Humanity, made in God's image

Then God said, 'Let us make humankind in our image, according to our likeness; and let them have dominion over the fish of the sea, and over the birds of the air and over the cattle, and over all the wild animals of the earth, and over every creeping thing that creeps upon the earth.'

(verse 26)

Right in its first chapter, the Bible teaches us that the oneness of humanity has its foundation in the creative desire of God, the Holy Trinity. The origin of human beings is not simply from the waters on the earth like the plants, fishes, birds and animals: it is 'in our image'. Adam and Eve were created as images of God in the world, and for the world, and all that God had created was called 'very good', free from evil, beautiful. Because Genesis 1 presents all the beauty of creation as existing by divine power and purpose, the unique place of human beings is also seen as within God's intention. This serene, wonderful world, in which all is ordered to human beings, and human beings are ordered to God, is a portrait of how God wills creation to be, and how it will be at the end, as Revelation 21–22 highlights at the end of the Bible. Beauty and love, creative purposefulness and oneness – these were the divine will from the beginning, part of the environment intended for the human community.

† *God, thank you for the reminder that we are your creation. Remind us to see ourselves and all others as imagers of God, and so to see our oneness in you and for your purposes. Amen.*

Genesis 9:1-7, 18-19

Renewal and reaffirmation

> **God blessed Noah and his sons, and said to them, 'Be fruitful and multiply, and fill the earth. The fear and dread of you shall rest on every animal of the earth, and on every bird of the air, on everything that creeps on the ground, and on all the fish of the sea; into your hand they are delivered . . .**
>
> **Whoever sheds the blood of a human,**
> **by a human shall that person's blood be shed;**
> **for in his own image**
> **God made humankind.'**

(verses 1, 2 and 6)

After the Flood, creation had the chance to begin again. The covenant God made with Noah and his sons echoes that given to Adam and Eve in Genesis 1. However, now there is an acknowledgement of another dimension existing between animals and human beings – fear – and between human beings, the evil of murder. This covenant is a precursor to the covenant made later with Moses at Sinai, embodied in the Ten Commandments; its laws are given to establish humanity's relationship with God, and then reflect that relationship in the human community. But despite the new dimensions added in the covenant with Noah, humanity is reaffirmed as images of God, and recommissioned – to fill the earth. Our God is a God who keeps his covenant; his qualities of love, justice, peace and righteousness are for all time, all places and all peoples, given so that we might live in relationship with God and others in the world made for us.

† *Lord, you are holy, and call us to reflect your holiness in the world. Speak to our hearts, renew our minds, and cleanse us to live together in your world as you intended. Amen.*

Acts 2:1-18

Pentecost's power

> **When the day of Pentecost had come, they were all together in one place . . . All of them were filled with the Holy Spirit and began to speak in other languages, as the Spirit gave them ability . . .**
>
> **'In the last days it will be, God declares,**
> **that I will pour out my Spirit upon all flesh,**
> **and your sons and daughters shall prophesy,**
> **and your young men shall see visions,**
> **and your old men shall dream dreams.'**

(*verses 1, 4 and 17*)

The word 'power' carries some negative associations of force, destruction, violence, domination. But the power that God sent at Pentecost brought unity, new ability, and amazement. Both the disciples and the onlookers recognised God as powerfully present, though the meaning was not yet understood. The disciples had known many different emotions since the crucifixion of Jesus: disappointment that Jesus had not turned out to be the powerful military leader they had expected in a Messiah; abandonment by their friend Jesus, with no clear strategy, no obvious next step; unity only in fear, weakness, confusion and loss. Then the promised Helper came. Power came to them and upon them, a power to transform them and the world. Not a power to keep for themselves, but to live within, to show and tell. God's power, proving God's presence beyond doubt, fear and isolation. A power available for everyone, everywhere, till the end of time.

† *Loving God, pour out your Spirit on us today, so that we may live with a deep sense of the presence of your power in us, with us and throughout your world, today and always. Amen.*

Them and us

> **The Spirit told me to go to them and not to make a distinction between them and us.**
>
> (verses 1, 2 and 6)

Seeing beyond the 'other', beyond the differences that make each one of us unique and beautiful in God's eyes, is not something that comes naturally to us. It is easy to speak and then, in just one more small step, to act and judge ourselves and others as superior or inferior, separating ourselves from one another by our own prejudice and preconceptions. But the gift of the gospel is the message of oneness by faith, oneness in Christ, oneness in God's love and compassion.

> **'If then God gave them the same gift that he gave us when we believed in the Lord Jesus Christ, who was I that I could hinder God?' When they heard this, they were silenced. And they praised God, saying, 'Then God has given even to the Gentiles the repentance that leads to life.'**
>
> (*verses 17-18*)

If God has made us one through faith, all needing forgiveness, love, peace and God's joy-filled presence, who are we to distinguish between 'us' and 'them'? Peter's vision radically changed everything for the Jerusalem church in the first century, and continues to have the power to open the eyes of our hearts, and empower lives and the church's mission, right through to today.

† *Help us to see all people through your eyes, Lord, to recognise that your life is for all, needed by all, and that we are all your beloved people. Amen.*

Acts 17:22-31

Searching and finding

> **'From one ancestor he made all nations to inhabit the whole earth, and he allotted the times of their existence and the boundaries of the places where they would live, so that they would search for God and perhaps grope for him and find him – though indeed he is not far from each one of us.'**

(*verses 26-27*)

There are echoes here of the words Mordecai chose in the book of Esther to encourage the faith-filled action of Esther. God, who has been working behind the scenes of world history since creation, who is the thread of the tapestry of each of our lives, has brought us all to where and who we are today 'for just such a time as this' (Esther 4:14). Created in God's image, we all have within us a desire to know the author of our lives, whatever our circumstances, place, relationships, jobs, or moment in history. We may all need to grope through a lack of seeing or hearing, misunderstanding or misdirection; we may all need to learn to recognise God's presence; and we all need to respond with loving gratitude and faithful repentance – but God is not far off. We live, as ever, known by God. And, at 'such a time as this', God calls us all to know ourselves in God.

† *Lord, may we know your living presence and recognise again that we live and move and have our being in you alone, no matter what or where or who we are today. For your glory, Amen.*

All

[T]he righteousness of God through faith in Jesus Christ for all who believe. For there is no distinction, since all have sinned and fall short of the glory of God; . . . to prove at the present time that he himself is righteous and that he justifies the one who has faith in Jesus.

(*verses 22 and 26*)

This week we have read of God's creation of humanity as image-bearers of God, and of our covenant-keeping God in whom we have always had our living, moving and being. We have read of our need to search for God, to see and know God, and of the power that God has given to enable and empower us to do this. But our God is a righteous God whose own laws cannot be broken. Humanity's separation from God, which we brought into existence and maintain with our choices, does not negate God's holy law, even with God's desire to be close to us. The separation has been dealt with through the life, death and resurrection of Jesus, but it requires a response and desire to draw near to God. The way is now open, but we all need to choose it. No one is exempt – all have sinned, all need to come right with God. God's loving arms and fullness of life await each one of us.

† *Lord of all creation, forgive us, every one of us, for our distance, our pride, our bad choices. We long to know you, long for your gift of grace and embracing love. Be known in us as you intended from the beginning. In Jesus' name. Amen.*

2 All one in God – barriers are taken away

Notes by Elisa Gusmão
based on the New International Version

Born in Brazil, Elisa belonged to the Presbyterian and Methodist Churches, before moving to the UK with her Scottish husband in 1987. Since then she has worked as a translator, while serving the United Reformed Church as an elder and lay preacher. Between them, Eric and Elisa have six grandchildren born in Switzerland, Canada, Mexico and Brazil.

Introduction

Since the beginning of the twentieth century we have been talking about ecumenism, and organising events promoting unity among Christian denominations. But we don't seem to have got very far in our endeavours, as today they still worship and serve God separately, taking different positions and working in different directions. Ecumenism in a larger sense also means a wider movement, promoting worldwide unity among different religions through greater co-operation and understanding. As we can see, given the present situation of global affairs, humanity hasn't gone far with this either.

Perhaps if Christians, united by love, had been more open and willing to work together in the world to which Jesus sent them, the whole situation would be different now.

Text for the week: John 17:21

'[T]hat all of them may be one, Father, just as you are in me and I am in you.'

For group discussion and personal thought

- Have you examined the issues that divide Christianity today?
- What is your/your church's position in relation to them?

Adam of death and Adam of life

> **Consequently, just as the result of one trespass was condemnation for all men, so also the result of one act of righteousness was justification that brings life for all men . . . so that, just as sin reigned in death, so also grace might reign through righteousness to bring eternal life through Jesus Christ our Lord.**
>
> (*verses 18 and 21*)

We often listen to news of wars and terrorism, and attacks of lethal viruses that can spread death all around. They seem small in comparison with the story of the Fall in Genesis, a catastrophe with an all-encompassing effect on the world and its inhabitants. Adam's deliberate rebellion against God brought a change to the human condition which we call sin. With sin, we all inherited death. So the news that Christ, the new Adam, brings incomparably more benefits to us than Adam brought evil (verses 15-17) sounds like music to our ears. We know evil is still around: social and racial injustice, thousands dying in unnecessary wars, fighting in our families, tensions at work, and so on. But we have the hope of a kingdom that is coming, and the certainty that death is only a physical event, a passage to another life!

† *Lord God, we thank you for the love you have shown us in Jesus Christ, our Saviour. We praise you for his life, sacrifice, and victory over sin and death for our benefit and salvation. Amen.*

1 Corinthians 12:4-13

Diversity within unity

There are different kinds of gifts, but the same Spirit. There are different kinds of service, but the same Lord. There are different kinds of working, but the same God works all of them in all men. Now to each one the manifestation of the Spirit is given for the common good.

(*verses 4-7*)

One Spirit, one Lord, one God – but each person of the Trinity is endowed with many gifts and ministries. Diversity begins in the triune God himself!

Detecting signs of self-centred competition among the Corinthians, Paul reproaches them with the helpful image of the body, which has its mystical moment in the organic unit of the Holy Supper. We are Christ's body, and together at the table we drink his Spirit (verse 13).

A healthy church has to be as diverse as a healthy body with its different parts, all of which have exactly the same importance. There is no place for prima donnas among Christians, as all our gifts have a common origin in God, and serve a common aim: the increase of his kingdom.

† *Christ has no body on earth now but yours;*
yours are the only hands with which He can do his work,
yours are the only feet with which He can go around the world,
yours are the only eyes through which His compassion can shine forth upon a troubled world.
Christ has no body on earth but yours.

(Teresa of Avila)

The gospel people

Human beings have always, in every spot on this planet, longed for God and sought him. 'My soul thirsts for God, for the living God. When can I go and meet with God?' (Psalm 42: 1). What has changed in time and space is our perception of God, and the events that gave birth to our faith. So at a crucial moment, when it was time to bring the boat of salvation to all nations, Yahweh – the ancient God of the Jews – became flesh in Jesus of Nazareth:

> **You are all sons of God through faith in Christ Jesus, for all of you who were baptised into Christ have clothed yourselves with Christ. There is neither Jew nor Greek, slave nor free, male nor female, for you are all one in Christ Jesus. If you belong to Christ, then you are Abraham's seed, and heirs according to the promise.**
>
> (*verses 26-29*)

A racial pedigree is no longer important for receiving the promise, but faith is. It is precisely because of God's continual action in history that we can now step out of the legalism of the Old Testament into the dispensation of grace of the New Testament. Each Christian, 'clothed . . . with Christ', is a fully qualified heir to the 'New Israel' – the gospel people.

† *Father, I am seeking: I am hesitant and uncertain, but will you, O God, watch over each step of mine, and guide me.*

(From *Praying with Augustine* by Valeria Boldoni, SPCK 2001).

Isaiah 2:1-4

The mountain of the Lord

I have a friend who lives near Chartres Cathedral in France. When I go to visit her, I arrive by train from Paris and can see – as pilgrims did in the distant past – the cathedral appear in all its glory in the middle of a vast green plain: a place of worship, where the faithful seek guidance from God. The Jewish people in Isaiah's time, around 650 years before Christ, also went in pilgrimage to their mountain temple. The prophet speaks of this place as the house of Yahweh, the universal king whose glory fills the earth (Isaiah 6:3). Isaiah's God is not only one who judges the nations, but also a God of peace and universal unity:

Many peoples will come and say,
'Come, let us go up to the mountain of the LORD' . . .
He will judge between the nations
and will settle disputes for many peoples.
They will beat their swords into ploughshares
and their spears into pruning hooks.
Nation will not take up sword against nation,
nor will they train for war anymore.

(*verses 4-7*)

† *My God and Father, forgive us because we forget your teachings and fail to understand the ways of peace and unity you established such a long time ago. Help us to respond to the news that 'For us a child is born, to us a son is given . . . and he will be called Wonderful Counsellor, Mighty God, Everlasting Father, Prince of Peace'* [Isaiah 9:6]. *Amen.*

The gospel people

> **After this I looked and there before me was a great multitude that no-one could count, from every nation, tribe, people and language, standing before the throne and in front of the Lamb. They were wearing white robes and were holding palm branches in their hands.**
>
> (*verse 9*)

Yesterday we looked at the Old Testament idea of different nations coming together at God's temple. Today, this same picture is drawn with the colourfulness and imagery that makes the visions in Revelation seem bizarre to some. The white robes and palm branches of the great old Jewish commemorations here acquire a unique Christian meaning.

> **And he said, 'These are they who have come out of the great tribulation; they have washed their robes and made them white in the blood of the Lamb.'**
>
> (*part of verse 14*)

Around the throne where the Lamb sits, we can find our own place. For this multitude is formed not only by martyrs, but by all of us human beings who, in the tribulations of life, suffer the effects of evil's war against God. In the final chapter of the things to come, God provides for his universal people in a way beyond anyone's dream, satisfying their every need, keeping them from every suffering.

> **'And God will wipe away every tear from their eyes.'**
>
> (*part of verse 17*)

† *Praise the LORD, all you nations; extol him, all you peoples. For great is his love towards us, and the faithfulness of the LORD endures for ever.* (Psalm 117:1-2)

Ephesians 2:11-22

The universal Church

[A]nd in this one body to reconcile both of them to God through the cross . . . Consequently, you are no longer foreigners and aliens, but fellow-citizens with God's people and members of God's household.

(*part of verse 16, and verse 19*)

There are indications that Ephesians was a circular letter, aimed at several Christian communities. For instance, the words 'at Ephesus' (Ephesians 1:1) are not found in the oldest manuscripts, and seem to have been inserted in the copy sent to the city of that name. Although Paul talks about the division between the two Christian groups of his time, Jews and Gentiles, this is a letter to all churches, at all times, with a forceful and clear message of union among them.

In 1967 I took part in the Ecumenical Fellows Programme at the Union Theological Seminary in New York. There a group of students of theology from different Christian denominations and different parts of the world, together with their families, lived in the same block, shared meals, looked after each other's children, and worshipped together. They anticipated a future where experiences like this would be common within Christianity . . .

Today, the church is a melting pot of races, nationalities, denominations, sexual tendencies, and many other differences. Still the message of Ephesians persists: Paul reminds us that enmities were eliminated at a very high price by the Lord, and have no place among his people.

† *O Father, help us to 'make every effort to keep the unity of the Spirit through the bond of peace'* [Ephesians 4:3]. *Amen*

Eucharistic Themes

1 Thanksgiving and thankful living

Notes by Philip Wadham
based on the New Revised Standard Version

Philip Wadham is an Anglican priest, now retired. During his career he has been extensively involved with the mission of the Church, working in Latin America and the Caribbean as well as England and Canada. He was an executive officer with the Partnership Programme of the Anglican Church of Canada and in this capacity travelled frequently to visit partner dioceses and churches. He and his wife now live on Vancouver Island in western Canada.

Introduction

The word eucharist comes from the Greek word meaning 'thanksgiving'. As we commence our reflections on 'eucharistic themes', the lessons for this week focus on thanksgiving and thankful living – underscoring the expansive generosity of the God of grace. Eucharist is about the liturgy of abundance for which we live a life of constant thanksgiving.

Text for the week: Matthew 10:42

'[W]hoever gives even a cup of cold water to one of these little ones in the name of a disciple – truly I tell you, none of these will lose their reward.'

For group discussion and personal thought

- Recall (and share with others) times in your life when you have been able to say, 'This is a holy time'. What made it holy?
- Christ comes to us in a special way in the Eucharist. But he is also to be experienced in the ordinariness of the world. Why is it so important to recognise the Christ who comes to us in this way? (Matthew 25:31-45 may be helpful.)

Psalm 116:1-4, 12-19

Faithful in death

Ross, aged 55, had complained of backache for some time before the intensity of the pain took him into emergency at a nearby hospital. An X-ray revealed a growth on his spine and a biopsy confirmed that it was cancer. Treatment by radiation was recommended, though it soon became clear that the disease had spread through much of his body. His church, Holy Trinity, prayed for him with an earnestness appropriate for one of its own. Ross, who had previously battled cancer and won, appeared confident that he would again be healed. But on a Sunday morning in spring Ross died, his final days of life filled with the compassionate care of family and hospital staff.

> **Precious in the sight of the LORD**
> **is the death of his faithful ones.**

(*verse 15*)

Ross's funeral filled the church. Tributes were paid to a good man, fond memories of a husband, a father and a friend. At the Eucharist the people heard again the familiar story of the One who gave up his life on the cross, as they shared in the brokenness of the day. The same One whose wounded, outstretched arms encircled Ross, one of his 'faithful ones', with a healing embrace that stretches into eternity.

† *Father of all, we pray to you for those we love but see no longer. Grant them your peace and let light perpetual shine upon them.*

In praise of God and human toil

'As you can see, Father, we have a school but we don't have a church. Our village needs a church.' The visiting priest was listening to the deacon in his riverside village in eastern Ecuador. What the priest heard was a request for money, so he tried to deflect the conversation. 'You use the school for worship; isn't that enough?' In unison of protest the villagers replied. 'No, Father, it isn't.' So an agreement was struck. The priest would supply roofing but the rest of the building would be the work of the people.

> **So then, whenever we have an opportunity, let us work for the good of all, and especially for those of the family of faith.**
>
> (*verse 10*)

And so it was that two months later, when the priest, accompanied by his bishop, visited the community, the people had been as good as their promise. In a prominent place overlooking the river below was the completed church. It was a modest construction, local logs and split bamboo, with benches for the congregation, a congregation now gathered to celebrate the consecration of their new worship centre. Having praised the people for this good work done together 'to the glory of God and in thanksgiving', all present shared in the Eucharist, God's gift and promise to the world, Jesus our Lord.

† *May we learn peace from the care we bring each other; may we learn justice from the holy food we share. Unite us in the mission of your Son whose saving love extends to every person, whose presence reaches into every place.*

(Extract from *Occasional Celebrations: Blessing of a Church*, Anglican Church of Canada)

Matthew 10:40-42

Uncommon gratitude

The journey had been difficult enough but Miguel complained that what he and his family had come to was little better than what they had left in El Salvador. The 1980s had seen an increase in violence from the Salvadoran authorities and a number of Miguel and Marta's friends had been killed. So they had fled. But here in Belize, their new country of residence, they experienced violence of a different kind. They were poorer than before and viewed with suspicion by neighbours. Familiar friends had vanished from their lives and they struggled with a new language. Loneliness was a constant companion.

> **'[W]hoever gives even a cup of cold water to one of these little ones in the name of a disciple – truly I tell you, none of these will lose their reward.'**
>
> (*verse 42*)

It was Marta who reminded Miguel that some positive things were happening. A local family, recognising the family's pain, had offered practical assistance: clothes for the children and food from their produce, and an invitation to meet with others at their community church. Worship on that first Sunday had been a shock, very different to their experience in El Salvador. But around the table of the Lord, as they broke bread together, they felt a common bond. It was the experience of being a part of the one body of Christ, diverse yet drawn together through his compassionate love.

† *Draw your Church together, O Lord, into one great company of disciples, together following our Lord Jesus Christ . . . and witnessing to his love.*

(Extract from 'Occasional Prayers: For the Mission of the Church', Anglican Church of Canada, *Book of Alternative Services*)

Luke 24:44-53*

Repentance, forgiveness, reconciliation

'Though we believed we were doing the right thing, looking back on it now we recognise how wrong it was.' So spoke a Canadian priest reflecting on the Anglican Church's involvement in residential schools for aboriginal children. For 150 years, between 1820 and 1969, native children were removed from their homes and communities to be educated in boarding schools. Here they were to learn the 'ways of the white man', so that they might live and work better within that culture. But in place of assimilation most students experienced alienation, divorced from their aboriginal roots and marginalised by white society.

> **'[R]epentance and forgiveness of sins is to be proclaimed in [Messiah's] name to all nations.'**
>
> (*part of verse 47*)

In August 1993 Archbishop Michael Peers, addressing a gathering of aboriginal peoples, offered a full apology on behalf of the Anglican Church of Canada. It included these words: 'I am sorry, more than I can say, that we were part of a system that took you and your children from home and family . . . that we tried to remake your image . . . that in our schools so many were abused physically, sexually, culturally and emotionally.' Thus began a process that should lead, with appropriate practical action, to reconciliation and healing. It is a eucharistic action, for we confess our sins and intend to lead the new life in Christ.

† *May God have mercy upon me, pardon and deliver me from all my sins, confirm and strengthen me in all goodness and keep me in eternal life; through Jesus Christ our Lord.*

(Modified from *The Book of Alternative Services of the Anglican Church of Canada*)

Matthew 26:6-13

O generous love

'And the majority of my estate, being the proceeds from the sale of my house, shall go to a medical research programme in Havana, Cuba, to be used in AIDS research.' So read the executor of Harold's will. The actual sum was quite considerable because the housing market in Vancouver, Canada, was booming. For those who knew Harold there was no surprise that the money would be directed towards finding treatment for AIDS. His son had died of the disease some fifteen years previously. But why Cuba?

> **[A] woman came to [Jesus] with an alabaster jar of very costly ointment and she poured it on his head . . . But when the disciples saw it, they were angry and said, 'Why this waste? For this ointment could have been sold for a large sum, and the money given to the poor.'**
>
> (*part of verse 7, and verses 8-9*)

In Cuba the representatives of the Anglican Church told the director of the AIDS research team about Harold's intention for the use of this money. 'Harold had travelled to Cuba many times. He had seen the good work of your doctors and received medical attention from them when he was sick. He knew that AIDS was a growing problem, that Cuba is poor and has little access to foreign drug suppliers and has to rely on its own resources. His gift is a way of supporting the Cuban people. He trusts that his generosity will be of benefit to them.' Though a complete cure for AIDS still eludes researchers, generous love has healing properties.

† *Loving God, your Son was anointed by the Holy Spirit not to be served but to serve. Receive all we offer you this day, that we who are called to serve you in the world may be effective ministers of your healing love*

(Prayer over the Gifts, *The Book of Alternative Services*, Anglican Church of Canada, p.618)

Thanks in giving

On the River Napo in Ecuador, South America, local villagers catch fish in a variety of ways. The most dangerous is to blast them with dynamite. Miguel is testimony to that danger. He lost both hands and almost his life when the explosive ignited prematurely. His wife Maria wondered how her family would now survive; she and Miguel had two young daughters. Villagers were kind, giving them food, but they too were poor and their gifts limited. A visiting pastor with two children of his own gave Maria clothes his girls had outgrown.

> **[Jesus] had compassion . . . Taking the five loaves and two fish, he . . . blessed and broke the loaves . . . and all ate and were filled.**
>
> (*part of verses 14, 19 and 20*)

On his next visit to the village, Maria, Miguel and their daughters greeted the pastor. The girls were wearing two of the dresses he had given them. Maria held out her hand: in it were two eggs for the pastor's supper. At the Eucharist that evening in the light of oil lamps, the villagers shared in the holy food of our Lord Jesus Christ. In the unison of voice and community they gave thanks and blessed the gifts they received in Christ and the gifts they were to each other.

† *Gracious God, we thank you for feeding us with the body and blood of your Son Jesus Christ. May we, who share his body, live his risen life; we who drink his cup, bring life to others; we, whom the Spirit lights, give light to the world. Amen*

(Prayer after Communion, *The Book of Alternative Services*, Anglican Church of Canada, p.214)

2 The shape of our life together

Notes by Iain Roy
based on the Good News Bible

Iain Roy is a retired minister of the Church of Scotland and former Moderator and Clerk of the Presbytery of Ardrossan. He was for many years industrial chaplain to the ICI Nobel Explosives Company at Ardeer. He has a long-standing interest in art, drama and music, sings tenor with Kilmarnock and District Choral Union, and preaches in local churches.

Introduction

Dom Gregory Dix wrote an authoritative and definitive work on the evolution of the Christian liturgy over the centuries, the Eucharist in particular, called *The Shape of the Liturgy*. I think, however, that he would also have approved of our study this week of the Eucharist as something given us by Christ to shape our lives and the life of the Church.

Text for the week: Acts 2:44

All the believers continued together in close fellowship.

For group discussion and personal thought

- What challenges do you think the sacrament of Holy Communion presents to your life and the life of the church today? How do you think these challenges can be answered?
- What do you believe that you get out of the Christian fellowship and are able to give to that fellowship? Are there things you and others could do to enhance the fellowship of your own church, especially to make it more welcoming?
- Reflect on your own spiritual life: are you feeding it on a regular basis through worship, study and prayer, with real food for thought and action?

Taken, blessed, broken, given

Our familiarity with the story of the Last Supper can easily make us forget how revolutionary an act it was. In the upper room Jesus appeared to be celebrating the Jewish Passover with his disciples. But with these simple words:

> **'Take and eat it', he said; 'this is my body.'**
>
> (*part of verse 26*)

Jesus changed the act from Jewish Passover to Christian Eucharist. He made himself and his love the focus of the act, and claimed implicitly that what unites us to each other and to all humanity is God's great love revealed in him and in his sacrament. The act of Holy Communion can therefore never be just an act of remembrance: it must also be seen as a challenge to us to live life as he lived it – with compassion for others, a readiness to forgive, and the ability to forget self and love others. In these things the Eucharist itself helps to guide us and inspire us.

† *Lord, let the ordinary table we sit at each day for our meals become sacramental, speaking to us of your love and your provision. Let it remind us of the love you have for us and the love we must have for each other.*

Luke 24:13-35

Broken bread, risen Saviour

We have to assume that the two who walked the Emmaus road with Jesus either stood at the cross themselves or, more likely, heard of his death as well as his Resurrection from others. Whatever, as yet, the cross had not opened their eyes to who Christ really was and what he had done for them. Indeed, there is in the words they speak to Jesus an element of despair and disillusionment.

> **'This man was a prophet and was considered by God and by all the people to be . . . powerful in everything he said and did . . . And we had hoped that he would be the one who was going to set Israel free!'**
>
> (part of verses 19 and 21)

There is nothing worse than dashed hopes, nothing sadder than the Christian who begins to lose faith or commitment. This incident is a gentle rebuke to us if this is our situation. Suddenly, in the breaking of the bread, the shut eyes were opened, the low spirits revived. The cross is a single act in human history, the sacrament a recurring act, given us by Christ because he recognises our human frailty, our need for reassurance.

† *Lord, all life and everything in life can be sacramental, speaking of your love and your truth. So let the things of every day speak to reassure us and let your presence strengthen our trust in you.*

Breaking bread together

The idea of the Christian ascetic, alone in meditation, has had attractions for some throughout the history of the church, but far more of us are attracted to the idea of the Christian fellowship: faith, worship and service as essentially a shared experience. This is what is seen here in this passage.

> **All the believers continued together in close fellowship . . . praising God, and enjoying the goodwill of all the people. And every day the Lord added to their group those who were being saved.**
>
> (*part of verse 44, and verse 47*)

An important criterion of any Christian fellowship is its openness to those who do not belong to it. The continuing tragedy of the Church is that so often the sacrament of Holy Communion itself has lacked this openness. Yet, all it takes is a few simple words to 'open the Table to all who love the Lord in spirit and in truth', words which capture the very essence of the openness of God's love in Christ to us.

† *Lord Christ, who in the breaking of bread and the giving of wine shared everything of yourself and your Father's love with us, show us how to share with each other the things of our faith, to welcome others as you welcome us.*

John 6:25-35

Bread that lasts

The Lord's Prayer and its petition, 'Give us our daily bread', remind us that even the well-fed have a necessity for bread. We do literally have to eat to live. The hunger of the well-fed however, is very different from the hunger of the starving of this world. Their hunger has a desperation about it which only they can know. Their hunger is an obscenity in a world so well resourced by God. Here, Jesus introduced his listeners to another kind of hunger, not physical but spiritual.

> **'I am the bread of life', Jesus told them. 'He who comes to me will never be hungry; he who believes in me will never be thirsty.'**
>
> (*verse 35*)

It is sometimes more difficult for us to remember to feed our souls than our bodies. The body has a way of telling us when we need to eat. The soul is less articulate. Too often we are in crisis before we realise that the cupboard is bare! Our study and prayer today is just one way of nurturing our inner selves, giving us something to fall back on in our day of need. The sacraments are another.

† *Feed us, Lord Jesus, with the truth we need to live by, with the love we need to sustain us, with the hope which constantly encourages us, and with the Presence which can see us through even the most difficult of days.*

Table manners

It is the custom in Scotland for the minister to be invited to sit beside the bride and groom at the top table at wedding receptions. It ensures that you are fed first. It comes as a shock on retirement, therefore, to sit at a table less exalted and have to wait! We are not actually told where Jesus was sitting at the Pharisee's table, only what he observed while he sat there.

> **Jesus noticed how some of the guests were choosing the best places, so he told this parable to all of them: 'When someone invites you to a wedding feast, do not sit down in the best place . . . go and sit in the lowest place . . . For everyone who makes himself great will be humbled, and everyone who humbles himself will be made great.'**
>
> (*verse 7, part of verses 8 and 10, and verse 11*)

There should be no reserved seats at the Eucharist. It should remind us of the equality that embraces all of us in the presence of Christ. The mother of James and John once asked for a special place for her two sons beside Christ (Matthew 20: 20-28). Her request was rejected. There can be no pulling of rank in Christ's presence. In the Scots phrase, 'We are all Jock Tamson's bairns', brothers and sisters in Christ, God's sons and daughters. Thus we should always approach the holy table with humility, and yet always rise from it with a sense of this worth God has placed on us through Christ.

† *Lord, help us even now to approach you humbly in our prayers, confessing our faults and sins and asking your forgiveness. Strengthen us where we are weak so that we may be worthy witnesses to your grace and favour in our lives.*

Acts 2:1-21

One in him

Much is made today of the divisive nature of religion, the beliefs which set people apart. The Acts of the Apostles, however, presents to us the unifying nature of religion.

> **'We are from Parthia, Media, and Elam; from Mesopotamia, Judea, and Cappadocia; from Pontus and Asia . . . Some of us are from Rome, both Jews and Gentiles converted to Judaism, and some of us are from Crete and Arabia – yet all of us hear them speaking in our own languages about the great things God has done!'**
>
> (*verse 9, part of verse 10, and verse 11*)

Pentecost was a remarkable phenomenon, and yet should we be surprised by it, we who participate in the Lord's Supper? For in the sacrament, in the last analysis, no words are necessary at all! Each of us from our own background, our own culture, our own tradition, our own language, can understand what Christ is saying to us through his sacrament. The bread and wine speak, even without the words, of the great outpouring of God's love for us in Christ. The sacrament is *word in action*. Every time we celebrate it we are united not only to all who believe but to the humanity Christ calls us to serve.

† *Let your Spirit fill us as it filled your first disciples. Make us one in your witness, for your sake, Amen.*

3 Living eucharistically

Notes by Kavula John
based on the New Revised Standard Version

Kavula John is a Methodist minister based in London. As well as having pastoral charge of two churches, she is Chaplain to a Methodist Homes residence. She was born and brought up in a village in Kenya.

Introduction

Being a minister of Word and Sacrament I place celebration of the Holy Communion at the centre of our Christian worship. Eucharist represents all that God has poured out for us without reservation. 'I am here for you' is the Eucharist's central message. And it doesn't end with the ceremonial act around the sacrament table; it follows us all our lives, bringing healing and wholeness in us individually and corporately as community. The Lord's Supper is an open table of grace, grace that is to be shared among all who respond and come, finding enrichment and enriching one another in this spiritual feast.

A year ago, after a church service one of the members gave me a gift wrapped in foil. It was not until I unwrapped it that evening that I discovered it was a home baked loaf of bread with a note: 'Please accept this bread which I baked for you.' I was very moved that someone thought of me, but more so as I sliced it and shared with the family for tea. The loaf was given to me not to keep in my study or treasure in the bread bin, but to feed on it and share it with those around me. It was in the sharing that this gift became a real gift.

Text for the week: 1 Corinthians 11:24

This is my body that is for you.

For group discussion and personal thought

- Our Lord shares his graces with you at the Eucharist. What do you do in response?

John 13:1-19

Servanting – the Jesus model

On this occasion, because Jesus was aware that he was soon to depart from his disciples, he took the opportunity in this private room to illustrate for them, his closest friends, the most important truths and principles of Christian living. He had loved them, and the washing of their feet was a sign of that love and the humility that accompanies true love. Jesus' action was also a way of touching and cleansing his friends so that through him they might be uncontaminated by all the evil, betrayal and other goings on around them and feel revived and refreshed.

> **[Jesus] got up from the table, took off his outer robe . . . poured water into a basin and began to wash the disciples' feet.**
>
> (*part of verses 4 and 5*)

Jesus' controversial act has two key lessons: allow Jesus to wash your feet, and in turn wash others' feet. Jesus' sacrifice cleanses us and his model helps us to serve others by helping them to experience his touch and cleansing. Our actions should help to heal our tired and hurting world. God's grace experienced in the Eucharist is grounded in this true love and sacrifice for all. Just as Jesus took off his robe to wash the disciples' feet, so he laid aside his divine prerogative to serve a lost humanity by dying on the cross: 'he loved them to the end' (verse 1).

† *Lord, I need refreshment in my daily busy life. I live in a world where I get negatively affected by unhealthy atmospheres. Wash and cleanse me, and in turn teach me to be a source of refreshment to my friends and all those who are around me. Amen.*

Remember me – memory and hope

The context of today's reading is a Corinthian congregation who were using the occasion of the Lord's Supper inappropriately; cases of gluttony, drunkenness and class distinctions had been reported. The Lord's Supper had been instituted to remember above all Christ's death, which is a supreme example of unselfish and sacrificial service.

'Do this in remembrance of me.'

(*part of verse 24*)

We remember lest we forget what the Eucharist represents: the measure of God's love for us, as well as our worth to him; remembering Christ's death with wondering awe that he, Christ, would pay so much for us undeserving people. And so thanksgiving becomes central to this eucharistic act. The act of breaking bread brings out an aspect of vulnerability: it is when the bread is in pieces that all can benefit. The cup has to be emptied out in order for anyone to drink. If the bread stayed whole and the wine remained in the cup, the sharing would not be possible. We need to remember lest we forget what God has done for us, and not only that, but also to continue proclaiming this truth until the Lord comes again.

† *Lord, remind me again and again that your love surrounds me day after day, and as I celebrate the Lord's Supper, may I understand more its meaning and celebrate appropriately. Amen*

Romans 8:18-25

Eucharistic ecology

As we celebrate Holy Communion we are reminded that Christ's incarnation, death and Resurrection were for our sake, and for the hope of a better life for humankind. What Christ started in the act of salvation carries on into the future whatever our circumstances. Hope for the world in Christ and all its meaning is affirmed in the Eucharist act.

> **[T]he creation itself will be set free from its bondage to decay and will obtain the freedom of the glory of the children of God.**
>
> (*verse 21*)

The entire creation shares in the futility of this present state and therefore needs healing and completeness, a restoration of what it was meant to be by its Creator. This emphasises that the whole world belongs to God and its liberation lies in the hand of God. The lesson for us is not to be resigned or look at the world around us with contempt because of all the bad things that are happening, but to do our best to live lives of sacrifice and service and hope that God will restore all to what it should be.

† *Help me, God, never to take for granted this world in which you have placed me. Give me the wisdom to care for the environment and to be loving and kind to your creatures. Amen.*

Getting the right balance

When I read this passage I can't help sympathising in a way with Martha. Our lifestyles require a lot to be done in preparation for visitors, or indeed just for general housekeeping, and somebody has to do the work. I am reminded of times when I have asked my two sons to take their turn in cooking or indeed cleaning the house.

> **'Martha, Martha, you are worried and distracted by many things.'**
>
> (*part of verse 41*)

It was the worry and distraction that Jesus addressed in Martha. The preoccupation with things to be done that could have waited with no harm at all. There are so many things to be done, so many places to visit, that these things can fill our time and leave our spirituality unnourished. We can talk a lot and forget to pray and seek God's wisdom and guidance. This story of two sisters represents two possible priorities for us: to serve or to listen to God. It is a matter of getting the priorities right. There are times when we take on tasks in the name of Christ but forget to consult him on what he would have us do. Just as the Eucharist is central to our worship, so it should be central in all we do. Our service has to be done around that centre: seeking Christ and his will for us.

† *Lord, I am surrounded by busyness and rushing all over the place to keep appointments. I am worried about the washing up which is still waiting to be done in the kitchen. Calm me down and help me to create a time to worship and seek you today. Amen.*

John 3:1-17

Born anew! Eucharistic calling

To meet with Jesus as Nicodemus wanted had to be done in the right context: recognising that Jesus comes from God and that his power and ministry originate from God. As Nicodemus had this attitude to Jesus, all that was left for him to do was to see and experience the revolutionary programme that God has launched through Jesus for all people.

> **'You must be born from above.'**
>
> (*part of verse 7*)

This new birth is the product of the transforming power of God's Spirit, giving us a new perspective of what life is about – that life brought about by the ministry, death and Resurrection of Jesus. We meet Jesus at the sacramental table as people who have been influenced by the spirit of God and whose perception of life has been changed by God's touch upon our lives. Eucharist draws together the body of Christ for transformation, healing and wholeness, so that it may be that one, holy and catholic body called the church of Christ in every age.

† *Lord I come to you as I am. Help me to yield to your remaking without reservation, ready for your healing touch to make me whole. Amen.*

Living eucharistically, in the Spirit

Our meditations all week are summed up in this weekend reflection: living eucharistically is living in the Spirit as one body brought together by the unity of Father, Son and Holy Spirit – the Trinity. This means that we truly live not by human standards, although we live physically in the world, but by spiritually assessing what is the right or wrong thing to do. This is the only true way to live. And by living this way we become members of God's family.

> **For all who are led by the Spirit of God are children of God.**
>
> (*verse 14*)

We become children in this wonderful family by God's gracious nature of acceptance of all, whoever we are and wherever we come from. And it is a dynamic family, where we are not called to be uniform but equal in the way God sees and relates to us all. The benefits of being members of this family are not only for the present but our future is also secured with God. And so when we come together to celebrate the Eucharist, let us remember to regard one another as brothers and sisters, lovingly and forgivingly, for it is by grace that we are invited and we are under obligation to God alone, not our physical demands or desires.

† *Thank you, Lord, for adopting me as your child and for the privilege of being in the church family. Give me love and understanding for others and courage to allow them to share in my life. Amen.*

3 Parables and healings

Notes by Emmanuel Borlabi Bortey
based on the New Revised Standard Version

Emmanuel Borlabi Bortey is a minister of the Methodist Church of Ghana. For 23 years he served the publishing house of the Christian Council of Ghana, first as editor and later as General Manager. From 2004 to 2007 he was Superintendent Minister of the Akosombo Circuit in the Eastern Region of Ghana and is currently serving the Adenta Circuit in Accra, the capital city of Ghana.

Introduction

This week we continue our readings from Mark's gospel and the privilege of gaining further insight into the person of Jesus, which is primarily what the gospels seek to do: to bring us to faith, or an affirmation of our faith, in Jesus. More specifically, this week's readings should enable us appreciate the limitless nature of Jesus' power and authority.

Text for the week: Mark 5:41-42

He took her by the hand and said to her, 'Talitha cum,' which means, 'Little girl, get up!' And immediately the girl got up and began to walk about (she was twelve years of age). At this they were overcome with amazement.

For group discussion and personal thought

- Is it possible to demonstrate or experience today, in our personal lives and in the Christian community, the power and authority of Jesus (in his teaching and in his authority over nature, evil spirits, illness, and death) which we encounter in the gospels? If no, why not? If yes, how can this be realised?
- Discuss what this week's readings teach us about Jesus, his person and his work.

Jesus' authority in teaching

> **Again he began to teach beside the sea. Such a very large crowd gathered around him that he got into a boat on the sea and sat there . . . in his teaching he said to them: ' Listen! A sower went out to sow. And as he sowed, some seed fell on the path, . . . Other seed fell on rocky ground . . . Other seed fell among thorns . . . Other seed fell into good soil . . . '**
>
> (*part of verses 1-5 and 7-8*)

Clearly the crowds loved to listen to Jesus! Why? Jesus used stories that people could understand – activities from their everyday lives such as the work of a sower. Such stories were easy to remember and would have stuck in the minds of his hearers for a long time. Earlier in this gospel the author remarked that the crowds 'were astounded at his teaching, for he taught them as one having authority, and not as the scribes' (Mark 1: 22). However, Jesus was under no delusion about the response he could expect from the crowds. He clearly expected a mixed response from his hearers: the *seeds on the path* – those who quickly ignore what they hear; the *seeds on rocky ground* who will not make room in their minds for what they hear; the *seeds among thorns* who allow distractions to crowd out what they hear from their minds; and the *seeds on good soil* who take time to ponder the words of Jesus so that they exert a positive influence on their lives.

† *Lord Jesus, grant me grace so to meditate on your word that it may continuously transform me to live righteously.*

Jesus' authority over nature

Jesus was travelling in a boat with his disciples. Then . . .

> **A great wind-storm arose, and the waves beat into the boat, so that the boat was already being swamped. But [Jesus] was in the stern, asleep on the cushion; and they woke him up and said to him, 'Teacher, do you not care that we are perishing?' He woke up and rebuked the wind, and said to the sea, 'Peace! Be still!' Then the wind ceased, and there was a dead calm.**

(*verses 37-39*)

How could Jesus fall into such a deep sleep in the midst of such a storm? This is one of the gospel stories which enables us to appreciate who Jesus is. If he were a mere mortal he would certainly have shared the disciples' worry; some of them were experienced fishermen and had no doubt they were in danger of death. That Jesus could still the storm by a simple word of command clearly reveals that he is lord over nature. Indeed, the Creator of heaven and earth has authority over his creation. This and similar incidents compel us as Christians to conclude that Jesus is God, come to live among mortals. And we believe that he still dwells with us in the power of the Holy Spirit, and therefore we have no reason to panic when 'storms' arise in our lives. We cannot always have fair weather and a smooth journey through life. Some turbulence may arise, such as illness, accidents, stress and scarce resources. Whatever the adverse moments which confront us, we can trust Jesus to pilot us safely through it all.

† *Lord, grant me grace to so trust in your authority that I may never lose hope when I face difficult moments in my life.*

Mark 5:1-20

Jesus' authority over evil spirits

> **And when he had stepped out of the boat, immediately a man out of the tombs with an unclean spirit met him. He lived among the tombs; and no one could restrain him any more, even with a chain. . . . They came to Jesus and saw the demoniac sitting there, clothed and in his right mind, the very man who had had the legion; and they were afraid.**
>
> (*verses 2, 3 and 15*)

To the modern (Western?) mind, the man described in today's reading as being possessed by an evil spirit, may at best be described as a mentally sick person. In many developing countries, including large parts of Africa, the traditional world view accepts the idea that such illnesses are caused by evil spirits. 'Healing and deliverance' are critical and much valued forms of ministry in many churches in Africa. Testimonies of wholeness (healing) after deliverance from demonic possession abound in many African churches and communities where a ministry of healing and deliverance is carried out in the name of Jesus.

However, we must quickly add that it is dangerous to attribute all illnesses and misfortunes in life to the activity of demonic forces. Obsession with demonic activity is an ever-present danger in churches which conduct healing and deliverance services. What is needed today is a recognition that the authority of Jesus over evil spirits includes the provision of a shield against every form of evil in the lives of all who abide in Christ and in whom Christ dwells. The church, especially in developing countries, needs to emphasise this teaching.

† *Thank you, Jesus, for your authority over evil spirits which guarantees my protection from every form of demonic activity.*

Mark 5:21-34

Jesus' authority over illness

> **Now there was a woman who had been suffering from haemorrhages for twelve years . . . She had heard about Jesus, and came up behind him in the crowd and touched his cloak, for she said, 'If I but touch his clothes, I will be made well.' Immediately her haemorrhage stopped; and she felt in her body that she was healed of her disease.**
>
> (verses 25 and 27-29)

This woman had been ill for so long that she was prepared to try anything that might bring her healing. Her strenuous effort to break through the crowd just to touch Jesus was one such desperate effort in search of healing. Even short bouts of illness can make people miserable; what a great pain, then, to suffer from an illness for twelve long years! For many African people (and perhaps people in other developing parts of the world) diseases which defy the skills of doctors must necessarily originate from witches and similar forces of evil. Many, therefore, tend to seek spiritual intervention during times of illness – from the church as well as from other faith communities. How wonderful, then, to know that Jesus' authority extends to illnesses and that in Jesus we can be healed no matter what illness plagues us. The numerous accounts of healing in the gospels should kindle in us a living faith which trusts that we can still receive healing today in the name of Jesus – including healing through the God-given skills of doctors and medication.

† *Lord, we bring before you today all who are going through the pain of illness. May your healing touch bring them relief; we pray in the name of Jesus. Amen.*

Mark 5:35 – 6:6a

Jesus' authority over death

> **'Why do you make a commotion and weep? The child is not dead but sleeping.' And they laughed at him . . . He took her by the hand and said to her, 'Talitha cum', which means, 'Little girl, get up!' And immediately the girl got up and began to walk about (she was twelve years of age). At this they were overcome with amazement.**
>
> (*part of verses 39-40, and verses 41-42*)

All the gospel accounts include examples of Jesus demonstrating his authority over death, including cases where there could be no shadow of doubt that the person resurrected was indeed dead (Lazarus, for example, had been buried for four days; John 11: 39). These resurrection stories were very important to the gospel writers because they reached their climax in the account of Jesus' own resurrection from the dead. These resurrection stories vividly demonstrate the limitless nature of the power and authority of Jesus: not even death could halt his overwhelming authority.

In today's reading, the mourners in the house of Jairus could not help laughing at Jesus; it seemed ridiculous to claim the child was not dead. For us modern readers of the gospel stories, we have enough evidence to compel absolute faith in Jesus. Such faith implies hope in all circumstances. For the believer in Jesus and his authority, no condition or situation can be declared hopeless. Wherever Jesus comes he brings a fresh zest for life. In Jesus, life can never be a dull business. Jesus quickens us to enjoy an exuberant life – abundant life, life in its fullness with no room for despair.

† *Lord, grant me grace to enjoy the fullness of life which you quicken in all who entrust their lives to you.*

Mark 6:6b-16

Jesus invests us with authority

> **He called the twelve and began to send them out two by two, and gave them authority over the unclean spirits . . . So they went out and proclaimed that all should repent. They cast out many demons, and anointed with oil many who were sick and cured them.**
>
> (*verses 7 and 12-13*)

Our readings for this week revealed the vastness of Jesus' authority over all things in the created world: over knowledge (in his teaching), nature, evil spirits, illness, and even over death. After exposing his disciples to the extent of his authority, Jesus now sends them out to replicate what they have seen him do, in the wider community.

As Jesus sent his first disciples into the world, so he sends us, his modern-day disciples, Christians, to extend his ministry throughout the world. Perhaps the best description of the church is 'the body of Christ' (1 Corinthians 12:27). The Church is Christ's presence in today's world. We must consistently and vigorously call the world to repentance from sin and to faith in Jesus. The first disciples ministered in power: preaching, exorcising evil spirits, and healing. Jesus has given us, the Church in today's world, the same mandate. The power of Jesus is still the same. We need to move forward in this faith and assurance and trust God to so work in us, with us and through us that everyone everywhere will acknowledge the lordship and authority of Jesus.

† *Lord, continue to empower us, your Church in the world, to so bear witness to your authority in our world that many may be drawn to believe in you. Amen.*

4 Stirrings of conflict

Notes by Philip Wetherell
based on the Good News Bible

Philip Wetherell has just ended seven years as the director of the ecumenical charity Christians Abroad, though stopping work is difficult, so he still acts as a consultant and recruits volunteers for Christian projects in Africa and Asia. While missing the lively multicultural worshipping community of his parish in London, the best bit about moving to a rural area of England has been the welcome and support within the local church, as he was diagnosed with a serious disability.

Introduction

Conflict comes in many ways. Christians always feel challenged. In some parts of the world there is physical or inter-faith conflict. Others are in conflict on moral issues, and sadly it is sometimes different strands of the Christian community who do not agree. Some find it difficult to work alongside those they disagree with. We are all challenged by this week's readings, which all have elements of conflict. Jesus himself is challenged.

Text for the week: Mark 7:37

All who heard were completely amazed. 'How well he does everything!' they exclaimed.

For group discussion and personal thought

- When is it right for us to be in conflict? Jesus is often challenged, but how does he deal with this? What are the principles we should follow?

Mark 6:17-29

The death of John the Baptist

We may or may not know about those who have died for their faith in our local situation, and the story of the death of John the Baptist may feel like a bit of horrible history. But we all have to deal with the challenges of guilt and deception which are the basis of the story. Herodias' guilt from John the Baptist's condemnation of her marriage becomes anger. This leads to the deception that ends John's life. Worse still, she encourages her dancing daughter to perform in order to win her deceitful fight with her weak husband.

> **So the girl went out and asked her mother, 'What shall I ask for?' 'The head of John the Baptist,' she answered.**
>
> (*verse 24*)

This story is a foretaste of what is to come. Jesus himself will evoke the same conflict – guilt at his words, which people know inside themselves are right; anger at his success in healing, preaching and attracting the unpopular and despised. Worst of all, much of this comes from those in positions of spiritual authority. Their jealousy motivates their demand for crucifixion and prompts the deceit which leads to the release of Barabbas.

Many questions are raised. How do we react when someone tells us something we know deep inside is right? How can our church leaders help us deal with the petty things that anger us and divide us? In personal terms, who or what makes us wrongly jealous?

† Lord, help me to be true to myself by listening to your voice.

Mark 6:30-44

The feeding of the five thousand

At first, it is difficult to see the conflict in this wonderful story of sharing and generosity – whether we see it as a physical miracle (the food magnifies itself) or as perhaps the even bigger 'miracle' of people revealing and sharing their hidden picnics. On the face of it this is a great story of people who just leave everything and follow Jesus, creating what seems to be Jesus' biggest group of followers. These are not modern-day city dwellers unable to deal with hardship, but people who know how to manage without food for a while. They don't ask for food.

> **When it was getting late, his disciples came to him and said, 'It is already very late, and this is a lonely place. Send the people away, and let them go to the nearby farms and villages in order to buy themselves something to eat.'**
>
> (*verses 35-36*)

Is there a hidden motive here? Are the disciples upset that the crowd is there, do they want to be alone with Jesus, or are they simply and stupidly unaware of the power and authority of Jesus? It is that power and authority that leads to Jesus' arrest and trial, because the religious leaders are scared that power and authority are being taken away from them. Apparently even good things can make people respond in a way Jesus never would.

Do we act like that when someone has a different idea? Can we understand and determine when God is working in our friends or leaders in church or state?

† *Lord, help me to see the good in others and see it as your work in them.*

Mark 6:45-56

Walking on water

Jesus goes to pray and tells his disciples to go on ahead of him. They were rowing against the wind and having huge difficulty making any progress. Their human reaction to this ghost-like figure approaching them in the dark in the early morning is understandable. Already feeling vulnerable, tired, and still thinking through how the 5,000 had been fed, how did they feel when Jesus spoke to them?

> **'Courage!' he said . . . 'Don't be afraid!' Then he got into the boat with them and the wind died down. The disciples were completely amazed, because they had not understood the real meaning of the feeding of the five thousand.**
>
> (*part of verse 50, verse 51, and part of verse 52*)

This is followed by healing of many people in Gennesaret, another story to show us the power and authority of this man. The disciples were with him constantly, had time to talk, listen to his words, and see all that he did – and yet they did not understand the origin or extent of what he could do. Are we any better after two thousand years of thinking, listening, and experiencing the good he brought into the world?

As we know from our own lives and within the countries where we live, we do not always experience or act in the ways Jesus would want. If we do, this may stir conflict that we do not want. How can we help to end this?

† Lord, help us to understand and respond to the power of Jesus for good in this world.

Man-made rules

Jesus is the centre of conflict when the Pharisees attack him for not washing his hands before eating. His reply is one of his most memorable:

> **'"These people, says God, honour me with their words,**
> **but their heart is really far away from me.**
> **It is no use for them to worship me,**
> **because they teach man-made rules**
> **as though they were God's laws!"**
> **You put aside God's commands and obey the teachings of man.'**
>
> (*part of verse 6, and verses 7-8*)

Jesus says two things here, both of which are, I am sure, part of the Pharisees' growing opposition to him. They are challenged over the way they use so-called religious laws on family inheritance to enrich themselves – but, more importantly, Jesus has hinted at where his own demands of justice in everyday life come from. Rules have to be made on principles, and tomorrow's readings tell us more.

Most of us live in a world where man-made rules predominate. The greed of those who are wealthy at our expense is the cause of much of the world's poverty, yet many churches accept donations without asking too much about where they come from. Do we conveniently misuse an idea that the wealthy are rewarded by God and the poor must be sinners? Do we manage to avoid the principle Jesus established here? The rules and laws God wants come from high principles and not human convenience and detail.

† *Lord, when we judge others, let us obey your principles, not the laws of man.*

Mark 7:14-23

In or out?

Where we live can earn a 'reputation'. This can be national or very local and can depend on anything from a good tourist report about wildlife to something more critical. I lived in an area of London which became known for its violence among black teenagers. While I enjoyed the community for ten years, that was how many other people saw the area. Some blamed lack of education or poor local opportunities for work. Others based their theory on race and concentrated immigration.

> **'It is what comes out of a person that makes him unclean. For from the inside, from a person's heart, come the evil ideas which lead him to do immoral things.'**
>
> (part of verses 20 and 21)

Did the reported violence in the area where I lived come from inside – due to human nature? Or from outside – due to lack of government investment? People were easily divided on the issue – but how do Jesus' words relate to this or any other community problem?

His list of sins is a starter. These are the background to both. Deceit, greed and the others are symbolic of selfishness. These can be as much the motivation of the poor as they can be behind those who have power. We should excuse neither, though in other places Jesus blames the rich and powerful more than those he sees as victims. But conflict will end and our communities be healed only when good things come from the hearts of all. How can our churches help us to do that?

† Lord, help us to examine our hearts.

How well he does everything

The first part of this section of Mark is very different from any of the other miracle healings. There is a challenge from a Gentile woman, whose daughter Jesus at first refuses to heal. We might see here a modern parallel in a mixture of racism (or at least ethnic/tribal preference) and gender discrimination (verses 24-30). The woman makes Jesus change his mind. The image of a group of people as 'dogs' seems particularly offensive. Some people are reluctant to recognise that here the 'perfect' Jesus seems to be wrong at first and is made to change his position.

> **So Jesus said to her, 'Because of that answer, go back home, where you will find that the demon has gone out of your daughter!'**
>
> (verse 29)

This may have been just a test of the woman's faith, but even if true it seems very offensive. But whether or not Jesus was wrong at first, the story is a good illustration of the verses we read yesterday. What comes from the heart rules for both the woman and Jesus. The woman who is unacceptable in Jewish eyes puts her daughter's future before her own fear of rejection and confronts Jesus. Jesus' heart is more important than any call to deal first with his own people and, with a little help from the woman, his good heart rules. And his healing continues, with his heart again at the centre as he meets the deaf-mute (verses 31-37), so that the people say 'How well he does everything' (verse 37).

† *Lord, help us to learn from others.*

Burden Bearers

1 Friends and supporters

Notes by Chris Duffett
based on Today's New International Version

Chris Duffett is a Baptist minister and evangelist who founded The Light Project, a charity that aims to demonstrate the Christian message actively in a relevant way and to train others in evangelism. He leads a team of 30 people involved in 25 youth and community projects, working with local churches. He and his wife Ruth have three children.

Introduction

I enjoy praying with others in many different ways, some quiet, some loud. Last week I was rather surprised to be asked to lie on the floor and then everyone grabbed a part of me and lifted me above their heads! For a minute they prayed for me and literally raised me up before God! This rather unorthodox method of prayer spoke powerfully to me about how dependent I am upon others to support and encourage me. I could not do what I do as an evangelist if it wasn't for close friends to encourage and value me as a friend and a child of God. It is not possible to walk the path of faith alone, and this week's readings are a reminder that we need one another.

Text for the week: 1 Timothy 5:1

Do not rebuke an older man harshly, but exhort him as if he were your father. Treat younger men as brothers, older women as mothers, and younger women as sisters, with absolute purity.

For group discussion and personal thought

- How can you let your friends know that you are grateful to God for them?

1 Samuel 18:1-4; 20:1-42

God can bring friends to us quickly!

It is remarkable how quickly the friendship is made in today's reading. David spoke to King Saul while still clutching the head of the slain giant Goliath; as soon as the conversation was over and without any prior mention of Jonathan, David and he

> **became one in spirit . . . and he loved him as himself.**
>
> (chapter 18, part of verse 1)

A clue as to how such a friendship was able to develop so quickly can be found in other translations of the Bible that refer to their friendship as the Lord 'knitting together' their spirits. While meditating on this scripture I couldn't help wondering what was the reason for this cosmic, almighty spiritual weaving? The text seems to suggest that to be used mightily by God, as David was in conquering the fearsome Philistine, we need friends. Friends keep our feet on the ground. Friends help us to have a healthy perspective on our own lives. Friends remind us not to be so heavenly minded that we are of no earthly use! The text continues at an alarming pace: as soon as David has his new friend he is promoted to leadership level in the king's army, and his success in fighting the enemies of Israel causes women to sing songs and dance as they declare how much better David is than Saul. Without a friend to ground David it could have all gone to his head!

† *Lord God, you are the giver of friends! Help me to be open to you speaking to me through those around me. Help me to be willing to make new friends today for your glory. Amen.*

Joshua 2

Whom will you allow to help you?

Rahab's occupation and lifestyle were far from holy; yet a holy and perfect God guarded his servants in the roof of her brothel and Jericho was conquered through her help and hospitality.

> **'[P]lease swear to me by the LORD that you will show kindness to my family, because I have shown kindness to you. Give me a sure sign that you will spare the lives of my father and mother, my brothers and sisters, and all who belong to them – and that you will save us from death.' 'Our lives for your lives!' the men assured her.**
>
> (*verses 12-13, and part of verse 14*)

The Bible declares Rahab to be a woman of faith, 'because she welcomed the spies, [she] was not killed with those who were disobedient' (Hebrews 11: 31). I wonder whether I would have been so keen to welcome help and friendship from someone who traded sex as their way of living. Rahab reminds us that first and foremost our God loves people. Despite mess and immorality in people's lives and how sin separates people from God, God is not separated from people. God led the spies to Rahab's den of iniquity to find help and ultimately to have their lives saved. He is able to speak to and use the most unlikely of people. Do you need to be ready to embrace those whom you have written off as beyond the pale for your Church?

† *Help me to see what you are doing in the lives of those around me.*
Help me to regard people with love, despite their sin and lifestyle.
Help me to welcome those whom you are calling into relationship with you.
In the name of Jesus, Amen.

Ruth 1:1-19

There are some relationships we need to fight for

Naomi was most insistent that Ruth and Orpah should leave her and return to their own mother's homes and find new husbands. Orpah kissed her mother-in-law good-bye but

> **Ruth clung to her . . . when Naomi realised that Ruth was determined to go with her, she stopped urging her.**
>
> (*part of verses 14 and 18*)

There may be periods in our lifetime when we need to choose to be like Orpah or Ruth. We don't know what happened to Orpah because the story isn't recorded, but we cannot assume that she made the wrong decision; we do not know why it was Ruth's responsibility to fight for this relationship and Orpah's to move on from it. As we know the end of the story (if you haven't read it yet, it has a happy ending!) it's easy for us to see why Ruth made the choice to fight for a relationship with Naomi. But Ruth wasn't to know that her fortunes were to change. May we have the wisdom to know which relationships we must fight for and which ones we should move on from.

† *Father, would you please take a close look at my relationships with different people. If I need to develop and change these relationships, help me to have your insight to know which ones need to grow and help me to show a greater commitment to those people. I pray this in the knowledge that you are Lord of all people and the chief giver of all friendships and relationships. Amen.*

Job 2

Five-minute friendships

When Job's three friends . . . heard about all the troubles that had come upon him, they set out from their homes and met together by agreement to go and sympathise with him and comfort him. When they saw him from a distance, they could hardly recognise him; they began to weep aloud, and they tore their robes and sprinkled dust on their heads. Then they sat on the ground with him for seven days and seven nights. No-one said a word to him, because they saw how great his suffering was.

(*part of verse 11 and verses 12-13*)

Jobs friends challenge me to the core, because I don't have time for my friends. I have friends with whom I will literally spend five minutes at a time as I rush from one church activity to another. Job's friends (despite how annoying and wrong Job found them to be later on) gave quality, planned time to sit with Job for seven days and seven nights! One New Year's Eve I was praying and reflecting upon the year and asking God what was my greatest achievement. I enquired of God whether it was the Alpha courses I had started, the community youth club I had set up, or the work with people who are homeless. As I pondered on what I had done through the year, a clear thought came into my mind of the afternoon I spent with a friend from church, 'plane spotting' at Manchester Airport. In that moment I felt God say that one of my greatest achievements was that I had valued my friend and given him of my time.

† *Carve out time in my diary for those that you give to me as friends.*
Shape me to be a person who values people by my time.
Mould me to be one who can sit and simply support my friends in their life.
Bind me in deeper friendships that give you glory.

Luke 8:1-3

Resource one another

The picture that some people have of Jesus is of a cowboy, Lone Ranger type of character, turning up at a village on a horse, performing great signs and wonders and then heading off into the sunset to the next village, alone and ready to do his miracles. However, Jesus was always around people, being supported and cared for by ever increasing circles of people around him. He had the first three disciples, then the twelve, and then the 72 whom he commissioned to heal the sick. In the midst of these groups of followers were a small, close group of women who made much of this mission activity possible. They resourced what Jesus was doing out of their own funds and time.

> **Jesus travelled about from one town and village to another, proclaiming the good news of the kingdom of God. The Twelve were with him, and also some women . . . These women were helping to support them out of their own means.**
>
> (*part of verses 1-3*)

This minor, often overlooked, text reminds us that even Jesus needed the support of others, not just materially but also through time and emotional encouragement. This scripture reveals two principles for us all as followers of Christ. Firstly, are there people whom we can support so that they can do what God has called them to do? And secondly, are there people whom we should ask to support us in prayer and friendship to help us achieve what God has called us to do?

† *Help me to resource others and to receive help from those around me. Freely I have been given, so freely I should give.*

John 13: 21-26; 21:20-24

You are the beloved

Picture the scene: you are at a dinner party with twelve friends. One of your friends is Jesus. You are sharing a meal together and, while none of the guests know it as yet, it is the last meal that you will enjoy as friends. Imagine yourself around the table; how close are you sitting to Jesus? Are you distant from him, perhaps not even at the table? Do you feel that you can talk to him? John was able to say about himself that

> **One of them, the disciple whom Jesus loved, was reclining next to him.**
>
> (*chapter 21, verse 23*)

Take a few moments to consider that today Jesus calls you his beloved, and he wants you to talk with him like John and recline next to him.

> **Leaning back against Jesus.**
>
> (*part of chapter 21, verse 25*)

John felt comfortable enough to lean against Jesus and talk with him. Even in the midst of betrayal and pain, Jesus allowed John to be close to him and share in a friendship that was close. Imagine leaning back against Jesus. What do you need to tell him? Despite Jesus' majestic, mighty power he allows us by his Spirit to lean on him and talk with him. He is our friend, and we can declare that we are his beloved.

† *Loving Jesus, I love you.*
Loving Jesus, you are mine.
Loving Jesus, I am yours.
Loving Jesus, I love you.

IBRA International Appeal

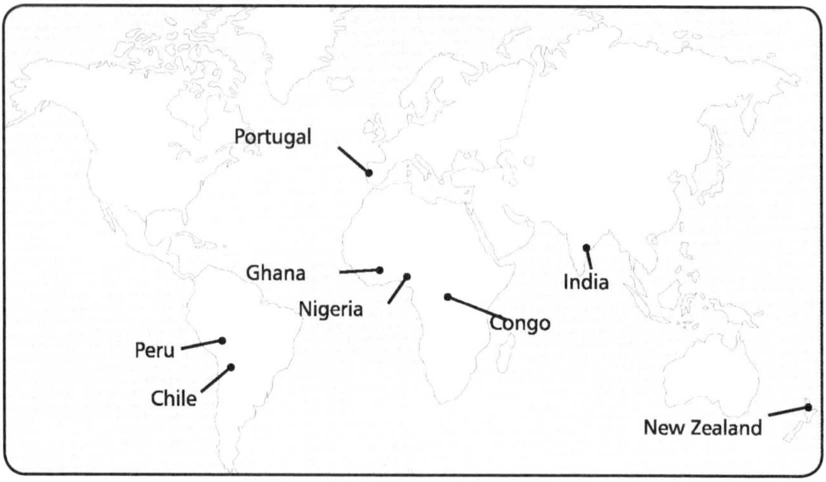

In five continents you will find Christians using IBRA material.

Some will be using books and Bible reading cards translated into their local language, whilst others use books printed in English. As well as our current overseas partners there are many more organisations who would like to print the books and cards themselves.

The IBRA International Fund works through churches, Christian groups and Christian publishing houses overseas to make these Bible reading resources available. Each year we receive more requests for help from the IBRA International Fund for assistance in producing these materials, but the only money we have to send is the money you give, so please help us again by giving generously.

Place your gift in the envelope provided and give it to your IBRA representative or send it direct to

The IBRA International Appeal
1020 Bristol Road
Selly Oak
Birmingham
B29 6LB
United Kingdom

Thank you for your help.

2 Mentors and teachers

Notes by Gloria Barrett-Sobers
based on the New International Version

Gloria Barrett-Sobers lives in Kingston, Jamaica, with her husband, Peter. She has recently retired as Registrar of the University of the West Indies and is adapting to being a full-time housewife and guardian to her two grandchildren, Ashlee and Jerome. A church leader and chorister at Providence Methodist Church in Kingston, she serves on the boards of the United Theological College of the West Indies and of Excelsior Community College.

Introduction

Many successful individuals will speak of people who have had great impact on their lives, often including a parent or teacher. All of us need friends, teachers, mentors and advisers to help us bear our burdens and meet our challenges. Relationships which provide encouragement, advice and critique are essential to our spiritual development and may come from unexpected sources. The Bible provides many accounts of such relationships. Our readings this week consider mentors or teachers of some of the prophets and leaders of Israel or heroes and heroines of faith in both Old and New Testaments.

Text for the week: 1 Timothy 1:18-19

Timothy, my son, I give you this instruction in keeping with the prophecies once made about you, so that by following them you may fight the good fight, holding on to faith and a good conscience.

For group discussion and personal thought

- What does Jethro's advice to Moses teach us about the necessity for applying commonsense to the management of church affairs?
- According to this week's readings, what are some key criteria to demand of those who seek leadership positions?

Exodus 18:1-27

Sound management advice from a father-in-law

Listen now to me and I will give you some advice, and may God be with you.

(*part of verse 19*)

In today's reading we find Moses extending himself all day, meeting his people, hearing their complaints, resolving their issues, teaching them God's ways and laws, all of which seems like very worthwhile and important work. However, Jethro, his father-in-law, a priest of Midian who had recently been converted to the worship of Jehovah, rebukes Moses for undertaking this task alone, pointing out that he would wear himself out. He advises him to select and appoint capable and trustworthy men who fear God, to handle the lesser disputes (verse 21). Jethro teaches his son-in-law how to delegate effectively, sound management practice applied over the centuries up to today. Moses does not seem to resent what some might perceive as Jethro's interference. Converted on the basis of Moses' stirring testimonies of Jehovah's goodness and providence, Jethro now seems to have successfully integrated his new-found faith into his thinking and shares his practical wisdom to the benefit of both Moses and the people of Israel. Often God uses family or other close relationships, where critique and challenge can be given and received in the appropriate spirit, to help us to become better Christian witnesses and leaders.

† *Help us to recognise and bless those who teach and mentor us along life's journey, and open our eyes and hearts to opportunities to share with others those insights and principles we have gained, so that we all may grow in your knowledge and wisdom and serve you better.*

Deuteronomy 31:1–29

Moses' charge to Joshua

> **Be strong and courageous, for you must go with this people into the land . . . The LORD himself goes before you and will be with you.**
>
> (*part of verses 1-3*)

From the time that Joshua, with his colleague Caleb, had returned from the land of Canaan with the minority positive report that although the Canaanites were giants and powerful, Israel should proceed and not be afraid to take the land, for 'the Lord is with us' (Numbers 14:9), Moses must have been keeping a special eye on him as a potential successor. God reveals Joshua as his chosen successor and Moses is now preparing the people and Joshua himself for the transition. All the people are encouraged to be strong, fearless and courageous as they take possession of the Promised Land. Joshua, as leader, must set the example, confident that God is with them. Moses does not restrain himself from warning them against rebelliousness and its dire consequences, but he encourages Joshua to continue to believe that God would be with him and to let that be the source of his confidence and courage. All of us have moments when we need direction, encouragement and support. God often provides a mentor just when we need one most.

† *Thank you, Lord, that you never leave us without friends and mentors who encourage us and provide guidance when we most need it.*

Judges 4

Deborah and Barak

I will lure Sisera, the commander of Jabin's army . . . and give him into your hands.

(*part of verse 7*)

Today's reading tells an interesting story of the strategic partnership between Deborah, an unusual woman of wisdom and influence, and Barak, who provides military leadership under Deborah's guidance. Together they accomplish a great victory for Israel over the Canaanites. Deborah, a popular prophetess and judge in Israel, commands Barak to take the field as Israel's commander-in-chief against Sisera. Barak consents, but only if she will accompany him into battle, which she does. As predicted by Deborah, the honour of getting rid of Sisera was left to a woman, Jael, and not to Barak, the military leader. Deborah plays a critical role in bringing about the success achieved by Barak. She initiates the operation, she accompanies and supports Barak in battle, but she also warns him that his failure to lead courageously and in full faith would deprive him of the highest honour. Most times a coach will encourage and guide us. Sometimes, however, we are warned when we are not prepared to take God at his word and trust him fully.

† *Lord, forgive our timidity and fear when faced with uncertainty and danger, even though you have promised to be with us and never to leave us alone.*

1 Samuel 3:1 – 4:1

Eli and Samuel

> **Go and lie down, and if he calls you, say, 'Speak, Lord, for your servant is listening.'**
>
> (*part of verse 9*)

Today we read how Eli teaches Samuel to recognise and respond to the voice of the Lord. We are told that 'Samuel did not yet know the Lord. The word of the Lord had not yet been revealed to him' (verse 7). That it is Eli who should teach Samuel to recognise God's voice and how to respond, is ironic, as Eli and his family are under God's curse because Eli had put his sinful sons before God. This curse is confirmed in the vision that came to Samuel that night. How terrible Samuel must have felt to be the one to proclaim the bad news to his priest and teacher! Samuel has evidently learnt valuable lessons from Eli, as we are told that the Lord 'revealed himself to Samuel through his word. And Samuel's word came to all Israel' (verses 3:21 and 4:1). Samuel, in contrast to Eli, goes on to be one of Israel's most important and successful prophets and judges. The Lord sometimes uses the least likely people to teach us important lessons.

† *Help us to learn the important lessons of life, regardless of the source, and help us readily to share the insights which we have, however unworthy we may feel.*

Luke 2:39-52

Mary, Joseph and Jesus

> **And Jesus grew in wisdom and stature, and in favour with God and man.**
>
> (*verse 52*)

This passage is the only biblical record of Jesus' youth and portrays him as a typical boy growing up in a typical family, and very much part of its traditions. Yet the reading also gives us an intimation that already Jesus had a clear consciousness of his identity and his mission. Jesus took advantage of the opportunity of being left behind in Jerusalem to engage the teachers in the temple court, respectfully questioning and listening to them, amazing them with the quality of his questions and his grasp of spiritual truth (verses 6 and 7). He returns home and continues to be obedient to his parents (verse 51). It is evident that both parents took seriously their role to teach and mentor their child, fully aware that he was special. Accordingly, he grew in wisdom and stature, and in favour with God and man (verse 52). In many parts of the world, my own country of Jamaica included, family life has broken down. One outcome is chronic crime and violence. Let us commit to building and encouraging family life such as Jesus knew.

† *Give us the caring and nurturing love of Mary and Joseph for all the children who come within our influence, so that they, like Jesus, may realise their identity and purpose in life.*

Paul and Timothy

> **Timothy, my son, I give you this instruction in keeping with the prophecies once made about you, so that by following them you may fight the good fight, holding on to faith and a good conscience.**
>
> (*1 Timothy 1:18, 19*)

Timothy was Paul's dearly loved companion and helper whom he first met at Lystra (Acts 16:1). He travelled with Paul on his missionary journeys and was sent by Paul from time to time on important missions. Paul left Timothy in Ephesus to check tendencies to false teaching and to supervise the affairs of the church there, and in this letter now writes to guide and encourage him in his work. Paul stands out as a teacher and mentor. The practical advice concerning church affairs and the preservation of purity of life and doctrine which he gives to Timothy is still valid and useful to us today. He stresses the need for love, a pure heart and a sincere faith (verse 5). Faith and a good conscience are worth guarding (verse 19). Let us give thanks for him and for all those who have helped us in our walk of faith by encouraging, admonishing, teaching and guiding us in times of need.

† *We thank you, Lord, for all those teachers and mentors who have helped us to get to know you and your ways better. Continue to strengthen our faith and our resolve to serve you better each day.*

3 Colleagues and peers

Notes by Peter Russell
based on the Revised English Bible

Peter Russell is a retired minister of the British Methodist Church. Much of his ministry was in training: training ministers in Nigeria and Zimbabwe (where he got into trouble with the Rhodesian government) and mission training in Selly Oak, Birmingham. He is a grandfather.

Introduction

God's servants cannot work alone. They need the help and support of others. In this week's passages we look at relationships where people work as helpers and companions, as equals rather than people of different status. Even Paul and Moses, heroes of the faith, needed help and support.

Text for the week: Exodus 4:15

[The Lord said to Moses] 'I shall help both of you to speak and tell both of you what to do.'

For group discussion and personal thought

- Do you have the support you need in your service of God? Where can you find support?
- Is there anyone doing God's work to whom you can give companionship and support?
- Were the heroes of the faith very different from the people you know?

Exodus 4:10-17, 27-31

Moses and Aaron

Moses has left Egypt and his fellow Israelites for fear of the Pharaoh, the king, and in his exile he has met the Lord who has told him to go back and speak to the Pharaoh and the leaders of the Israelites, and to lead the people into freedom. Moses thinks he is a poor speaker and a nobody, so he feels quite inadequate for this task, and asks the Lord to choose someone else. Instead, the Lord promises him the help of his brother Aaron, who is a man of ready speech.

> **'Who gives a man speech? . . . Who makes him keen-sighted or blind? Is it not I, the LORD?'**
>
> (*part of verse 11*)

Moses is the hero of the Exodus, the escape of the Israelites from slavery in Egypt, so this part of his story is rather surprising: heroes should not feel inadequate! The story suggests that Moses was an ordinary man who was helped by God and did what he did because God was with him.

† *Dear God, be with me so that I can love and serve you.*

2 Samuel 23:8-39

David's heroes

This passage is one of three appendices to the history of King David told in 2 Samuel 9-20. There are stories of famine and war, and three songs of David. Then follows this list of heroes, men who were with David when he was an outlaw in the reign of King Saul. It consists chiefly of a list of names, but there is the story of men who fetched water from Bethlehem for David. David does not feel worthy to benefit from the courage of the men, who had risked their lives for him, and so he pours out the water as an offering to God.

These are the names of David's heroes.

(*part of verse 8*)

The passage reads like an official list to which somebody has added notes about particular outstanding actions. Much of the history of David is to do with war against the enemies of Israel, and so these are mostly stories of brave deeds that helped David to victory. The name of David was and still is well known, and this passage reminds us that many people played a part in his work. Someone has made sure that their names are not forgotten, but there were many more whose names have vanished. This is the case in many of the great achievements of humanity – thank God for the many heroes who have made the world a better place, but whose names have been forgotten.

† God, let me take my place in the company of your servants.

2 Kings 2:1-18

Elijah and Elisha

In 1 Kings 19:16-19 God tells Elijah to anoint Elisha to be prophet in his place. Now the time has come for Elisha to take over.

> **Elijah said to Elisha, 'Tell me what I can do for you before I am taken from you.' Elisha said, 'Let me inherit a double share of your spirit.'**
>
> (part of verse 9)

The double share is the share of an eldest son and heir. Elisha wants to be the true heir of Elijah, and the cloak with its wonderful power is the symbol of this (verses 13-14). Elijah has been taken to God, but the work goes on.

We are part of the great succession of workers for God; from Jesus through the apostles, through their disciples, down through the generations, down to us, there are people, remembered and forgotten, who have carried on the work of Christ. For most a time comes when they realise that they can no longer go on as they have done. We get tired, we have said all we have to say and done all we can do, we feel called to some other work, our minds and bodies show signs of age, and like Elijah we have to hand over the things, big and little, that we do for God. We have to leave to others our work in the church, our work for charity, our kindnesses to our neighbours. God sees that the good work goes on.

† *Loving God, may I be worthy of my place in the great succession.*

Luke 10:1-9

The seventy-two sent out in pairs

Jesus too relied on people to help him and here he sends them to the places where he is intending to go. He cares for their need for support and fellowship by sending them in twos, and encourages them to accept hospitality. The Greek word used here for 'send' is the root of the word 'apostle'. Apostles are people who are sent, and in the law of Jesus' day what sent people did and what was done to them was reckoned to be done by or to the sender. So the 72 go as Jesus' commissioned representatives, sent by the One who is sent by God (see John 17:18).

'The kingdom of God has come upon you.'
(*part of verse* 9)

The disciples go to say that the kingdom of God has come, and to pray for people's peace. 'Peace' meant more than tranquillity or the absence of war. It meant all that is good – total well-being. It is the gift of God to his people, what they have when the kingly rule of the God of peace and love has come to them. The words of verse 12, addressed to the people of Chorazin and Bethsaida, are not a threat but a warning. People may reject God and so lose his peace.

† God of love, let me share your kingdom and your peace.

Paul and Barnabas

Paul has had his encounter with the risen Christ, and now preaches Christ as the Son of God. The change from persecutor to disciple causes surprise, and suspicion. Barnabas (whom we meet first in Acts 4:36) apparently knows about Paul's experience and is able to accept him, and introduce him to the Christian fellowship in Jerusalem. Then Paul is sent for his own safety to Tarsus, his home town. Barnabas is sent to Antioch to be with the growing church there, and fetches Paul to be his companion in the work of teaching and evangelism. Later they travel together as missionaries.

> **[T]he two of them lived in fellowship with the church there, and gave instruction to large numbers.**
>
> (*part of verse 26*)

This is a story of friendship. Barnabas apparently sees Paul's trouble and rescues him, teaching the Christians that Paul is no longer to be feared. In Antioch he brings his friend Paul to share his work, and they become companions in Christ's service.

† *Thank you, God, for friends in Christ: may your blessing rest on our friendship.*

Galatians 1:13 – 2:14

Paul and Peter

We read in the Acts of the Apostles of the controversy over the place of Gentiles, non-Jews, in the Christian fellowship. Should they be admitted at all? Should they be bound by the laws that Jews obeyed, such as the laws about food and circumcision? Paul had a strong vocation to evangelise Gentiles and was convinced that they should be free of the parts of the law that did not concern love of God and neighbour, sharing a freedom that Jesus enjoyed and taught (see Mark 7:19):

> **for the same God who was at work in Peter's mission to the Jews was also at work in mine to the Gentiles.**
>
> (*chapter 2, verse 8*)

In spite of Paul's strong disagreement with Peter, there is no sense that he feels that Peter had no place in the plans of God. In the church there has to be room for different callings and different views.

Cephas, or better *Kephas*, is the word Jesus would have used for 'Man of Rock'. Greek speakers used *Petros*, from *petra*, meaning 'rock', and we have turned it into *Peter*.

† *Father of all, teach your people how to disagree with love and understanding.*

4 Challengers and critics

Notes by Marian Strachan
based on the New Revised Standard Version

Marian Strachan is the wife of a Baptist minister serving with both a city centre church and a village church in Devon, England. They have also worked for the United Reformed Church and in a university chaplaincy. Marian has taught in Papua New Guinea, Samoa and England. She currently works with both adults and children in the church.

Introduction

We learn and grow through living and working with others. Our relationships with those around us can be challenging, rewarding and fulfilling, but they can also be painful and demanding. We need 'critical friends' who will question and challenge what we do and say, and who will also reflect positive feedback to encourage and support us. The challengers and critics in this week's readings made life uncomfortable for some and a joy for others.

Text for the week: 1 Kings 10:1

When the queen of Sheba heard of the fame of Solomon . . . she came to test him with hard questions.

For group discussion and personal thought

- Challengers and critics of your faith journey – can you think of any who have been especially helpful? How did they help?
- In your Christian life and church life, how do you manage criticism, both positive and negative?
- How can your church listen to the community around it, as well as speak to it?

2 Samuel 12:1-14

(Note that some translations include the beginning of this story at the end of chapter 11.)

Truthfulness in relationships

In Britain we sometimes talk about 'home truths'. This is information about us that is true but uncomfortable to hear: for example, when a friend mentions that we've said or done something that is unkind, selfish, or wrong. We do not like to be told home truths, but we can learn from them. Even leaders and kings need those who will speak truths that are uncomfortable and challenging. The prophets of the Old Testament were God's messengers, who spoke out when they saw injustice and wrongdoing.

Nathan, the chief prophet in the court of King David, is remembered especially for his courage in confronting his king. When David took Uriah's wife and killed Uriah, it was a terrible stain on David's character. David had mostly lived to please God, so his wicked actions must have saddened and horrified his chief prophet. Exposing David's wrongdoing showed that Nathan was loyal both to God and his king.

> **But the thing that David had done displeased the LORD, and the LORD sent Nathan to David. He came to him, and said to him . . . 'Why have you despised the word of the Lord, to do what is evil in his sight?' . . . David said to Nathan, 'I have sinned against the Lord.'**
>
> (*part of verses 1, 9 and 13*)

David made no excuses, he acknowledged his sin immediately. Repentance brings God's forgiveness. But David had to face up to the truth and effects of his wrong actions.

† Dear Lord, give us those who will speak your word, to challenge, guide, encourage and help us.

1 Kings 10:1-10

Questioning relationships

Between the ages of six and eight, children's favourite words seem to be 'why' and 'how'. This can be stimulating for their teachers and exhausting for their parents! Jesus often asked questions and people also questioned him. Do we welcome questions as an opportunity to talk with others and find out what they think? Or do we find questions threatening?

> **When the queen of Sheba heard of the fame of Solomon, (fame due to the name of the LORD), she came to test him with hard questions . . . and when she came to Solomon she told him all that was on her mind. Solomon answered all her questions; there was nothing hidden from the king that he could not explain to her.**
>
> (*verse 1, part of verse 2, and verse 3*)

The queen, who probably traded with Solomon, travelled from southern Arabia to Jerusalem. There she saw how prosperous Solomon's people seemed to be and how well he ruled. Having heard of his wisdom, she was eager to question and discuss many things with him. These two rulers appear to have trusted and respected each other, and valued the opportunity to talk, learn from each other, and share ideas.

We all benefit from sharing ideas, and we need others to help us question and think about what we say and do.

† *Loving God, I pray for wisdom to serve you well, and for willingness to learn from the insights of others.*

1 Kings 21

Relationships and consequences

King Ahab was weak. He allowed his wicked wife Jezebel to do as she pleased. Jezebel encouraged idolatry and many atrocities in the kingdom. Ahab's desire for Naboth's ancestral property led to theft, lies and murder. God sent Elijah to challenge the king.

> **Ahab said to Elijah, 'Have you found me, O my enemy?' He answered, 'I have found you. Because you have sold yourself to do what is evil in the sight of the LORD, I will bring disaster on you . . . When Ahab heard these words he tore his clothes and put sackcloth over his bare flesh; . . . he fasted . . . and went about dejectedly. Then the word of the LORD came to Elijah the Tishbite, 'Have you seen how Ahab has humbled himself before me?'**
>
> (*verse 20, part of verses 21 and 27, verse 28, and part of verse 29*)

Ahab's sorrow and humility over his shortcomings saved him. But Jezebel's evil deeds had terrible consequences. The Old Testament writers believed that the disastrous lives of Ahab's children were God's punishment for the sins of their parents. The God and Father of our Lord Jesus Christ didn't behave in this way, but in Old Testament times people thought he did.

In our own time we know that some children have terrible lives because of their parents. Irresponsible, uncaring parents cause harm and suffering to their children's lives and futures.

† Lord, we pray for parents. Show us how we can support them.

Relationships and responsibilities

God's people had been created to serve him and be a blessing to others. When they disobeyed, God sent his prophets to help and guide them, but they were ignored. Even worse, in Jeremiah's time the people and leaders rejected God and turned to the evil practice of child sacrifice as part of their worship of other gods. Jeremiah had a sad and difficult task. He had to tell the people that they could not commit sin continually and still think that God would bless and use them. They would be punished for their idolatry, pride, and injustices

> **Thus says the LORD of hosts, the God of Israel: I am now bringing upon this city and upon all its towns all the disaster that I have pronounced against it, because they have stiffened their necks, refusing to hear my words.**
>
> (*chapter 19, verse 15*)

We might have expected that Pashur, a temple priest, would have supported Jeremiah. But he lied and said only what others wanted to hear.

> **Now the priest Pashur son of Immer, who was chief officer in the house of the LORD, heard Jeremiah prophesying these things. Then Pashur struck the prophet Jeremiah, and put him in the stocks.**
>
> (*chapter 20, verse 1 and part of verse 2*)

Leaders have great responsibility. If they say only what others want to hear, and hide or ignore the truth, as Pashur had done, it not only hurts them but also others in their care.

† *Pray for world leaders and their advisers.*

Matthew 15:21-28

Challenging relationships

We all need companions, friends, challengers and critics on our journey of faith and so did Jesus. He went away with his disciples, perhaps to be quiet and rest. They were disturbed by a Canaanite woman who asked for help. The disciples wanted to send her away. The woman was a Gentile, and Jesus said his mission was to the Jews.

> **He answered, 'I was sent only to the lost sheep of the house of Israel.' But she came and knelt before him, saying, 'Lord, help me.' He answered, 'It is not fair to take the children's food and throw it to the dogs.' She said, 'Yes, Lord, yet even the dogs eat the crumbs that fall from their master's table.' Then Jesus answered her, 'Woman, great is your faith! Let it be done for you as you wish.' And her daughter was healed instantly.**

(*verses 24-28*)

This woman did not give up easily. Even if Jesus' mission was to the Jews, surely he must have a few crumbs of compassion and healing for her daughter. Was she pleading with Jesus, or was she challenging him? Some think she challenged Jesus to expand his vision, ministry and mission to include those outside Judaism – to be the Saviour of all who came to him in faith. Or was Jesus challenging her, hoping and looking for that kind of persistence and faith that he could use to help others?

† Persist in prayer and grow in faith – I can, with your help, Lord.

Acts 15:1-20

Challenge and co-operation

In Antioch, the gospel had been received by both Jews and Gentiles, who lived together as Christian brothers and sisters. Visiting Jews from Judea argued that Gentiles should only come into the church if they first accepted Jewish Law. After many discussions, Paul and Barnabas were sent to the headquarters of the church in Jerusalem to consult the leaders there. Peter shared his own experiences of mission to the Gentiles and said:

> **God, who knows the human heart, testified to [the Gentiles] by giving them the Holy Spirit, just as he did us, and in cleansing their hearts by faith he has made no distinction between them and us . . . we believe that we will be saved through the grace of the Lord Jesus, just as they will.'**
>
> (*verses 8 and 9, and part of verse 11*)

James, the much respected leader of the Jerusalem church, confirmed what Peter had said and showed how the prophets had spoken about all peoples seeking the Lord. So the Gentile believers were welcomed into the church.

In today's passage we read how the great leaders of the early church faced up to dissension over one of the most important and divisive issues that faced them. It began with argument and disagreement. But by working together, sharing experiences, supporting one another, and being willing to listen to each other, the early Church finally recognised where God was leading.

† *Pray for leaders of the Church, as they help us to understand what God is wanting us to say and do today.*

Ezekiel

1 The call of Ezekiel

Notes by Corneliu Constantineanu
based on the New International Version

Corneliu Constantineanu is a Romanian Christian pastor. He is Associate Professor and Academic Dean at the Evangelical Theological Seminary in Osijek, and President of Elim Evangelical Theological Seminary in Timişoara, Romania. Married to Ioana, they have two daughters, Anamaria and Carmen.

Introduction

The book of Ezekiel was written in a very tumultuous time for the people of Jerusalem and Judah. The prophet speaks to the exiles in Babylon and condemns the religious abominations that led them there. But the people left behind continue in their disobedience which will eventually lead to the destruction of Jerusalem and prolonged exile. Ezekiel, himself an exiled priest and prophet, uses arresting visions and powerful symbolic actions to bring a clear message from God: he will judge and cleanse his sinful people but, faithful to his promises, will ultimately restore them, so that everyone will see 'the glory of the Lord'. Ezekiel's call is grounded in 'the glory of God'. Only a proper understanding of this will explain the impending judgement.

Text for the week: Ezekiel 3:17

'Son of man, I have made you a watchman for the house of Israel; so hear the word I speak and give them warning from me.'

For group discussion and personal thought

- Have you sometimes felt like Ezekiel, sent to accomplish a very difficult task for which you feel totally inadequate? What significant lessons have you learned from the way he responded to God's call?

Ezekiel 1:1-28

The foundation of Ezekiel's call

Today's text is by no means obvious and straightforward, with its images of windstorms and living creatures with four faces and wings, glowing metal and wheels, fire and the roar of rushing waters, a heavenly throne and brilliant light, and so forth. At a closer reading, however, Ezekiel seems to be trying very hard to give us at least some hints of something so powerful and wonderful that it defies simple description: a vision of the glory of God, the Almighty. No one has ever seen the invisible God and so no biblical writer ever attempted to describe him. All they can do, like Ezekiel, is to try to portray what appeared to be a likeness of his glory:

> **Like the appearance of a rainbow in the clouds on a rainy day, so was the radiance around him. This was the appearance of the likeness of the glory of the Lord.**
>
> (*verse 28*)

Despite the difficulty of putting it into words, the message of the vision is rather clear: the sovereign God is above all people and all things; his Word is everywhere, reaching out to all his people, reassuring them of his presence. This vision of God's glory also represents the foundation of Ezekiel's call and the message he will be called to proclaim. Only by catching a glimpse of the glory of the Lord could Ezekiel speak of it and proclaim it; and only in the light of God's holiness and glory can his impending judgement be understood.

† *Our heavenly Father, give us a glimpse of your glory to shine on our path always, but especially when we go through our darkest moments. And may your glory inspire us to share it with the people who cross our way.*

Ezekiel 1:28b – 3.3

(The reading begins in the second half of verse 28)

The call and the challenge defined

Contrary to our common human expectation, when people have rebelled against and rejected their God, God does not abandon them but calls a prophet to speak to them! True, God's presence causes Ezekiel to fall on the ground (1:28b) unable to stand by himself, aware of the greatness, splendour and glory of God. In a situation of rebellion and helplessness, God calls Ezekiel and sends him to speak his words:

> **'Son of man, I am sending you to the Israelites, to a rebellious nation . . . You must speak my words to them, whether they listen or fail to listen.'**
>
> (*part of verses 3 and 7*)

Both Ezekiel and his call are thus a reminder of God's faithfulness. The call of God, however, carries many challenges. Given the difficulty of his task, Ezekiel feels profoundly the challenge of fear and rejection. God knows it and encourages him no less than three times, 'do not be afraid' (verse 6). When God calls us, he encourages and empowers us to respond to that call. The Spirit of God enters into us, making us stand and respond (verse 2). It is this that empowers us, gives us courage to overcome fear, and enables us to respond to God's call.

† *Lord, we ask for your strength and your Spirit as we respond to your call. Help us to be faithful to your call whatever challenges come on our way.*

A watchman to Israel

God warns and prepares Ezekiel for the rejection that will follow the message (verses 4-7), and yet he has no choice but to obey and speak to them (verses 8-11). God is determined to send Ezekiel to speak to his people despite their clear disobedience and stubbornness – the greatness of his love and patience amazes and shocks.

> **'Son of man, I have made you a watchman for the house of Israel; so hear the word I speak and give them warning from me.'**
>
> (*verse 17*)

Much responsibility is laid on the 'watchman' – he must warn people against the judgement of God, and their salvation or perdition depend on him. He will be responsible for their life (verse 20). A huge responsibility for a mortal! However, the text shows clearly, again and again, that it is the Spirit of God who makes Ezekiel's task possible (verses 12, 14, 24). If God call us to a specific ministry, he will empower us with his Spirit so that by divine authority we can carry out his task. And if we are called then we must make the message our own and deliver it so that our hearers can be saved and brought back into relationship with the Father. If we find ourselves as 'watchmen [or women] on the wall', Ezekiel reminds us that we have a double duty: to *watch* – listen, discern, hear the words of the God and take them in; and to *warn* of any danger and testify to God's message.

† *Lord, make us your watchmen or women for a lost and desperate world which perishes without you. Enable us to hear you clearly and then strengthen us and give us courage to speak for you, to witness to your goodness and love.*

Ezekiel 4:1-17

Embodying the call and bearing sin

Ezekiel pays a great price as he answers God's call. Being a prophet is not simply to speak in the name of God but also to bear the sins of his people:

> **Then lie on your left side and put the sin of the house of Israel upon yourself. You are to bear their sin for the number of days you lie on your side . . . I will tie you up with ropes so that you cannot turn from one side to the other until you have finished the days of your siege.**
>
> (*verses 4 and 8*)

The prophet is one of the people, identifying himself with them as he takes upon himself the burden of sin and guilt of the nation. Though his action is symbolic, it suggests a true spiritual experience for Ezekiel and requires real endurance. He has to lie on his side every night (verses 4-6), be tied with ropes for many days (verse 9), limit his food and drink (verse 10), bake his bread over cow manure (verse 15). He has to illustrate and embody his message by sharing the pain, shame and suffering of the sins of God's people.

We too are called to embody God's message to our own people – not from a safe and comfortable distance but experiencing their pain and anguish, understanding and carrying the burden of their sin and guilt. Only then can we properly present God's message of grace and forgiveness.

† *Dear Lord, help us to embody your message in our everyday life and to bear the sin and guilt of others towards redemption. Make us instruments of your grace and forgiveness.*

The judgement of Jerusalem

It is very uncomfortable and difficult to hear a message of judgement from God! We are so accustomed to hearing and speaking about God's love, forgiveness and grace that we easily forget or neglect the other aspect of God's work: judgement. Jerusalem, the great city of God, was supposed to be a light to the nations but would become a shame and ruin among the nations because of its moral corruption. This was unbelievable and shocking, unthinkable to everyone: those who were supposed to manifest the glory of the Lord among the nations had themselves fallen into darkness!

> **I will make you a ruin and a reproach among the nations around you, in the sight of all who pass by. You will be a reproach and a taunt, a warning and an object of horror to the nations around you when I inflict punishment on you in anger and in wrath and with stinging rebuke. I the LORD have spoken**
>
> (*verses 14-15*)

It is no accident that for many people one of the most urgent and important tasks of churches around the world is to repent of their misdeeds and *be* the communities of redemption they were meant to be. A self-sufficient, arrogant and unrepentant church will experience the judgement of God and become a spectacle to all. The judgement of Jerusalem in Ezekiel's time is a great and timely reminder for us.

† *Lord Jesus, we ask your forgiveness for not being what we were meant to be. We repent before you of our shortcomings and ask you to give us strength to become communities of love, faith and hope, a sign of your kingdom in this broken world.*

Ezekiel 8:1-18

A vision of God

We began this week's readings with the 'glory of the Lord' as the foundation of Ezekiel's call, and appropriately we end with another vision of God. Before he was ready to see the 'abominations' of the people of Israel and the consequences of their choices, Ezekiel had to be exposed to the overwhelming presence and manifestation of God:

> **[T]he hand of the Sovereign LORD came upon me there. I looked, and I saw a figure like that of a man. From what appeared to be his waist down he was like fire, and from there up his appearance was as bright as glowing metal.**
>
> (*part of verse 1, and verse 2*)

Only from the perspective of God's consuming fire and radiant glory could Ezekiel understand and interpret the awful sin he would see in the elders of Jerusalem. In the light of God's vision he was able to discern and comprehend the magnitude of sin and the consequences of abandoning God. The vision of fire represents the wrath of God against sin and God's way of eradicating evil. However, Ezekiel is enabled to see beyond the consuming fire of God into his radiant presence, glory and goodness. As we are daily exposed to sin, injustice and rebellion against God, we need to have the vision of God always before us, a God who is a consuming fire but also serene radiance. Only from God's perspective will we be able to bring a message of hope to this world.

† *Heavenly Father, grant us your vision and enable to live and act in the light of your holy presence and glory.*

2 Words of warning

Notes by Lesley George Anderson
based on the New Revised Standard Version

Lesley G Anderson is the President of the United Theological College of the West Indies (UTCWI), Jamaica, and Chair of the Praesidium of the Caribbean Conference of Churches (CCC). He is also a member of the World Council of Churches (WCC) Pentecostal Joint Consultative Group.

Introduction

Ezekiel, prophet and visionary, was a man chosen by God to proclaim with power and conviction that he was a just and mighty God. Instead of destroying the people of Israel for their sins as he did other nations, he permitted only their captivity. He warned them to repent of their rebellious ways. He continually instructed them that he was their God. The phrase 'they shall know that I am the Lord' occurs approximately thirty times in chapters 6–39. God informed them that neighbouring nations who rejoiced over their downfall would be judged (25:1 – 32:32). They must live in hope that Israel would have a Davidic king and be restored.

Text for the week: Ezekiel 13:1-2

The word of the Lord came to me. Mortal, prophesy against the prophets of Israel who are prophesying; say to those who prophesy out of their own imagination: 'Hear the word of the Lord!'

For group discussion and personal thought

- Read again Ezekiel 13:1-16. Why is it that with all our sophistication some people are still gullible to listen and follow those who 'prophesy from their own imagination'? What are some of the manifestations of these in your society? Who are those who preach not the Word of God? In what way do you see yourself being an Ezekiel?

Ezekiel 11:13-25

Keep hope alive

Hope had grown dim. The promises of God appeared lost. The exile was a dominant humiliating event in the experience of the people of Israel. Conquered by King Nebuchadnezzar, the elite and the marginalised suffering poor of Judah's society were all together in Babylon. Ezekiel, the son of a priest named Buzi, whose name means 'God will strengthen', was there too. In the midst of the desolation he gave the people hope. This is what he said:

> **I will gather you from the peoples and . . . I will give them one heart, and put a new spirit within them.**
>
> (*part of verses 17 and 19*)

I went to visit a young woman dying from cancer at the University Hospital in Jamaica. With her was her only son. In her predicament she never felt as if she was in exile. She had the assurance that God was with her. Death was near, but God was nearer. In her weakness, she felt his strength. In her moments of pain and despair, he provided her with hope.

Jerusalem, God's holy city, was a ray of hope. The people believed God was there. However, Ezekiel warned them that both the city and the temple would be destroyed, but they must keep faith and hope in God. Because Ezekiel was certain of God's restoration promises, he made God's glory in the midst of desolation and sadness his central message (verses 22-23).

† *Almighty God, many of us have been sustained through illnesses, hardships and the trials of life because you cared. Give us courage to live in hope. Amen!*

Ezekiel 12:1-20

See and hear

At the beginning of this passage, the prophet again speaks:

> **The word of the LORD came to me: Mortal, you are living in the midst of a rebellious house, who have eyes to see but do not see, who have ears to hear but do not hear.**
>
> (*verses 1-2*)

In the Caribbean there are two sayings appropriate to this story: 'What you do not see will not trouble you', which means attend to your own affairs. And 'If you do not hear you will feel', which means that when you are rebellious or disobedient to God, your parents or anyone in authority and do not listen, you will bear the consequences of your actions. The prophet speaks when he is called by God to speak or he must remain 'speechless' (silent). Ezekiel faced two basic challenges: firstly, the people had eyes to see Ezekiel's acted-out prophecies: they had seen him bound and starving; they had seen him growing thinner and weaker; they had seen him with nagging sores; they had seen him dramatise the fall of Jerusalem, but they refused to see in his actions a sign from God. Secondly, they had ears to hear the truth but were not prepared to hear because they were both unbelievers and rebellious. The consequence of Israel's rebelliousness was that the prince and people would be carried into exile with broken hearts, for there would be no postponement of the judgement.

† *Teach us in your wisdom, O Lord, how to see and to hear your word. Amen.*

Ezekiel 13:1-16

Beware of false prophets

Again the prophet speaks:

> **The word of the LORD came to me. Mortal, prophesy against the prophets of Israel who are prophesying; say to those who prophesy out of their own imagination: 'Hear the word of the LORD!'**
>
> (*verses 1-2*)

Ezekiel's ministry was becoming very challenging and difficult. Speaking only when led by the Spirit of God, he made a clear distinction between himself and the false prophets: he was a prophet of God, they were not; he spoke on behalf of God, they spoke on behalf of men; he was inspired by the Spirit, they were inspired by their own spirit. They were spiritually blind prophets. They could 'not see' themselves as deceivers. They 'misled' the people and prophesied 'lies' to them. They spoke of peace when there was no peace. They were not in communion with God so they had no message from him. Ezekiel did and prophesied against them.

Some preachers today give the impression that they are true prophets. Some are exceedingly rich and popular, preaching their own inspired word to cheering, dancing and clapping crowds of people. Think and reflect: Is God's word being proclaimed in all of these?

† O Lord, my God, help and guide me in all your ways. Amen

Assume personal responsibility for your sins

Ezekiel, having received a word from the Lord, speaks again:

> **What do you mean by repeating this proverb concerning the land of Israel, 'The parents have eaten sour grapes, and the children's teeth are set on edge'? As I live, says the LORD God, this proverb shall no more be used by you in Israel.**
>
> (*verses 2-3*)

This proverb was exceedingly popular because it was easier to blame someone else for one's own sins. In this case, the exiles blamed their plight on the sins of their 'parents', but their judgement stems from their own sins (see Lamentations 5:7). Parents do have a responsibility to guide their children's upbringing. I visited a graveyard recently and many of the dead were boys from eleven years of age up. Many died from violence and gang wars. Who is to be blamed: the parents or the children? On the other hand, some young boys living in the same environment have grown up to assume responsible citizenship and leadership in their community. Was their success due to their parents or to their own efforts?

Determinism cannot dictate anyone's outcome in life. In the end, having freedom of choice and free will, we must each take responsibility for our sins.

† *In assuming responsibility for my life, help me to depend on you, O Lord. Amen.*

Ezekiel 18:19-32

Seek the way of the lord

Once again Ezekiel was compelled to speak:

> **Therefore I will judge you, O house of Israel, all of you according to your ways, says the LORD God. Repent and turn from all your transgressions; otherwise iniquity will be your ruin.**
>
> (*verse 30*)

The sins and rebelliousness of the kings, leaders and people of Israel were judged as a nation. Of course, individuals too had to assume responsibility for their own sins. Now it was important to have a personal relationship with God. Those who sin and rebel against God would die! Those who kept the covenant and had 'a new heart and a new spirit' (verse 31) would live. Those who responded to God, turned from their transgressions and walked in his ways would live.

Sometimes we become stumbling blocks to others by the things we say and the way we behave. Let us repent of our sins and turn to Jesus Christ. He is the Son of the living God and our greatest example! He is loving, merciful and forgiving. Let us walk with him all the days of our lives.

† *Give me a new heart, and a new spirit, and a new mind in Christ, O God, and in your mercy, cleanse me from all unrighteousness. Amen.*

Ezekiel 22:23-31

Depart from evil

Evil had penetrated the whole of society. False prophets continued to mislead the people. The princes stole from the people. They made married women widows. The holy was violated and wickedness prevailed. In the midst of it all was general corruption. The prophets, priests and princes were all sinful and God was angry. Ezekiel warns:

> **You are a land that is not cleansed, not rained upon in the day of indignation.**
>
> (*part of verse 24*)

This means there will be no rain to replenish the land. It will remain dry! Hurricane Dean came to Jamaica. Many homes were damaged. Trees were uprooted. Flooding was everywhere. Electricity was cut. Water was at a premium. But in our suffering, God was present. The life of the land was renewed.

The trees are now once again bearing fruit. The birds are singing and we are rebuilding. God is good – all the time, but we must not take him for granted. We must take him seriously. He loves us but dislikes our sins.

† *O God, I repent of my sins. Be merciful to me, a sinner, and forgive me my sins. Amen.*

3 Words against foreign nations

Notes by Chris Duffett
based on Today's New International Version

For Chris' biography see p.172.

Introduction

We serve a God who knows all things. Through this week Ezekiel reminds us of four truths about the God we serve. Firstly, God is not confined to the four walls of our church buildings but is the God 'out there'. Secondly, God sees everything, from the fiscal activities of entire nations to the hearts of leaders. Thirdly, God has an opinion. He considers all walks of life, from kings to shepherds, and has something to say to each of us. Fourthly, God is a judge. It is he who pronounces judgement over all; he is the arbiter over all and announces that which will come to pass.

Text for the week: Ezekiel 34:15-16

I myself will tend my sheep and make them lie down, declares the Sovereign LORD. I will search for the lost and bring back the strays. I will bind up the injured and strengthen the weak, but the sleek and strong I will destroy. I will shepherd the flock with justice.

For group discussion and personal thought

- Keep a 'leader list' this week of every president, prime minister, king or queen that you read or hear about in the news. Pray for every person on your list that they may have humility and godliness in leadership. (If for any reason you can't make a list, http://rulers.org provides a vast selection of world leaders to pray for.)

Prophetic action

Ezekiel's wife, the delight of his eyes, dies (verse 16). God uses this sudden tragic death and Ezekiel's response to it as a message to his people, telling them how they must behave in the midst of their loss and grief.

> **'Ezekiel will be a sign to you; you will do just as he has done. When this happens, you will know that I am the Sovereign LORD.'**

(*verse 24*)

Ezekiel would have had every right to make a loud public display of wailing to show his mourning at the loss of his beloved. He could have dressed and eaten in the customary fashion that would have very openly shown his loss; however, God instructed him to groan only quietly and dress as normal (verse 17). What can we see in this heartbreaking story when we read it with New Testament eyes? I believe that this tragic account challenges us to live out the story of our beloved who died, but who now lives for evermore as our eternal bridegroom. Just as God gave Ezekiel a message to share through his actions, so he calls us to embody the gospel message. Today's story calls us to live out the words of God; not to simply pass them on to others on printed paper but to show the story in the way we live.

† *Lord Jesus, I wonder whether today you will lead me into a situation where I can show someone your life and Resurrection through my actions. If you do, please help me to respond. Amen.*

Ezekiel 27:1-25

God's inventory of imports and exports

Ezekiel reveals in this chapter that our God is the God who is omnipotent and omnipresent over every nation. Nothing, large or small, escapes his attention – including finance and trade. Through Ezekiel's prophecy over Tyre, God reveals that he has an opinion on these matters. For example he notes that

> **'Greece, Tubal and Meshek did business with you; they traded human beings and articles of bronze for your wares.'**
>
> (*verse 13*)

Later on in the chapter God declares through Ezekiel that such will be the destruction of all that is traded in Tyre that the entire nation will come to a horrible end (verse 36). Look at the labels on your clothes today. Where were they made? If you can, follow these three steps to help you pray for the nations of the world that export huge quantities of clothes and goods.

1. Ask God to give special attention to the nations whose names are on your labels.
2. Ask yourself whether you think the clothes you are wearing today were made fairly. Did the factory worker receive a fair wage? Could child labour have been used to make the clothes?
3. If you can, research the nations in which your clothes and or household items were made and pray for the people of that nation. Your public library or http://www.operationworld.org are good places to start.

† *Thank you, heavenly Father, for your care for the nations. Thank you that you know what is bought and what is sold everywhere. Help me to engage with your world. Amen.*

Ezekiel 28:1-19

Pray for your leaders to be humble.

'In the pride of your heart
you say, "I am a god;
I sit on the throne of a god
in the heart of the seas' . . .
Through your widespread trade
you were filled with violence,
and you sinned.'

(*part of verses 2 and 16*)

God cannot abide proud leaders. Some leaders today, like the leader of Tyre in Ezekiel's time, are so proud that they liken themselves to a god. For the health of the nation in which we live we need meek servants who lead knowing that it is God alone who has given them their position of power and authority.

Read through the following prayer and, if you feel you can, replace the word *'leader'* with the name of the political leader of your own country.

† *Lord God, thank you that your Word declares that you appoint kings and others in power. I lift to you in prayer our own leader of this nation. Today, Lord God, please speak to 'leader' and let him/her know that you know his/her affairs and conduct. Let 'leader' know that you are the one who sees the heart and knows the motive. Please humble 'leader' so that he/she will know that you alone are God, that you watch all trade, and economy and policy, and that it is you, Lord God, who will be lifted up and exalted. I pray this in the mighty name of our sovereign leader, the Lord Jesus Christ, Amen.*

Ezekiel 29:1-16

Jealous God

We serve a God who desires a relationship with us and to be the number one in our lives, a God upon whom we can depend. Ezekiel delivered God's message of grievance against Egypt, a heartfelt cry to his people to stop turning to Egypt for help. The irony was that instead of finding help from Egypt they found injury:

> **'Egypt will no longer be a source of confidence for the people of Israel but will be a reminder of their sin in turning to her for help. Then they will know that I am the Sovereign LORD.'**
>
> (*verse 16*)

Where does your confidence for help lie? Is it in a family member, a minister or a spouse? The Old Testament, especially the Psalms, declares time and time again that it is God alone who will offer help to his people: 'People of Israel, you must trust the Lord to help and protect you' (Psalm 115:9). Spend a few minutes thinking about the help God offers and ask your chief helper for special attention where you are in need.

† *Father, you are my Lord and I look to you for help. Amen*

Timber!

Ezekiel delivers a message that if summarised in one word would simply say 'Timber!'– the cry that announces the felling of a tree. He bravely declares that despite the beauty of the tree of Egypt,

> **You, too, will be brought down with the trees of Eden to the earth below . . . This is Pharaoh and all his hordes, declares the Sovereign LORD.'**
>
> (*part of verse 18*)

Even in recent times there have been leaders who have had great power only to be suddenly felled – Saddam Hussein, for example, and the apartheid regime in South Africa.

Today's reading is a reminder to us to be people who watch the leaders of our nations. Do you know of leaders who, in their greed, are oppressing the people they have been called to lead? We must pray that God, who was able to chop down Pharaoh and his friends, will be able to do the same to those who are cruel and unjust. People who do not honour our Lord God run the risk of being removed from positions of power and god-given authority as quickly as a tree is chopped down.

† *Thank you that you are the God of justice and the God of grace.*

Thank you that you are the God of wrath and the God of peace.
Thank you that you are the God of judgement and the God of mercy.
Thank you that you are the God of love. Amen

Ezekiel 34:1-16

The lost are found by God

God's complaint against the shepherds of Israel was that they were shirking their pastoral responsibility for the well-being of his own people. Ezekiel delivers a message that has many New Testament parallels:

> **I myself will tend my sheep and make them lie down, declares the Sovereign LORD. I will search for the lost and bring back the strays. I will bind up the injured and strengthen the weak, but the sleek and strong I will destroy. I will shepherd the flock with justice.**
>
> (*verses 15 and 16*)

Jesus echoes Ezekiel's prophetic word when he declares himself to be the good shepherd (John 10:14). When the teachers of the law and the Pharisees grumbled at Jesus for spending time with sinners, he tells the story of the man who had a hundred sheep but one had gone astray. When he returns, having found the sheep, the man in the story declares: 'Let's celebrate, I've found my lost sheep!' (Luke 15:6). You and I are part of the body of Christ and he has chosen us to be the ones who, in his name and as his ambassadors, search for the lost and bring back those who are broken and astray.

† *Jesus, you are the Good Shepherd. Please use me to be your hands and feet today, so that through me you may find the lost and bring them home to you. I would like to be used by you in this way. Let it be for your glory!*

IBRA
International Bible Reading Association

1020 Bristol Road, Selly Oak,
Birmingham B29 6LB, UK

Order form for 2010 books

Name: ______________________________

Address: ______________________________

____

____

______________________________ Postcode: ______________

Telephone number: ______________________________

Your order will be dispatched when all books are available. Mail order only (post included).

Code	Title of Book	Quantity	Unit Price	Total
	UK customers			
AA0922	Words For Today 2010		£8.50	
AA0921	Light For Our Path 2010		£8.50	
AA0923	Light For Our Path 2010 large print		£12.00	
	Overseas customers in Europe			
AA0922	Words For Today 2010		£11.00	
AA0921	Light For Our Path 2010		£11.00	
AA0923	Light For Our Path 2010 large print		£16.00	
	Overseas customers outside Europe			
AA0922	Words For Today 2010		£13.50	
AA0921	Light For Our Path 2010		£13.50	
AA0923	Light For Our Path 2010 large print		£17.50	
		Total cost of books		
		Donation to IBRA Fund		
		TOTAL DUE		

Payments in pounds sterling, please.
Please allow 28 days for delivery

☐ **I enclose a cheque (made payable to IBRA)**

☐ **Please charge my MASTERCARD/VISA/SWITCH**

Card Number: ☐☐☐☐☐☐☐☐☐☐☐☐☐☐☐☐ **Issue Number:** ☐☐

Expiry Date: ☐☐ ☐☐

Security number (last three digits on back): ☐☐☐

Signature: ______________________________

Website: www.ibra.org.uk Email: sales@christianeducation.org.uk
Tel: (+44) 0121 472 4242

The INTERNATIONAL BIBLE READING ASSOCIATION is a Registered Charity

Please, tell us about yourself…

Age: ☐ Below 30 ☐ 30-49
☐ 50-64 ☐ 65-80 ☐ Over 80

Gender: ☐ M ☐ F

Denomination ______________________________

Do you attend Church? ☐ Every Sunday ☐ Frequently
☐ Occasionally ☐ Rarely

How long have you read IBRA? ____________________ years

Do you read the IBRA notes:

☐ Every day ☐ Frequently
☐ When feel the need / time allows ☐ Very occasionally

Would you like to see:	More	Same	Less
Whole OT Books / Gospel / Epistle	☐	☐	☐
Weeks using poetry	☐	☐	☐
Wide variety of writers	☐	☐	☐
Commentary rooted in personal experience	☐	☐	☐
Critique based on academic study	☐	☐	☐

Other comments

What national Christian periodicals do you look at?

☐ Reform magazine ☐ Woman Alive
☐ Methodist Recorder ☐ Families First (Home and Family)
☐ Magnet ☐ Christianity magazine
☐ Baptist Times ☐ Universe
☐ Church Times ☐ Third Way

Other ______________________________

THANK YOU

LFOP

4 Words of hope

Notes by Meeli Tankler
based on the New International Version

Meeli Tankler lives in Pärnu, Estonia. She is a psychologist, and teaches part-time in the Theological Seminaries of the Methodist and Lutheran Churches of Estonia. In 2001-06 she was President of Europe Continental Area in the World Federation of Methodist and Uniting Church Women. Married to a Methodist pastor, she is a local preacher, Sunday school teacher, choir leader, a mother and grandmother

Introduction

Hope is an attitude of expecting good things to happen even in difficult circumstances. People who always expect a positive outcome are sometimes called naïve, and not taken quite seriously. As people of God we can be somewhat 'naïve', for our hope is not some unrealistic dreaming, it is based on our faith. We are given glorious promises of hope by God. God does not change and God's promises are still valid, so we can trust them. And for God no situation is hopeless – God can reshape the most difficult circumstances and bring something good out of utter misery.

Text for the week: Ezekiel 34:26, 30

There will be showers of blessing . . . Then they will know that I, the LORD their God, am with them and that they, the house of Israel, are my people.

For group discussion and personal thought

- According to this week's readings, what does God want his people to remember?
- How personal are God's promises for you? Do you dare to put your hope entirely in God?
- Is there a difference between trusting God and thoughtlessness? How would you describe it?

Ezekiel 34:17-31

Showers of blessing

The prophet Ezekiel begins by pointing out serious problems concerning the 'sheep in God's flock', but he immediately goes on to proclaim a wonderful promise of God's abundant grace. Even though the people have been disobedient, God is still willing to be present and visible in and through their life. He is concerned about the situation, and his concern leads to a positive outcome: there will be a new shepherd and a new covenant – a covenant of peace. And the future of a blessed and properly tended flock depicted here is wonderful: there will be showers of blessing for people and places, a peaceful life in total security, and a land renowned for its crops. All this will be provided for the people of Israel by God, in order that

> **'they will know that I, the Lord their God, am with them and that they, the house of Israel, are my people.'**
>
> (*part of verse 30*)

What does this say to us today? The Bible keeps reminding us that God does not change with time. So we can believe that he is still willing to be present and visible among his people – among us. Even when we have not always been obedient, God keeps his promises. But without acknowledging God's authority over us we may be in serious danger of missing these promises.

† *God, give us faith to lean onto your promises; help us to grow in obedience to you, and send us your showers of blessing for we are willing to be your people. Amen.*

Ezekiel 36:1-12

Branches of fruit for my people

An interesting message is proclaimed here – a message not addressed primarily to people but to places. God sends his prophet out to proclaim his word 'to the mountains and hills, to the ravines and valleys, to the desolate ruins and the deserted towns' (verse 4). And the purpose of this message is to prepare everything in the land for the homecoming of God's people. God cares for his people, and in order to take good care of them, he makes preparations – or rather he proclaims the need for the fields, orchards, towns, and so on, to prepare. Isn't it interesting that God's promises of abundance and fruitfulness are given not to people who will profit from these fruits, but to the land itself?

> **'I am concerned for you and will look on you with favour; you will be ploughed and sown, and I will multiply the number of people upon you . . . I will settle people on you as in the past and will make you prosper more than before.'**
>
> (*verse 9, and part of verses 10-11*)

Everything is in God's hand: people and places, time and space. It is encouraging to see how wisely God guides his whole creation – and how much he cares for everything. We as his people are dear to him, but so is the whole creation. We should remember this more often.

† *Sovereign Lord, we thank you for your concern and care for the whole creation. Help us to be responsible inhabitants of the earth you have created. Amen.*

Ezekiel 37:1-14

And you will live

I have always found this Bible passage one of the most puzzling. It is very powerful, but it is also quite frightening, and the image of dead bones coming together with 'a rattling sound' is not one of my favourite images in my meditation time. But it has an important message that we should not lay aside too easily: a message about God's ability to bring life even into a hopeless lifelessness.

God is the creator of life. All life originates from him, and he has the final word about every living soul. Only he can say 'Return to dust, O sons of men' (Psalm 90:3). And in situations when, according to our human assessment, there is no more life, God's assessment can still be different. For God there is always hope. Someone who seems to be dead – and according to certain measurable indicators is dead – is nevertheless not a 'hopeless case' in the eyes of God. Someone who is spiritually dead can become alive by God's grace, for he is able to restore life both physically and spiritually. You will live – by God's will and by his acting upon you. Today's reading is about dead bones, about dead bodies – but in the end, it tells us about God's Spirit who gives real life, spiritual life. The source of all life is with God, and he hears our prayers for life even today.

'I will put my Spirit in you and you will live.'

(*part of verse 14*)

† *Restore us, O Lord God Almighty, make your face shine upon us, that we may be saved. Amen. (*Psalm 80:19*)*

Ezekiel 40:1-4; 41:15b-26

(The second half of this reading begins halfway through verse 15.)

The table before the Lord

Ezekiel's vision of the new temple is interesting. In the beginning he is told to look and listen very carefully and to report everything back to his people. He is guided through important areas of the temple, and his memory is wonderful about all the details. But not much explanation is given. Ezekiel's heavenly guide makes only a few comments, one of which is:

> **'This is the table that is before the LORD.'**
>
> (*part of chapter 41, verse 22*)

Why is it so important to point out this place in particular? Perhaps the table is important because it is the connecting point between God and his people. And that's what the temple is all about – to make the connection between God and his people visible and real, to create a holy space for those who seek the Lord. Everything else in the temple is pointing towards this most holy moment of God meeting his people there, at the table. So the table embodies the promise of God's presence. For us, the New Testament people, the table before the Lord is even more the symbol of the meeting place with God, now approachable for all believers. We rejoice in those holy moments when God's table is prepared for those who long to meet him.

† *Lord, we pray for the people who come to your table, and for the people who serve at your table. May your holiness be evident, and your presence manifested at your table. Amen.*

Ezekiel 43:1-12

The glory of the Lord

Here Ezekiel's vision takes an unexpected turn. After carefully measuring the walls and learning the design of the temple, Ezekiel suddenly experiences it becoming alive with God's glory:

> **And I saw the glory of the God of Israel coming from the east . . . The glory of the LORD entered the temple through the gate facing east.**
>
> (*part of verse 2, and verse 4*)

It is no longer just a mighty but empty building. It becomes a house of God in a real sense. Ezekiel can both hear and see God's glory as it enters the temple and completely fills it. No more attention is paid to measurements or exact details – there is only this thrilling and overwhelming experience of God coming down and being very real and present. This is a most holy moment. And God gives his promise to live among his people.

In our daily life there is not much holiness left. Our days are mostly filled with casual activities and thoughts. We are often in a hurry, and even our worship can lapse into a hurried routine without much space for quiet time or reflection. We very much need the experience Ezekiel had of God coming down – of God entering our worship space so that it is filled with his glory. God is willing to give us such experiences – are we willing to ask him into our worship space?

† *Lord, let us experience your presence in our church. Let us feel the touch of your holiness. We want to be open to your presence, and we ask you to enter our midst as we gather. Amen.*

The river that brings life

Ezekiel's vision finally leads him out of the temple. And now he can see the water coming out of the temple, more and more water. For God's glory does not end inside the walls of the temple. Its influence goes, and should go, much further. The water from the temple finally forms a river, and the river flows towards further places as a life-giving flood. Ezekiel's heavenly guide explains that

> **'where the river flows everything will live.'**
> (*part of verse 9*)

There will be large numbers of fish in the river, and on its banks will grow trees that bear fruit every month, with leaves that are for healing, 'because the water from the sanctuary flows to them' (verse 12).

In our readings this week, God's promises have come to us as different pictures. Today's is a really challenging one. We have this water from the sanctuary that does not stay inside the sanctuary; the water that is life-giving and brings freshness and healing. We can experience the glory of God in his temple – but we should remember that God's glory is poured out for all people. It is not limited to us. So we should let this water flow through our lives.

† *Thank you, Lord, for being so generous. Thank you for your abundant blessings and life-giving presence in our lives. Help us to enable your river to flow freely and reach people who still do not know you. Amen.*

5 Training the disciples

Notes by Sheila Giffard Smith
based on the New International Version

Sheila Giffard Smith is a retired teacher of children with special needs, specialising in dyslexia. She is an active member of her local church and leads a Bible study group. Some years ago she took an intensive correspondence course and set up and led a Sunday school in the village where she then lived. She has written three devotional books, and lives in Surrey, England.

Introduction

Although the disciples had been with Jesus for a good while, they still had much to learn. It may sometimes seem to us that they were slow learners! Indeed, Jesus himself sometimes sounds exasperated by their failure to grasp what he is teaching them, Of course, they did not have our advantage of the New Testament to study, to give them the broader view which helps us in our understanding. They were being offered completely new concepts, and they did not have the trained minds with which some of us are blessed. So there is no cause for criticism of them, or for pride in ourselves.

Text for the week: Mark 8:34

'If anyone would come after me, he must deny himself and take up his cross and follow me.'

For group discussion and personal thought

- Why did Peter and the other disciples find it so hard to accept the idea of Jesus' death and Resurrection?
- What caused Peter, James and John to be so frightened at the Transfiguration?
- What do you think the disciples learned from the events in these passages?

Spiritual food is more satisfying than bread

Would you set out on a long walk to listen to an itinerant preacher without taking food? Clearly the crowd had not expected to stay so long, but what an astonishing experience to see and hear Jesus at work with such authority! Spiritual hunger overcame physical needs. But Jesus recognised these.

> **'I have compassion for these people; they have already been with me three days and have nothing to eat. If I send them away hungry, they will collapse on the way.'**
>
> (verse 2, and part of verse 3)

Was the teacher out of his mind, expecting the disciples to deal with the situation? Where was their faith? Jesus knew what to do, and asked the disciples to distribute what was available. We ourselves can help a needy world by sharing what we have; however little it is, God can make it enough.

The Pharisees demand more signs, but Jesus recognises that they are simply testing him and trying to undermine his authority. Are we, or people we know, among those who will not be convinced of the truth, whatever the evidence? The Pharisees see and believe only what will prove that Jesus was not the Messiah. We, too, need to beware of interpreting things according to our preconceived ideas, so there is a lesson for us here.

† *Lord, give us an ever greater hunger for your truth, and help us to trust when we cannot understand.*

Mark 8:14-26

Seeing is believing; believing is seeing.

Jesus often used ordinary things to bring alive his teaching. Everyone would be familiar with the properties of yeast. In this passage the disciples take the reference literally: is he criticising them for having no bread for the journey back after the feeding miracle? No – they still have much to learn.

> **'Be careful,' Jesus warned them. 'Watch out for the yeast of the Pharisees and that of Herod.'**
>
> (*verse 15*)

Those people were guilty of hypocrisy (see Luke 12:1). They were fermenting evil and trouble amongst Jesus and his followers — 'the yeast of malice and wickedness' (1 Corinthians 5:8). We can sense a rebuke in verses 17 and 18: 'Are your hearts hardened?' he asks. Are they deaf and blind to what Jesus has just been doing? Their spiritual blindness is followed, appropriately, by the healing of a physically blind man! Unusually, the cure is gradual, just as the disciples are learning only gradually what Jesus is teaching them.

When we are reading a passage in the Bible we need to stop and ask ourselves, 'What is God saying to me here? What difference will it make to my life today?' Only by applying what we read in a practical way will we be able to spread the gospel like yeast to those around us.

† *Lord, open our eyes that we may see and understand more and more fully what you want to teach us.*

Mark 8:27 – 9:1

A shocking revelation

Jesus asks his disciples,

> **'Who do people say that I am?' They replied, 'Some say John the Baptist, others Elijah; and still others, one of the prophets.'**
>
> (*part of verse 27, and verse 28*)

Both Elijah and John the Baptist were indeed seen as forerunners of the Messiah. Peter's answer is inspired:

> **'You are the Christ.'**
>
> (*part of verse 29*)

Matthew tells us that Peter was blessed for this revelation from God; but a shock soon follows: Peter is rebuked for contradicting Jesus! To him, as to the other disciples, the suffering he described had no place in their conception of the Messiah. This part of Mark's account is centred upon the divinely predetermined destiny of Jesus: he would be triumphant, but would also suffer. And we are to be prepared to suffer, too. What does it mean for us to deny ourselves and take up our cross? That cross, I believe, is not the inevitable ills of all earthly life, but suffering willingly accepted for the sake of Christ. Most of us do not have to suffer persecution or death for our faith, like many Christians. But, at the very least, we are to put the welfare and interests of others before our own, and proclaim Christ, at whatever cost, if not in words then by our way of life. But there is encouragement: God's ultimate purpose is the saving of souls, and this means eternal life.

† *Lord, give us courage to follow you, whatever the cost.*

Mark 9:2-13

A high-point experience

What a privilege for these three disciples! How exciting to see Moses and Elijah with Jesus! But the men are frightened, unable to think clearly how to respond to such an awe-inspiring event.

> **Then a cloud appeared and enveloped them, and a voice came from the cloud: 'This is my Son, whom I love. Listen to him!'**
>
> (*verse 7*)

Those words are perhaps the most important in this whole episode – for the disciples, and for each of us. How often do we listen to Jesus? Do we leave enough quiet space to hear him if he speaks to us? Do we 'listen' carefully to what we read in the Bible, and in church meetings?

Most of us will have had some 'mountain-top' experience, when Jesus felt especially close. And, like the disciples, we want it to last. But we cannot hold on to it for ever; we have to come down to the ordinariness of life on earth. For the puzzled disciples, sworn to secrecy, it is an unbearable contrast: once again Jesus is referring to the distressing truth that he is to die, and they do not yet understand about rising again.

The issue raised in verses 11-13 is difficult. Jesus gives an answer, but there is no space for further explanation here. I myself am content to recognise the wonderful way in which the Old Testament often foretells the coming of the Messiah.

† *Lord God, help us to listen more often and more carefully to Jesus speaking to us.*

Mark 9:14-29

The importance of prayer

The nine disciples not present at the Transfiguration may have felt hurt. When a sick boy was brought to them, no doubt it was a welcome opportunity to heal him and make an impression on the crowd, especially the teachers of the law. But they failed. When Jesus returns from the mountain he asks what is going on and hears the father's story.

> **'O unbelieving generation . . . How long shall I put up with you? Bring the boy to me.'**
>
> (*part of verse 19*)

It is not clear to whom Jesus is expressing his exasperation, but probably the humiliated disciples would have been stung by it.

The father's confession of incomplete faith is touching – how many of us do not experience doubt at times? But one thing he knows: Jesus is compassionate. He pours out his troubles, begging him to help 'if he can'. That 'if' prompted heartening words for us all:

> **'"If you can"?' said Jesus. 'Everything is possible for him who believes.'**
>
> (*verse 23*)

When the disciples ask Jesus privately why they had failed, he emphasises the importance of prayer in driving out 'this kind', so presumably it was true demon possession.

Can we learn something for ourselves from this episode? Experience reminds us that we have sometimes prayed for a person in faith, yet our prayer has apparently not been answered. Had we failed to prepare the way by prayer?

† *Lord, may we remember to pray earnestly before seeking to help the needy, and to believe in your power.*

Mark 9:30-37

A lesson in humility

Jesus now needs to be alone with his disciples to discuss, for the third time, his coming passion. They still do not understand, yet they are afraid to ask him. Why is this, do you think? So they change the subject on the way back, secretly discussing personal ambition – at a time like this! But Jesus hears. Tactfully, he waits till he can sit down and talk to them.

> **'If anyone wants to be first, he must be the very last, and the servant of all.'**
>
> (*part of verse 35*)

This is not what they want to hear, and perhaps few of us today find it easy to contemplate. It is a human trait to want recognition and status. A child in the time of Jesus had no status, no rights, so it was natural for Jesus to turn to the children gathered around him.

> **'Whoever welcomes one of these little children in my name welcomes me; and whoever welcomes me does not welcome me but the one who sent me.'**
>
> (*verse 37*)

We read serious words in Mark 10:15: 'I tell you the truth, anyone who will not receive the kingdom of God like a little child will never enter it.' We may be adult in years, but let's turn back the clock spiritually so that we are not excluded from the kingdom.

† *Lord, thank you that you died for us. Help us to serve humbly as you taught us.*

6 Going up to Jerusalem

Notes by Anthea Dove
based on the Jerusalem Bible

Anthea Dove is a great-grandmother, a retired teacher, retreat-giver and writer, at present working on her eleventh book. She is a Roman Catholic with a strong commitment to justice and peace and to ecumenism in its widest sense. Anthea has lived in India and France and several parts of England, but has now settled with her husband in a cottage near the sea on the north-east coast of England.

Introduction

This week we are nearing the time when Jesus enters Jerusalem and begins his journey towards death. He is still teaching the disciples, and they are still slow to understand. Most of us Christians are 'slow learners' too, and these teachings of Jesus are helpful to us today. It is not only his words but also his actions that enlightened his disciples and enlighten us too: this week we see the tenderness of Jesus towards children and his readiness to heal blind Bartimeus.

Text for the week: Mark 9: 50

'Have salt in yourselves and be at peace with one another.'

For group discussion and personal thought

- Nearly all of this week's readings are concerned with the teachings of Jesus. Which of these teachings are relevant for you?
- In what ways does Jesus reveal his humanity in these texts?
- Why do you think Mark placed the story of the healing of the beggar who had lost his sight immediately before his account of the entry of Jesus into Jerusalem where he begins to face torture and death?

Mark 9:38-50

Jesus getting his point home!

When people hear this passage, they are sometimes dismayed at what seems to be the severity and the ferocity of Jesus and the horrific nature of the punishments for sin. We need to understand that in the time of Jesus it was usual for anyone trying to make a point to exaggerate in extreme and often colourful language. Jesus wants the disciples to realise how wrong it is to lead others astray or weaken their faith, but we surely know enough about him to be certain that he would never in reality ask them to cut off a foot or tear out an eye. He ends this section of his teaching with the wonderful phrase:

> **'Have salt in yourselves and be at peace with one another.'**
>
> (*part of verse 50*)

Salt brings out the taste in food to make it good, so Jesus is challenging us to bring out the best in ourselves and at the same time be gentle and merciful towards others.

† *Lord Jesus, teach us to follow you in all things. May we always be sensitive to the way our words may influence others, and realise the hurt we may do by speaking thoughtlessly. Help us to inspire and encourage our sisters and brothers.*

Mark 10:1-12

The question of divorce

To his disciples Jesus said,

> **'from the beginning of creation God made them male and female. That is why a man must leave father and mother, and the two become one body.'**
>
> (*verses 6-7*)

It seems that as long ago as the time of Jesus, and even further back in the time of Moses, people were confused about the subject of divorce. So perhaps it is not surprising that many of us still feel uncertain today. Some people believe that divorce is always absolutely wrong. Others think that sometimes a marriage is so unhappy that the only answer is for the couple to split up. Some wives and husbands say that however miserable they are with each other, they should soldier on for the sake of the children, while many believe that a badly failing marriage is in itself seriously damaging to children. Jesus said that Moses found the people unteachable; perhaps that is how we are too, as we struggle in our day to find the answer to such complex problems. But two things are certain: first, it is a mistake to enter marriage lightly, and secondly, each person in a marriage should do their utmost to pursue the welfare and happiness of their partner.

† *Dear Lord, be present to us as we struggle to keep our marriages loving and strong. Help us to consider every aspect of the welfare of our partner without losing confidence in our own worth.*

Mark 10:13-22

The humanity of Jesus

Today we are looking at two separate incidents in the life of Jesus which strike us as being very different from each other. In the first, we see Jesus being quite angry with the disciples, then very loving towards the children:

> **'he put his arms round them, laid his hands on them and gave them his blessing.'**
>
> (*verse 16*)

In the second incident we see Jesus being drawn towards the rich young man, and then disappointed when he goes away sad. What both events have in common is the way they show the humanity of Jesus, how he felt things keenly and sometimes changed quite quickly from one mood to another. We also see his humanity in the natural way he touched the little children; Jesus was not afraid to touch people, even lepers. The rich young man was unhappy because he was unable to bring himself to give up his possessions; Jesus, who had looked at him steadily and loved him, must also have felt sad when he walked away. It is important to remember how profoundly human Jesus was, like us in all things but sin.

† *Lord Jesus, when we try to relate to you through scripture or in prayer, help us to understand how well you can identify with us in our human frailty. Help us to remember that you are our friend and brother and that we can always place our trust in you.*

Mark 10:23-31

The worried disciples

One of the most consoling teachings of Jesus is this:

> **'For men' he said, 'it is impossible, but not for God, because everything is possible for God.'**
>
> (part of verse 27)

This must have been reassuring for the disciples, who even towards the end of Jesus' life are still astonished and puzzled by the things he says. In this passage, Peter, so often the spokesman for the group, anxiously asks what is going to happen to them since they have left everything to follow him, and surely the words of Jesus must have comforted them all. But earlier they had a concern which is common for many of us today. We ask, 'Is it sinful to be rich?' 'What does it mean, to be rich?' 'Ought I to sell all my possessions and give the money to the poor?' Each person must answer these questions according to his or her conscience, but I don't think there can be any doubt that we should be aware of the huge and growing gap between the rich and the poor in the world. Nor is there any doubt that we should try, in our own way, to do something about it.

† *Dear Lord, let us never forget the poor in our own country and in other lands. Free us from valuing material possessions too highly and teach us to be willing to share wherever there is need.*

Mark 10:32-45

The disciples: still learning

In this part of Mark's gospel, we are nearing the day when Jesus enters Jerusalem, yet his disciples still have a lot to learn. They still don't understand what is happening: they don't seem to be able to take in what Jesus is telling them. Moreover, they still have not learnt how to behave! James and John completely fail to realise that selfish, greedy demands are hardly the first thing on the mind of Jesus when he knows he is on the way to his death. The other ten disciples, far from being tolerant towards their brothers, are angry with them, resenting the idea of special privilege awarded to James and John. Jesus will have none of it. He makes the deliberate gesture of calling them all close, and says emphatically:

> **'This is not to happen among you. No, anyone who wants to become great among you must be your servant.'**
>
> (*verse 43*)

This is a teaching he will make even more explicit when, only a short while afterwards as they are celebrating the feast of Passover, he kneels to wash his disciples' feet. Now we are his disciples, so often quarrelsome, selfish and ambitious. When will we ever learn?

† *Dear Lord, have pity on us because we are so slow to learn and understand. Open our eyes to receive your message and act upon it. Teach us not to be ambitious for worldly power but to be truly humble, to live our lives in the service of others.*

The blessing of light

There is something particularly engaging about the character of Bartimeus. From the words of Mark in this passage, we can sense his excitement, his eagerness and his determination. So many of us, in the face of affliction, lie down and give up. Our courage fails and we feel we can't make the effort. We lose all hope of improvement. Not so Bartimeus.

> **'Courage,' they said, 'get up; he is calling you.' So throwing off his cloak, he jumped up and went to Jesus.**
>
> (*part of verse 49, and verse 50*)

People often ask, 'Is it worse to be born blind, or to lose your sight?' We can't know the answer, but it certainly must be terrible when those who, like this blind beggar, have experienced light, beauty and colour are suddenly deprived of all these things and have to fumble along where they once strode or danced. We might expect that Jesus, apprehensive and afraid before his last entry into Jerusalem, would hardly want to be approached by yet another poor creature in need of healing. But of course, Jesus stopped. He asked Bartimeus what he wanted, and immediately his sight was restored. His desire then was to follow Jesus.

† *Lord Jesus, I ask that whatever my situation, and however great my difficulties, I may hold on to my trust in you, act with courage and never lose hope. I pray for those who are blind and for all who are physically, mentally or emotionally disabled.*

Idols

1 The many guises of idolatry

Notes by Elizabeth Bruce Whitehorn
based on the Contemporary English Version

Elizabeth Bruce Whitehorn grew up in Edinburgh. After many years spent working as a teacher and adult educator, she was Senior Editor for NCEC (now Christian Education) and IBRA until the end of 2005. She then 'retired' to Cambridge where she has been able to revive and develop various interests, including French, reading and music. She is a member of the United Reformed Church and, at the time of writing, was embarking on a year-long course on prayer.

Introduction

Idolatry may seem a rather old-fashioned word today. In the Bible it means not just the worship of statues representing gods in human or animal forms, but also excessive love for material things. Today, in the Western world at least, we see undue preoccupation with not just material things but also people such as pop or film stars and footballers. As Christians we are constantly faced with choices; what we choose reflects our priorities and the importance of God in our daily living.

This week's notes are written in the form of personal reflections to encourage you to examine your own priorities.

Text for the week: Ezekiel 14:5

When they hear my message, perhaps they will see that they need to turn back to me and stop worshipping those idols.

For group discussion and personal thought

Each day's reflection contains several questions for personal thought. Take time to ponder them prayerfully.

- What action(s) do you need to take, individually and together?
- How can you help and encourage each other?

Being famous

> **[People] said: Let's build a city, with a tower that reaches to the sky! . . . We'll become famous.**

(*part of verse 4*)

I'm not concerned about the world's tallest building, whether it is in Taipei or Dubai.

I don't want to be famous, although some people say that that's their ambition in life.

So what does the story of the Tower of Babel say to *me* here and now?

I do care about what people think of me.

I do want to have a good reputation, to make a good impression...

Is that more important than my relationship with God?

Perhaps God comes nearer when I stop striving, struggling to measure up, trying to maintain the edifice of my life, putting on a calm and cheerful exterior.

Perhaps confusion and brokenness, which seem to make a mockery of all my efforts, are opportunities for me to find God in new ways.

† *God of confusion and of mercy, I confess . . .*
Please help me to reassess my priorities and to be more concerned about your good name than my own.

Genesis 30:25-43

One-upmanship

[Jacob said to Laban] You didn't have much before I came, but the LORD has blessed everything I have ever done for you. Now it's time for me to start looking after my own family.

(*verse 30*)

There's nothing wrong with wanting to provide for my family, is there?
Surely it is more wrong to neglect them for the sake of my work?
But the end doesn't necessarily justify the means.
Laban tried to ensure that Jacob wouldn't get many animals.
Jacob took steps to ensure a higher than average birth-rate of speckled and spotted animals.
And so the game of one-upmanship proceeded.
So what does the story of Laban and Jacob say to *me* here and now?
God's blessing doesn't necessarily mean I will be better off than other people.
Do I ever push the boundaries of honesty?
Do I put others down to make myself seem better?
Do I measure my success by comparing myself with others?
Do I get a kick out of doing better than someone else?
Am I secretly pleased when someone else gets into trouble?

† *God of justice and of mercy, I confess . . .*
Please help me to reassess my priorities
and to treat other people with respect and honesty.

Priorities

> **When they hear my message, perhaps they will see that they need to turn back to me and stop worshipping those idols.**
>
> (*verse 5*)

But I don't worship idols!

That belongs to other times and cultures – doesn't it?

I go to church, read my Bible and pray.

I try to live a good Christian life.

And yet, here and now, I can't hear God's voice:

no words of comfort or challenge, no sense of God's prompting.

So what does Ezekiel have to say to *me*, here and now?

Perhaps God's silence is actually my deafness.

Have I unconsciously allowed my priorities to change?

Has the culture in which I live subtly influenced my attitudes?

Have I adapted my way of living to be acceptable to the people around me?

Do I really want to live God's way?

What obstacles have come between me and God?

† *God of judgement and of mercy, I confess . . .*
Please help me to reassess my priorities and reopen the channel of our communication.

1 Timothy 6:3-10

The love of money

> **The love of money causes all kinds of trouble. Some people want money so much that they have given up their faith and caused themselves a lot of pain.**
>
> (*verse 10*)

But, I want to object, my faith is far more important to me than money!

I have not always had enough and to spare, but neither have I done wicked things in order to get more.

So what does Paul have to say to *me*, here and now?

How important is money in my life?

Do I use what I have to help others?

Am I willing to pay a fair price for the food I eat and the clothes I wear?

Perhaps my desire for a bargain robs someone else of a fair wage?

Perhaps what I regard as careful stewardship is verging on miserliness?

To what extent are my wants affected by advertising and the prevailing fashion?

What would be a Christ-like attitude to money in my situation and culture?

† *God of generosity and of mercy, I confess . . .*
Please help me to reassess my priorities
and make good use of the resources you have given me.

Self-love

You can be certain that in the last days there will be some very hard times. People will love only themselves and money.

(*verse 1, and part of verse 2*)

Hard times bring out the best in some people, but the worst in others.

In news stories we learn of ordinary people doing extraordinary things in times of crisis.

But sometimes the stories are of ordinary people committing terrible atrocities to try and save themselves.

So what does this passage have to say to *me*, here and now?

I cannot foretell how I would react, but I can pray for God's help and preparation in the challenges I face each day, however small they may seem.

How can I love my neighbour as I love myself?

How do I use whatever power and influence I have over other people, men and women, old and young?

Is my faith superficial or does it affect every aspect of my life?

† *God of truth and of mercy, I confess . . .*
Please help me to reassess my priorities
and let your love permeate every aspect of my life.

Luke 12:13-21

Self-absorption

Then [Jesus] said to the crowd, 'Don't be greedy! Owning a lot of things won't make your life safe.'

(*verse 15*)

I can't help feeling sorry for the man in this story.

There is no suggestion that he acquired his wealth unjustly.

Many people would regard him as providing wisely for the future, making sure he could enjoy life – yet Jesus called him a fool.

So what does Jesus have to say to *me*, here and now?

Perhaps I am so focused on my own plans and desires that I forget about other people and their needs?

Perhaps I think that the big issues that face the world (global warming, sex trafficking, slave labour . . .) are just too big for me to be concerned about?

Do I unconsciously think that owning a lot of things will make my life safe?

Do I live as though I am in charge of my life, forgetting that I am answerable to God, my maker?

What preparations am I making for the day when I will appear before God myself?

† *God of challenge and of mercy, I confess . . .*
Please help me to reassess my priorities
and live each day in readiness to appear before you.

2 Making the appropriate choice

Notes by Anthony Loke
based on the New International Version

Anthony Loke is an ordained minister with the TRAC Methodist Church in Malaysia and a lecturer in Old Testament in the Seminari Theoloji Malaysia, the largest ecumenical seminary in the country. His wife, King Lang, holds an M.Theol in Christian Education. They have two children, Charis and Markus.

Introduction

Idols and idolatry are given much attention in the story of the people of God. The selected readings for this week point to some of the guises of idolatry with which the biblical writers wrestled.

Text for the week: Deuteronomy 30:19

Choose life!

For group discussion and personal thought

- Why do we find it so difficult to give God our undivided loyalty?
- What are some of the things in our lives that constitute idolatry? How can we get rid of them?

Matthew 6:19-24

Heart and eye: God or mammon

> **'The eye is the lamp of the body. If your eyes are good, your whole body will be full of light.'.**
>
> (*verse 22*)

Some people find it hard to throw things away. We have lived in our house for nine years and accumulated quite a bit of stuff. Spring-cleaning and throwing away what we do not need is a difficult chore. What we have kept all these years is like treasure to us. In verses 19-21, Jesus speaks about the futility of storing treasures on earth, compared with the usefulness of storing treasures in heaven. Where your heart is, there will be your treasure – and where your treasure is, there your heart will be also (verse 21). This verse reminds us that we often set our hearts on what we count as most important, and this allegiance determines the future direction and content of our lives. It is the same with the 'eye' (verses 22-23). If we can 'see' with singleness of purpose and undivided loyalty, then the rest of our body is sound.

It is in this context that Jesus went on to speak about God and mammon (verse 24). 'Mammon' here refers to 'money, wealth or profit'. Loyalty to God must be undivided. We can work for two employers but no slave can be the property of two owners. Since we belong to God and not mammon, we must put our single-minded trust in him. It is impossible to combine devotion to God and devotion to mammon, as each demands our utter loyalty. Idolatry is allowing something else to have a share of our devotion.

† *Teach me, O God, to have space in my heart only for you.*

Luke 12:22-32

What is life?

> **Therefore I tell you, do not worry about your life, what you will eat; or about your body, what you will wear.**

(*verse 22*)

The pastors of the Methodist church to which I belong undergo an annual medical check-up. I used to dread taking the test, not wanting to know whether my cholesterol level is on the high side or my blood pressure is above normal. Nevertheless, annual medical check-ups are important as they provide a helpful monitor to our physical health and well-being.

When Jesus told his disciples that they should not worry about what to eat or wear, he was not saying that they should go out and enjoy themselves regardless of their health and their personal well-being. Rather, he was asking them not to allow these earthly concerns to take the rightful place of God in their lives. There are some people who allow such earthly concerns to become the controlling factors in their lives. Their whole lives revolve around eating, drinking and deciding what to wear. They either over-indulge themselves with these things or worry themselves to death over them. Surely life is more than just these basic human necessities. Jesus reminded us that God will take care of these small things if we allow him to be our prime concern. If we place God first in our lives and seek his kingdom, all the little things will fall into line (verse 31). Idolatry is when we allow our concerns for the basic necessities of life to take first place in our lives.

† *Teach me, God, to seek first your kingdom concerns and not to worry about the others.*

Acts 17:16-34

Foreign gods

> **'Therefore since we are God's offspring, we should not think that the divine being is like gold or silver or stone – an image made by man's design and skill.'**
>
> (*verse 29*)

I grew up in a typical Chinese home where my mother worshipped the gods of Chinese folk religion. Each child was dedicated at birth to a god or goddess. I was dedicated to the god of war, a sister to the goddess of mercy and a brother to a tree! The Chinese pantheon had many gods and goddesses and even inanimate objects of worship. The apostle Paul found Athens similarly full of idols (verse 16), and even found an altar dedicated to an unknown god. Perhaps the ancient Greeks made this altar in case they forgot a deity, or had a nagging doubt whether they knew all the gods and goddesses; was there one more deity they had not yet worshipped?

Paul proclaims that he knows this unknown God (verse 23). This is the creator God who made the universe, and every nation and family (verses 24-28), the God to whom we owe our very existence and breath. This God cannot be represented by any image or idol (verse 29). If in the past God had overlooked our human ignorance of this fact, he now demands that we repent and worship him (verse 30). We know this God is true because he has raised Jesus from the dead (verse 31). This can only have one consequence: there can be no idols in our lives in place of the living God. Idolatry is not knowing this true God and replacing him with our human-made images and idols.

† *Search me, O God, and see if there are any idols in my heart.*

1 Corinthians 12:12-26

Perfection and the body image

Now the body is not made up of one part but of many.

(verse 14)

There is a modern retelling of the story of the body parts. One day there was a contest between the members of the body about who was the greatest. They all made their claims: the eye gave vision to the rest of the body; if the mouth did not eat, the body would starve; if the hands did not bring the mouth food, it could not eat; without the feet, the body would not be able to get the food. Finally, one very insignificant member of the body chipped in to declare himself the greatest, but everyone laughed at him in disbelief. So he went on strike. The others ignored him and continued their argument. After many days, the other members began to feel the effects of the strike: the eye drooped, the mouth trembled, the hands shook, and the feet had no strength. Finally, they all came to the least significant member and declared unanimously that he – the bottom – was the greatest after all!

Greatness is not in any one part but in all. There should not be anyone 'greater' than the others; we all have our part to play. When we exalt one or put down another, we lose sight of our corporate nature. The only one greatest in the Body is Christ the head. He holds all the parts together and we all grow up together into unity in Christ. Idolatry is when we begin to see ourselves as more important than others and forget the one who is by far the most important.

† *There is one Lord, one faith, one baptism, one God and Father of all, who is over all and through all and in all.* (Ephesians 4:5-6)

Deuteronomy 8:1-10

Eat your fill and bless the Lord

> **When you have eaten and are satisfied, praise the LORD your God for the good land he has given you.**
>
> (*verse 10*)

It is a human tendency to grumble and complain. We grumble and complain when we do not have and we grumble and complain even when we have! The people of God were just the same as they travelled in the wilderness. Moses led them out of Egypt to the Promised Land of Canaan. Along the way, the people grumbled and complained against Moses and God about food and water. Finally, when the older generation chose not to obey God's word to enter and take the land, they were condemned to wander in the wilderness for forty years (Numbers 14). One by one, the older generation died and were buried in the desert sands. A new generation arose to take their place and Moses began to speak to them when they reached the plains of Moab at the edge of Canaan.

Moses' speech was a timely reminder not to forget God. For forty years God had provided for all their needs: they had manna from heaven and water from the rock, and their clothes and shoes did not wear out (verses 3-4). And God would continue to do this for them in the Promised Land, where the people would literally 'lack nothing' (verse 9). So when they have eaten their fill and are satisfied, they must not forget God but continue to praise and thank him. Idolatry is forgetting to thank God for all the good things he provides for us.

† *Lord, when I am full and satisfied, may my mind continue to remember you and my mouth continue to praise you.*

Choose life!

> **Now choose life so that you and your children may live . . . For the LORD is your life.**
>
> (*part of verses 19-20*)

The people were on the verge of entering and possessing the Promised Land after the forty years in the desert. Moses chose to end his teaching of the Torah to the new generation of Israelites with a solemn warning: when the people enter the Promised Land, it will be easy to forget God. Surrounded by all the good things in a land 'flowing with milk and honey', they may forget that all these blessings come from God, not their own efforts.

In our modern world, we are spoilt for choice. Too many choices often make choosing difficult, but God does not ask for the impossible. Moses commanded the people to do one thing (verses 11-13): to choose between 'life and prosperity' or 'death and destruction'. Who in their right mind would deliberately choose death and destruction? But death and destruction will follow if the people's hearts are turned away and enticed by idols (verse 17). Choosing to follow God may seem very simple but often it is not. As Moses made very clear, to follow God is to 'love the Lord your God, to walk in his ways, and to keep his commands, decrees and laws' (verse 16). It is a conscious choice that the people must make and keep. As their subsequent history showed, they often failed to keep that promise. Idolatry is the failure to keep our promise to God.

† *Lord, help us to make this life-giving choice to obey you, listen to your voice, and hold fast to you.*

3 Countering idols and idolatry

Notes by Selina Samuel
based on the New International Version

Selina is from New Delhi, India. She is a housewife and a freelance editor.

Introduction

How can people of faith – those who walk the Jesus way – counter the grip of idols and idolatry? Idols are not just carved images but also material things, work, money, achievements, physical beauty, and so on, that are perceived as giving satisfaction in life. The problem is not that these things do not give satisfaction but that they take the place of God. They are idols because the desire for them is greater than the desire for God. Can we counter idolatry? This week's readings help us to see God's provision for enjoying life, all we need to stay focused on God and not on self. The Spirit works from within us; his rules for life are not forced on us, they are a joy to obey.

Text for the week: Galatians 5:16

So I say, live by the Spirit, and you will not gratify the desires of the sinful nature.

For group discussion and personal thought

- The letter to the Romans says, 'Do not conform any longer to the pattern of this world, but be transformed by the renewing of your mind' (Romans 12:2). What is the 'pattern of the world' in your society? What can you do to resist it and 'renew your mind'?

The Jesus way

> **'If anyone would come after me, he must deny himself and take up his cross daily and follow me.'**

(*part of verse 23*)

Our cultures are so absorbed in consumerism and instant gratification of desires that we find it difficult to accept Jesus' words. Yet they are words that call us to life. This call is, firstly, to 'deny self', deny all my rights to self-rule, and refuse to allow anything but Jesus to take the uppermost place in my heart. Secondly, we must take up the cross. Unless we have encountered the love of Jesus and his forgiveness on the cross, taking up the cross daily makes no sense. A daily taking up of the cross is important to keep sin at a distance. Thirdly, following Jesus is an everyday lifestyle. To deny self and take up the cross is not by itself the call, but to follow Jesus is the essence of life. Our walk with the Lord must always be fresh and the experience of God a daily event.

To be free from the shackles of self-rule and an inclination to allow idols to step in and control my life, I need to deny all rights to my self, allow the cross to be a daily part of my life, and follow Jesus. It's not my will that counts any longer, but what Christ wills.

† *Lord, help me to say no to idols and let you take control of my life. Amen.*

Romans 12:1-8

The renewed mind

Do not conform any longer to the pattern of this world, but be transformed by the renewing of your mind.

(*part of verse 2*)

This is a two-way command: not to be 'conformed', and to be 'transformed'. J B Phillips' translation says it well: 'Don't let the world around you squeeze you into its own mould, but let God re-mould your minds from within, so that you may prove in practice that the plan of God for you is good, meets all his demands and moves towards the goal of true maturity.'

Our framework for life, the basis for our character, needs total transformation and not just minor corrections. It's like the caterpillar becoming a butterfly.

The ways of the world look good, harmless and attractive, but the command is to be transformed and this requires discipline. We need to study the Word of God to seek his will, meditate on it and allow the Word to shape us. Lack of study starves the mind – how do you feed your mind? Spending time in prayer also builds our relationship with him, and meeting with fellow Christians gives mutual encouragement.

† *Lord I do not want to be an artificial Christian. Help me to be transformed in my mind, attitudes and actions and show to the world that your will is 'good, acceptable, and perfect'. Thank you. Amen.*

Life in the Spirit

So I say, live by the Spirit, and you will not gratify the desires of the sinful nature.

(verse 16)

We are slaves to whatever controls us. We can choose either to live to satisfy the desires of the sinful nature, or to live by moral standards, or to live by the Spirit. The law is the moral standard but it does not equip us to live a truly righteous life. Living by the Spirit frees us from legalism and immoral and self-centred lives. We are called to live by the Spirit, to a life of freedom and love in total obedience to the Holy Spirit who now indwells us. The acts of sinful nature have no place (verse 19).

Living by the Spirit undermines the power of the flesh. We deceive ourselves when we think that God is too holy and will not walk with us, or that we are too messed up for him to want to walk with us. But in Jesus we are invited to see God's willingness to walk with us. He gives us the Holy Spirit to equip us to live by the Spirit. The fruit of the Spirit listed in verse 22 gives a beautiful picture of someone walking in step with the Spirit.

† *Lord, I want to walk in step with you. Help me to have the freedom to walk in the Spirit and to love and serve generously. Amen.*

James 2:1-17

Faith and faithfulness

> **Mercy triumphs over judgement! . . . faith by itself, if it is not accompanied by action, is dead.**
>
> (*part of verses 13 and 17*)

One of the common charges against the Church today is that it is full of hypocrites. We can joke and say there is room for one more, come join us, but it is a sad predicament. The letter of James warns us that faith and action are bound together. One without the other is dead. In this passage James talks of favouritism, specifically in relation to economics. The glitter of gold makes people forget God. Wealth is an easy idol to have. It gives a false assurance of total self-sufficiency. The Church over the ages sometimes seems to have had a problem resisting the lure of riches, good looks, charismatic people, success and so on. We forget that the gospel is for all, irrespective of our background. How dare we judge others when we ourselves have received our salvation by mercy!

Christian faith is an action word and it is about faithfulness to God in our character. To love our neighbour, to be a compassionate person, is to say no to hatred and prejudice. It is not just our churches but even our homes that need to be protected against this kind of evil.

† *Father, help me to put my faith into action, showing mercy and loving without favouritism or prejudice.*

Living with enough

**He guides me in paths of righteousness
for his name's sake.**

(*part of verse 3*)

This psalm never fails to comfort. It covers all areas of life and all of life's experiences, the refreshing times and the dark valleys. In all of life, the Lord as my shepherd is constant and so I lack nothing. As someone said, 'The Lord is my shepherd. He is all I really want.' Many of us know him as saviour but few of us allow him to be our shepherd. He is our creator, our saviour and is our best guide and shepherd on a daily basis. Like sheep, we all have a tendency to stray. It may not always be to indulge in sinful acts. We may have allowed some good things to become idols, such as serving people, or church involvement, and the danger is that we become preoccupied with that and not with God. In turning to him we experience restoration. 'I shall not want or lack, even though I walk through the valley of the shadow of death' – surely this is a far cry from the green pastures and still waters. But this must also be the path of righteousness because he is with us, guiding us through it. He leads us for his own name's sake and so we can trust him completely. He is a shepherd whose presence is constant, guiding, restoring and providing.

† *Lord, help me to know that in you is all my sufficiency.*

James 3:13 – 4:3, 7-8a*

Living the go(o)d life

> **But the wisdom that comes from heaven is first of all pure; then peace-loving, considerate, submissive, full of mercy and good fruit, impartial and sincere.**
>
> (*verse 17*)

James talks about two different sources for wisdom, earthly and godly. We have two different paths for life, righteous and wicked. Wisdom is a character that cannot be hidden. It is evident by the way we live and is defined by whom we worship. The Christian life shows the world the character of God by the way we care, love, submit, and so on. This wisdom is pure not just in doctrine but in actual living. It is impartial and peace-loving. There is no place for feelings of superiority – we all need his mercy. Wisdom from above helps us to live and do our good works in humility, but envy and selfish ambition destroy this and give rise to bitterness.

The world, the flesh and the devil have a lot of attractive idols to bring our way. We pursue them, envy those who have them, and covet and kill, but only get momentary pleasure. Sin makes us run from God, not wanting to be anywhere near holiness. But it is only in submitting to God that we can resist the devil. If we draw near to him, he will draw near to us.

† *Father, help me to obey you so much that the world will see your character evident in my life and worship you.*

7 Jesus in the temple

Notes by Iain Roy
based on the Good News Bible

For Iain's biography see p.144.

Introduction

There are two occasions in the gospels when we find Jesus in the temple. The first is as a young lad sitting at the feet of the teachers, asking questions and learning. The second occasion is here, where Jesus not only confronted the spiritual leaders of Israel but was also confronted by them. This confrontation saw the beginning of the most decisive week in his ministry, which would lead directly to his death. It is a crucial week also for our understanding of our faith.

Text for the week: Mark 11:18

The chief priests and the teachers of the Law heard of this, so they began looking for some way to kill Jesus. They were afraid of him, because the whole crowd was amazed at his teaching.

For group discussion and personal thought

- Reflect on the worship in which you take part. What positive contribution does it make to how you lead your life as an individual or a group?
- On Thursday the notes comment on the Parable of the Tenants in the Vineyard, a story which brought Jesus into confrontation with the authorities. Look at some of the other familiar parables (e.g. Good Samaritan, Luke 10:25-37; Lost Sheep, Coin and Son, Luke 15; and the Rich Man and Lazarus, Luke 16:14-31): why did they bring Jesus into conflict with the Jewish leaders?

Mark 11:1-11

The beginning of crisis

I remember as a youngster in Sunday school taking part in a dramatised version of this incident. It is not difficult to see why our teachers chose this method to impress it on our minds. It is a dramatic story and appears in all four gospels.

> **The people who were in front and those who followed behind began to shout, 'Praise God! God bless him who comes in the name of the Lord!'**
>
> (*verse 9*)

Mark's account differs in one important respect from the other three gospels. It gives no hint of the hostility Jesus is about to face in Jerusalem. Mark seems more preoccupied with the crowd's reaction to Jesus' apparent re-enactment of the prophecy of Zechariah (Zechariah 9:9). This act was to end in his death. But there was no hint of that yet in the people's praise, only perhaps in the fact that at the end of this incident Jesus felt the need to retreat to the quiet of Bethany. It is a reminder to us that in meeting the crises of our own lives we need places of quiet in God's presence to strengthen our resolve.

† *Lord, help us to be still in your presence so that we may order our thoughts and strengthen our wills and our spirits to meet what life demands of us.*

Mark 11:12-26

Fruits of the Spirit

The fruitlessness of the fig tree echoes in nature what Jesus found in the Scribes and Pharisees in the temple. They lacked the fruits of the Spirit, spiritual insight.

> **He then taught the people: 'It is written in the Scriptures that God said, "My Temple will be called a house of prayer for the people of all nations." But you have turned it into a hideout for thieves!'**
>
> (*verse* 9)

We need to recognise the real anger Jesus had for the Scribes and Pharisees' distortion of the Jewish religion. They were concerned with the formal observance of their faith in the temple, hence their tolerance and even perhaps encouragement of the commercial activity associated with the temple sacrifices. Jesus demanded a deeper worship, in spirit and in truth, a worship leading to a life in society that was full of forgiveness and compassion. This is the kind of worship we need to aim at ourselves in private and public devotion.

† *Lord, keep us from just going through the motions of worship. Help us to internalise our worship in our lives so that we may externalise it in our living, especially in our relationships to each other and to you.*

Mark 11:27-33

Confrontation

Jesus may have been the one to confront them first, but now the Scribes and Pharisees were actively seeking to confront him. He had questioned *their* authority, now they question *his*:

> **As Jesus was walking in the Temple, the chief priests and the teachers of the Law, and the elders came to him and asked him, ' What right have you to do these things? Who gave you this right? '**
>
> (*part of verse 27, and verse 28*)

What emerges from this confrontation is the deep sense of insecurity of the leaders of Israel. Spiritual authority is not something conferred by office, but earned by the integrity of a life that reflects God's love and truth. The leaders of Israel questioned Jesus' authority but not their own faith and witness. They felt threatened, but that threat existed because the worship of the temple was no longer driving their moral imperatives and their spiritual insights. Worship must always be a humble act, making us more aware of God's love but also more aware of our need of forgiveness and redirection.

† *Lord God, bless us by your presence in our worship, so that in it we may see the greatness of your love for us and also gain the insights we need to live our lives humbly, quick to confess our shortcomings and to learn from Christ's truth.*

Mark 12:1-12

A story with a purpose

Any idea we may have that parables are nice cosy little stories must surely be dispelled by this parable of the Tenants in the Vineyard that Jesus told. This is story as polemic, with the purpose of confrontation.

'The owner sent another slave, and they killed him; and they treated many others the same way . . . Last of all, then, he sent his son to the tenants. "I am sure they will respect my son," he said. But those tenants said to one another, "This is the owner's son. Come on, let's kill him, and his property will be ours!"'

(*part of verses 5-6, and verse 7*)

Jesus knew he was in a great line of succession – the servants of God whose message had been rejected, most particularly by those who should have known better. The difference now was that Christ himself was more than the messenger. He was *the message*. God himself was speaking directly to his people through his Son. They were being asked to choose *for* him or *against* him. It is the choice before us every day, not just ethically but spiritually: to live our lives *with* God or *without* him.

† *Lord God, help us to make the right choice in life, to live our lives with you, not without you, whatever each day may bring.*

Mark 12:13-27

Questions with a threat

The heat was on. The leaders of Israel were becoming bolder. Jesus was no longer a teacher to debate with. He was an enemy to be eliminated. The questions they now put to him are laced with threat.

> **Some Pharisees and some members of Herod's party were sent to Jesus to trap him with questions.**
>
> (*verse 13*)

They wanted Jesus to condemn himself with his own words. They had also shifted the grounds of their attack on him from religion to politics. There is always a real area of debate between obedience to God and obedience to the state. The German theologian, Dietrich Bonhoeffer, was only one of many who had to address this problem not only in his writings but in his life. In his case, as in that of Jesus, it led to his death. This may not be so for us, but there are times still when the Church and its people need to have the courage to question what the state does. A healthy democracy should never be fearful of that kind of debate between church and state.

The other question the Pharisees and Herodians put to Jesus was of the kind that every minister of the gospel encounters all too frequently: a question that appears to seek clarity of theology but is in fact only a peg on which to hang rejection of the gospel, an evasion of the challenge God's love makes to our lives.

† *Lord, we pray for those who have hard decisions to make in states where there is corruption, violence and persecution. Help your children in their choices.*

Those not against us but for us

One of the most telling episodes in the gospels is the story of the Healing of the Ten Lepers, only one of whom came back to give thanks (Luke 17:11-19). There is something of that same feeling in this incident of the teacher of the Law who, instead of condemning Jesus' teaching, commends it. Who was he? Could he have been Nicodemus who in St John's Gospel came to him by night? Could he have been Joseph who gave the disciples a tomb in which to lay his body? Whoever it was, he had an honesty and courage that the others lacked.

> **The teacher of the Law said to Jesus, 'Well done, Teacher! . . . It is more important to obey these two commandments than to offer animals and other sacrifices to God'. Jesus noticed how wise his answer was, and so he told him, 'You are not far from the Kingdom of God.'**
>
> (*part of verses 5-6, and verse 7*)

Of how many other people may this have been true down through the centuries and even today – folk 'not far from the Kingdom of God', fellow-travellers? Sometimes in the Church we fail to recognise that, as well as those who actively criticise the Church and our faith, there are many who have a great goodwill towards us, sharing many of the Church's convictions on how to live life, and trying to meet the demands these make on them. If Jesus could appreciate and value such people, so should we!

† *Lord Christ, give us that magnanimity of spirit that can work with all people of goodwill to establish in society what reflects your love and mercy and compassion. For your sake, Amen.*

8 The days are coming

Notes by Alec Gilmore
based on the New Revised Standard Version

Alec Gilmore is a Baptist minister, Senior Research Fellow at the International Baptist Theological Seminary in Prague, and his most recent book is *A Concise Dictionary of Bible Origins and Interpretation* (Continuum).

Introduction

Instead of seeing these stories as a series of climactic events in a few weeks leading up to the Crucifixion, try reading them as a selection of events over two or three years, brought together by a compiler to demonstrate the inevitability of what was about to come next. Imagine two worlds. In the one you have the establishment and the traditionalists, mostly accepting without question what they have been brought up to believe. In the other you have a few individuals, more interesting and exciting, but potentially threatening and always in danger of being taken too seriously by the general public. Think of some examples. In which of the two worlds do you see yourself?

Text for the week: Mark 13:1-2.

As [Jesus] came out of the temple, one of his disciples said to him, 'Look, Teacher, what large stones and what large buildings!' Then Jesus asked him, 'Do you see these great buildings? Not one stone will be left here upon another; all will be thrown down.'

For group discussion and personal thought

- What would your feelings and reactions have been if you had been present at these events?
- What tricky questions do you think Jesus might be asking if he were around today?

Throw down the gauntlet

Anyone threatening to bring down the temple must have been regarded as either extremely arrogant or a fool. This man is not living on the same planet. Reputation he might have had – once. Some good things he might have done – or so they say. Certainly there was a time when he really did give hope to many. But not now. Unless he has his tongue in his cheek, he is crazy.

But try a less literal approach. Think of the large stones as a symbol of the mighty and the powerful – the people who control everything, always have and always will. Power-hungry rulers and dictators. Religious leaders who cannot bear to be questioned.

No wonder Jesus struck fear not only among 'the large stones' but also in the hearts and minds of many contemporaries. This was putting firecrackers under everything. To those who are over-awed by it all Jesus points in a different direction. We need a new understanding of who matters and what counts.

> **As he taught, he said, 'Beware of the scribes, who like to walk around in long robes, and to be greeted with respect in the marketplaces' . . . Truly I tell you, this poor widow has put in more than all those who are contributing to the treasury.**
>
> (*verse 38, and part of verse 43*)

One big stone gone and the echo can still be heard.

† *Father, give me the imagination to stop and think, the courage to ask the question, and the grace to face the consequences.*

Mark 13:1-13

The disbelieving and the anxious

To share the vision of Jesus for a different world and a different way of organising society is one thing. To see it ever happening is another. No wonder the disciples say, 'Yes . . . but when? And how will we know what to look for?' Jesus has some clear and precise answers.

- First, don't be taken in by people who pop up offering quick and easy solutions. Suchlike will always be around but the world is not changed like that.
- Second, be prepared for conflict. It's not that people will go on fighting for a very long time and then one day everything will be different. Rather, conflict is the prerequisite of change. It doesn't have to be violent (though where feelings are strong violence at times will break out) and, properly handled, might even be constructive until we discover how destructive violence can be contained or redirected. Learn how to handle conflict in love.
- Third, a word of advice and encouragement for those moments when we are most conscious of our inadequacy:

'When they bring you to trial and hand you over, do not worry beforehand about what you are to say; but say whatever is given to you at that time, for it is not you who speak, but the Holy Spirit.'

(*verse 11*)

† *Father, when the going is at its worst, help me simply to do or say what I feel to be right and grant me the grace to leave the rest to you.*

If not now . . . when?

In the musical *Fiddler on the Roof*, when their village is being razed to the ground and the people who had built their homes and made their life there find themselves refugees yet again, a young man says to the rabbi, 'Rabbi, we were always taught that in a time of crisis and suffering Messiah would come. Wouldn't it be a good time for him to come right now?' And the rabbi says something like, 'Maybe it would . . . but I suspect now we'll have to wait for him some place else.'

That young man was echoing what the disciples were feeling and what many people feel today; but there is no quick fix, and the faithful need to beware of those who like to think that there is. Even if the Messiah were to come tomorrow, there is no evidence that everybody would fall at his feet any more than they all rushed to fall at the feet of Jesus. The new world Jesus has in mind comes only after much suffering and tribulation. So for now his simple message is:

> **'Be alert, I have already told you everything.'**
>
> (*part of verses 5-6, and verse 7*)

What has he told us? That after the bad times come the good, and when they do, the elect will be those who recognise it.

† *Father, when I see goodness emerging from situations of suffering and privation, help me to see you there at the heart of it, and give me patience to wait and watch for its fulfilment.*

Mark 13:28-37

Reading the signs

By this point Jesus seems to sense that the disciples have still not got it. It's all so vague and intangible. Like anyone striving to find a true, loving and lifelong relationship they want to know when, and if they are not to know when, they do need to know how they will know when they have got it right. 'How will I know when I meet Mr (or Miss) Right?' may not always be expressed but is often somewhere there, lurking in the background at least. All Jesus can say is:

> **'From the fig tree learn its lesson: as soon as its branch becomes tender and puts forth its leaves, you know that summer is near. So also, when you see these things taking place, you know that he is near, at the very gates.'**
>
> (*verses 28-29*)

What things? The signs of something new when everything looks dead. When the branch shows signs of tenderness, the leaves begin to shoot, colour gives hope. Sensitive observers know that this is only the beginning. There is more to come before the fruit can be enjoyed. At this stage you cannot even know how much there will be or what it will look like, but something tells you that it will come unless someone wilfully destroys it. Those who fail to see it may be looking in the wrong place.

† *Father, keep alive within me the capacity to see, to read the signs and to nurture the shoots when they appear.*

Mark 14:1-9

God provides . . . a way through the sea

Just as a picture is worth a thousand words, so a person is worth a dozen theories. In case the disciples have forgotten where all this started (with the destruction of the big stones and the large buildings), the compiler pops in a human story which seems to answer all their questions about when, and where, and how. Even more to the point, the incident includes the notion of doing what you believe is right and facing the consequences.

Trevor Dennis makes the point that this incident happened in a place where Jesus should never have been – in the house of a leper, engaging in something he should never have done – eating with a leper, with a woman who should never have been there – interrupting a group of men who were eating, and with something precious being squandered (*The Book of Books* (Lion, 2003), pp. 377-9). What a waste! What a disaster! Whatever was going on? But then, could this be an example of the sign of the fig tree – tenderness, sensitivity, adding colour to life, and pointing to a wholly new world? If it were, only Jesus seems to have seen it that way.

> **Jesus said, 'Let her alone; why do you trouble her? She has performed a good service for me.'**
>
> (*verse 6*)

For everybody else, it broke all the rules and conventions.

† *Father, if I am to recognise your signs, teach me to look in unfamiliar places.*

Mark 16:9-20

The doubt of disbelief

Reading the signs is bound to be difficult for those who live by the rule book, for the arrogant, the know-alls and those who have already decided what they are going to see. Perhaps that is why the Resurrection caused problems. These verses are not found in some of the earliest authorities, but alongside the other Resurrection stories they carry the ring of authenticity and point us to three specific places where the signs of new life are recognised.

- First, a woman who had a personal experience of his healing touch.
- Second, a couple who have given up and are walking away from it all.
- Third, a group of men whom you might have expected to be the first to spot what was happening, but who were prevented by 'their lack of faith and stubbornness' and whose fixed position was so fixed they even had difficulty seeing it when others pointed it out to them.

Yet it was to these Jesus said:

> **'Go into all the world and proclaim the good news to the whole creation.'**

(*part of verse 15*)

† *Father, forgive me the blindness that prevents me from seeing . . . and even more, the stubbornness and certainty that prevent me from believing what people are trying to tell me. But thank you for giving me the charge to share with others what I do know and what I can believe. I know now what you meant about the widow's mite.*

1 Creating abundant life

Notes by Anthea Dove
based on the New Jerusalem Bible

For Anthea's biography see p.239.

Introduction

In this week's readings we are reminded of the generosity of God and the wonderful world he has created for us, full of beauty and variety. When we marvel at all that God has done for us, we cannot help asking the questions: How have we responded? What are we doing with the gifts of our generous God?

Text for the week: Isaiah 9:1

The people that walked in darkness have seen a great light.

For group discussion and personal thought

- After reading this week's Old Testament passages, what differences and similarities do you notice between ancient Jewish society and our own today?
- Who do *you* think were 'the people who walked in darkness'?
- How do you think we can best respond to God's generosity?

Psalm 104:14-23

God's creation

In this psalm we have a wonderful, ecstatic description of creation. It reminds me of my own walks in the hills near my home, where there is so much to delight our eyes and ears and all our senses: flowers, birds, streams, hills. Like the psalm's writer I am entranced by the different animals: the rabbits, the timid hares, and the shy deer. I love to stand still to listen to the skylark's song. In other countries of course there are far more exotic creatures and plants to amaze us, and even those of us who live in the middle of dense cities don't have far to go to glimpse the glory of sunset or sunrise and the gentle loveliness of the moon. But as the psalm reminds us, God is not only concerned with creating a beautiful world for us; he also gives us the means to provide for ourselves:

for cattle you make the grass grow,
and for people the plants they need,
to bring forth food from the earth,
and wine to cheer people's hearts,
oil to make their faces glow,
food to make them sturdy of heart.

(*verses 14-15*)

† *Lord God, I praise and thank you with a full heart for all your many gifts and blessings. Let me never take for granted the beauty and usefulness of nature. I pray that I may treat others with ungrudging generosity.*

Genesis 2:8-15

Paradise?

Today's reading is a description of Paradise. It reminds me of something else I read recently in a book of guided walks. The author wrote, 'A walk of extreme beauty, but the first 2¾ miles are veritably a journey through Paradise.' It was a lovely stretch of countryside, but nowhere on earth can compare to the Garden of Eden. So it comes as a dreadful shock to discover that the part of the world described in the Bible's story of Creation, the land where the Tigris and the Euphrates flow, is none other than the country we know as Iraq.

> **Yahweh God took the man and settled him in the garden of Eden to cultivate and take care of it.**
>
> (*verse 15*)

Thinking of this, of God's loving intention and humankind's response, we are dismayed to realise what we have done to our inheritance. Iraq is now a devastated country, its history in ruins, its people divided. Many thousands of ordinary men, women and children have lost their lives. In other countries too, people have destroyed whole forests, rivers and coral reefs in pursuit of wealth. God has given us abundant life; our response has all too often been to destroy it.

† *Lord, as your child, part of the family of men and women you have created and showered with blessings, I ask forgiveness for my part in the rejection and destruction of your wonderful gifts. Help me to work for harmony and restoration.*

Deuteronomy 6:1-9

Loving God

In today's reading, Moses is speaking to the people after he has revealed the Ten Commandments to them. He says:

> **'You must love Yahweh your God with all your heart, with all your soul, with all your strength.'**
>
> (*verse 5*)

Moses then adds, 'Let the words I enjoin on you today stay in your heart.' Nowadays we see all sorts of mottoes, slogans, logos everywhere: printed on tee shirts, posted on hoardings, even tattooed on people's bodies. But wouldn't it be good if we took the command of Moses to heart, and took his words as our inspiration? Jesus asserts that these words are the greatest commandment of all. To love anyone with all your heart, all your soul and all your strength is a huge and lasting commitment. It is the way our God loves each one of us; but most of us, most of the time, make only a feeble effort to love like this. It seems to demand too much of us and requires us to abandon our own interests for those of other people. We can only truly love God if we care for our brothers and sisters; any other kind of love would be a sham.

† *Dear loving Father, fill me with love that is true and pure and strong, love for you and for all the people in my life. Help me to be sensitive to the needs of others.*

Deuteronomy 5:12-15

Rest and relaxation

This section from Deuteronomy is all about our need for rest on the Sabbath day.

> **'You must not do any work on that day, neither you nor your son, nor your daughter, nor your servants – male or female – nor your ox, nor your donkey, nor any of your animals, nor the foreigner who has made his home with you; so that your servants, male and female, may rest, as you do.'**
>
> (*parts of verses 14-15*)

For many of us, and especially those living in Western countries, this picture of life seems pretty strange. I do not have an ox or a donkey or a servant or even a foreigner living with me. Even so, I wish that in my country the Sabbath, or Sunday, was still observed as far as is reasonably possible. Our world becomes more and more relentlessly frenetic and noisy and full of stress. So often we hear people saying 'We simply haven't the time.' Perhaps we should all make time, at least once a week, not only to rest and relax, but to make time for God, to think about him, pray to him, think about what he might be asking of us, and to enjoy the blessings of his creation.

† *Dear Lord, stop me in my tracks. Make me take time to be with you, to rest my body and my mind, to take pleasure in the world around me, in all you have given me.*

Leviticus 25:1-13

Jubilee

Whatever we read, be it scripture, or history, a love story or crime fiction, our minds inevitably switch from time to time to situations in our own lives, or things that happened to us once.

> **'The jubilee will be a holy thing for you.'**
>
> (*verse 12*)

When I read this extract from Leviticus my thoughts flew at once to a little badge which lies somewhere in my 'clutter drawer'. It commemorates Jubilee 2000, which was the campaign in the year 2000 for the cancellation of debt in the poor countries of the world. This is not an entirely irrelevant thought, for the great lawgivers of the Old Testament proclaimed a year of freedom for all the people every fiftieth year, and we read in Deuteronomy that every seven years there was to be a cancellation of debt. The lawgivers of Israel had very high ideals of the sort that in our day we often fail to implement. Jubilee was a great celebration, heralded by the blowing of a trumpet. We will have cause to celebrate too when those debts of the year 2000 are properly cancelled, and on the day when poverty really does become history and people everywhere are freed from the ravages of war.

† *Lord God, help us not to falter in the work for justice, or to lose faith in the power of the people who strive on behalf of the oppressed and the victims of war.*

The kingdom

There are many beautiful and uplifting passages in the writings of Isaiah, but this one is outstanding and very moving. It is also full of promise.

> **The people that walked in darkness**
> **have seen a great light.**
>
> (*verse 1*)

But every Christmas, when I listen to this first line being read, I ponder and I wonder. Who were, who are, the people who walked, who walk nowadays, in darkness? Were they sinners, wicked people, outcasts, strangers? And who are they today? Are they, perhaps, the very poor whose children die of hunger? Are they the lonely? The unloved? Are they those who huddle in doorways, homeless and stupefied by drugs? Are they the ones who know nothing of God? If you walk in complete darkness, any light seems like a miracle, seems like salvation. But this was a *great* light. It was Jesus. Isaiah is foretelling the birth of the son of God: Jesus born like one of us, Jesus in the Eucharist, Jesus who will turn our lives upside down if we let him. When he extends his dominion in boundless peace, then God's kingdom will come at last, and nobody will walk in darkness any more.

† *Dear Lord, help me to look out for the people who walk in darkness, and to recognise their need. I thank you for the great light you bring into our lives and for the abundant love you shower on all your children.*

2 The vision of abundance: for ourselves and for others

Notes by Kate Hughes
based on the New Revised Standard Version

For Kate's biography see p.74.

Introduction

Individuals were often given their own personal visions of what abundant life might mean for them personally. 'Abundance' could be imagined in many forms, but it was always relevant to their circumstances, giving them strength for that moment and hope for the future. Although the 'vision of abundant life' was personal, it was also often prophetic, in that it was a foretaste of an even greater abundance promised, but not yet given – a promise in which others would share. And there were some who were so gripped by the vision of all that God longed to give the people – and that the people failed to receive because of their disobedience – that they were moved to proclamation and action: above all, Jesus himself, who announced that the promise was fulfilled.

Text for the week: Luke 4:18, 21

'The Spirit of the Lord is upon me, because he has anointed me to bring good news to the poor' . . . 'Today this scripture has been fulfilled in your hearing.'

For group discussion and personal thought

- What would 'abundant life' mean for you personally?
- What would 'abundant life' mean for your local community?

Genesis 12:1-5

Setting out

Abraham's family came from Ur of the Chaldees, in what is now Iraq. His father Terah had once set out for the land of Canaan with his family, but got no further than Haran, in modern Turkey (Genesis 11:31). But Abraham (or Abram as he still was) had a call from God, and more reason to make the journey to Canaan. The Lord promised Abraham many descendants, a great nation; a great name, power and influence; and the continuing support of God. For a family in the ancient Middle East, this was abundance indeed. So it was no surprise that Abraham obeyed the Lord and set out with his family, his slaves and his possessions. Yet we mustn't underestimate the scale of Abraham's obedience. He never seems to have questioned God's commandment. Apparently he left Haran without a backward glance, although he probably had a comfortable life there and he could lose everything on the journey. God said 'Go', and Abraham went, trusting in the promise of abundance and of becoming a blessing to many.

> **So Abram went, as the LORD had told him.**
>
> (*part of verse 4*)

Jesus promises us abundant life (John 10:10); but like Abraham, we have to have the courage to journey towards it, risking all we have but trusting God's promise.

† *Lord, you have promised us abundant life. Give us the courage to trust your promise and set out on the journey with you.*

Genesis 21:8-19

Hope in the wilderness

Things couldn't have looked worse for Hagar. Because of Sarah's jealousy, she had lost her position in Abraham's household; she had been thrown out with just some bread and water, with no clear idea of where she was going or what she was going to do. Eventually the water was finished, the sun was beating down, she and her son seemed to be miles from any settlement, and everything seemed hopeless. Hagar and Ishmael were going to die. And then the Lord intervened. God had 'heard the voice of the boy' lying in the shade of a bush. His promise that Ishmael would found a great nation must have seemed incredible to Hagar, but his practical help of providing water meant that she and her son could survive. And where there was a well, there would be people, a place for them to stay. I love the picture of Hagar and her little boy walking hand in hand to the well. Hagar must have been dazed by the sudden change in their fortunes; the promise of greatness in the future probably didn't mean much, today's abundance of water was far more important, but above all she was given hope and the promise of God's continuing care and blessing.

> **'Do not be afraid . . . Come, lift up the boy and hold him fast with your hand, for I will make a great nation of him.'**
>
> (*part of verse 17, and verse 18*)

† *Thank you, Lord, that you bring the water of life into our desert, giving us both immediate help and the hope of future abundance.*

Proclaiming freedom

For many people, abundance means an abundance of things: good harvests, security, wealth, plenty to eat. But for those who are enslaved, as the Israelites were in Egypt, abundance means only one thing: freedom. The freedom to move around, make choices, work for oneself and one's family – all these are parts of the abundant life that we often take for granted if we have them. Freedom for the Israelites did not come from their own efforts – no slave uprising here – it was entirely the work of God. God actively intervened: the verbs he uses in verses 7-8 are all 'doing' words: I have observed, I have heard, I know, I have come down, I will deliver and bring out. Human beings cannot free themselves by their own efforts, whether from physical bondage, or from bondage to sin. God has to intervene, and has promised to do so. Freedom is part of the abundant life God promises to all.

> **Then the LORD said, 'I have observed the misery of my people who are in Egypt; I have heard their cry on account of their taskmasters. Indeed, I know their sufferings, and I have come down to deliver them from the Egyptians, and to bring them up out of that land to a good and broad land, a land flowing with milk and honey.**
>
> (*verse 7, and part of verse 8*)

† *Lord, according to your promises, free your people from all that imprisons them, so that we can receive the abundant life you offer to all.*

Isaiah 25:6-10

The land renewed

The land of Israel was surrounded by more powerful neighbours. If the Israelites were not being invaded and occupied by the Assyrians, Babylonians, Greeks or Romans, they had foreign armies marching across their land to fight each other. So understandably, their vision of abundant life in the future included Israel defeating its enemies and being top dog for a change. But it also included the renewal of the land, so that it would produce food and drink in abundance, with no more struggling against drought, floods, locusts and invading armies. Abundant life meant the freedom and security to feast together, enjoying the fruits of the earth. Above all, it meant the presence of God; it is he who prepares the feast, and, in a wonderful phrase, destroys 'the shroud that is cast over all peoples', the shroud of death. He tenderly wipes away his people's tears.

But the Israelites had to do their part. They had to *wait* for God to act and not, as they were prone to do, rush around looking for salvation from other gods or other nations. They had to *believe* that God would keep his promises. They had to *trust* in his power. If they did that, then the abundant life would come.

> **It will be said on that day,**
> **Lo, this is our God; we have waited for him, so that he might save us;**
> **This is the LORD for whom we have waited;**
> **Let us be glad and rejoice in his salvation.**

(verse 9)

† *Lord, help us to wait, believe and trust in you, so that we may in your time receive your abundant life.*

Jeremiah's vision of plenty

What a glorious vision of abundant life! Singing, dancing, feasting, people streaming to Zion from all the points of the compass, then walking beside streams on easy paths, between flourishing vineyards and olive groves. But there is also an underlying theme in Jeremiah's visions. In chapter 30 he spells it out: 'I will by no means leave you unpunished' (verse 11), 'because your guilt is great, because your sins are so numerous' (verse 14). The Israelites were in exile in Babylon because they had disobeyed God. The abundance God promises them in chapter 31 depends on them learning to be obedient. God is steadfast in his relationship with the Israelites; they are his people, he will never finally give up on them, he will always love them and care for them. But for the Israelites this relationship involves duties as well as rights, and this was a lesson they were very slow to learn. They cannot do exactly what they like, secure in the knowledge that God will never desert his people. They have to co-operate with him and show their love in their obedience. Then God will pour upon them the abundant life described in today's reading.

I have loved you with an everlasting love;
Therefore I have continued my faithfulness to you.

(*part of verse 3*)

† *Lord, it is wonderful to know your steadfast love for us. Help us never to take it for granted.*

Luke 4:14-21

God's abundance

Throughout this week's readings, we have seen that abundant life – of whatever kind, now and in the future – comes about through God's intervention. He calls, reassures, gives hope and practical help, promises and encourages, and acts. But for the people of the Old Testament, abundant life was something in the future, something to journey towards, hope for, glimpse in visions. Now, in today's reading, Jesus says that the waiting is over. First he defines abundant life in the words of Isaiah:

> **'The Spirit of the Lord is upon me,**
> **because he has anointed me**
> **to bring good news to the poor.**
> **He has sent me to proclaim release to the captives**
> **and recovery of sight to the blind,**
> **to let the oppressed go free,**
> **to proclaim the year of the Lord's favour.'**

(*verse 12*)

Good news, release, freedom, sight, the favour of God – abundant life indeed. But it is no longer a promise for the future:

> **'Today this scripture has been fulfilled in your hearing.'**

(*part of verse 21*)

Jesus does not just proclaim that abundant life is available. He *is* that life, the living proof that God keeps his promises and loves his people. In Jesus we see how God's abundant life is incarnated in a human being. And it is for us too: 'I came that they may have life, and have it abundantly' (John 10:10).

† *Father, thank you for the abundant life we can have in Jesus. Make us as open to receive it as you are to give it.*

3 Abundant life for all

Notes by John Oldershaw
based on the Good News Bible

John Oldershaw is a Minister of the United Reformed Church. He works with churches in the north-west of England to help them discover new ways of serving and worshipping God. His wife is a teacher and they have a son who is a transport planner and a daughter who is a research psychologist.

Introduction

God gives abundant life. The big questions have always been about how widely it should be shared and who is included in the blessing. This week's Bible passages reflect on this debate. We discover that the love of God is so vast that there is enough of his bounty for everyone; sufficient for every depth of need. In realising that God's wealth is to be shared by all, our task is to live with generosity and trust, confident in giving and receiving.

Text for the week: Psalm 67:6

The land has produced its harvest; God, our God, has blessed us.

For group discussion and personal thought

This is a saying from the Jewish collection of teaching called the Talmud:
'A man will have to give account in the judgement day of every good thing which he might have enjoyed and did not.'

- What are the ways to enjoy the abundance of God without being selfish?
- What are the ways in which we can enjoy the abundance of God without feeling guilty?

Genesis 9:1-17

The universal covenant

Having survived the Flood, Noah and his family receive promises from God and instructions about how they should live their lives. The plan is that Noah's family will have many descendants and live all over the earth. This is abundance beyond measure.

However, memories are often short and so God sets a sign in the sky; but it is a clever sign. It is not there all the time and so there is no danger of familiarity breeding contempt. It is the rainbow, seen when rain and sunshine are both present. Interestingly though, the sign is not there for the benefit of people, it is for God so that he remembers what he has promised.

> **When the rainbow appears in the clouds, I will see it and remember the everlasting covenant between me and all living beings on earth.**
>
> (*verse 16*)

It is also important to note that the promises that God makes are for *all* the inhabitants of earth. So right at the beginning of the Bible we encounter a God who has no limit to his generosity, and who is determined never to forget the promises he makes.

† *Thank you, God, for the signs of your love and the signs of your promises. Help me today to remember that your generosity is not limited to some, but is for everyone. Help me to respond with gratitude and demonstrate a generosity of spirit in my life.*

Leviticus 19:9-18

For the whole community

Leviticus is a collection of rules and regulations for the people of ancient Israel, and yet it is amazingly relevant for us centuries later. Today's Bible passage is absolutely wonderful, and it ends with a verse which is regarded as the second most important of God's commandments:

> **'love your neighbour as you love yourself. I am the LORD.**
>
> (*part of verse 18*)

It is all very well to be able to recite an important commandment, but what does it mean, practically? How should it be lived out? This passage demonstrates that the great commandments of God are made real in everyday tasks, not simply in grand gestures.

In this set of rules it is clear that the harvest is for the benefit of the whole community: not just for those who own the field, not only for those who are able to work all day. The fruit of the land belongs also to those who are the weakest; the most vulnerable should have their opportunity to gather crops for themselves. The message is that there is enough for all, if it is shared with the whole community.

† *Lord of creation, you set challenging rules for us to live by, but in this way of living you show that creation is your gift to us all. Help me to make today a sharing day in my community, and with the people I meet.*

Isaiah 11:1-9

For all creation

At times of political turmoil and uncertainty, grand prophetic oratory uses poetry and imagination to set a vision for the future. This is such a passage. The pictures painted are not realistic, but the mind and heart are drawn into a landscape where life is dramatically different.

> **Wolves and sheep will live together in peace,**
> **and leopards will lie down with young goats.**
>
> (*part of verse 6*)

Isaiah, a prophet in the eighth century BC, is setting out his concept of a world under God's rule. In so doing he is attempting to change everyday life so that the law of God is honoured and thus people live at peace with themselves and with neighbouring countries.

The description, however, is not just about people. The whole of creation, every living thing, is at peace, and this is possible because all creatures acknowledge the love and law of the Creator. God's concern is for all that he has created, and his blessing knows no bounds.

> **On Zion, God's sacred hill,**
> **there will be nothing harmful or evil.**
> **The land will be as full of knowledge of the Lord**
> **as the seas are full of water.**
>
> (*verse 9*)

† *Father God, you are the Creator of life and love. Thank you for your creation; today may I play my part in caring for it. Forgive me for the times when I have selfishly misused what you have given to us.*

Given freely – for joy

In these verses the prophet Isaiah is puzzling about why life is as it is, and he speaks God's question: why do people spend their time and money on things that are simply transitory and which do not satisfy, whilst all the time, and all around, there is evidence of God's presence and the promise of things which bring lasting satisfaction?

Yet there is mystery too, for, try as we might, we will never understand all that God offers, because we do not see things his way.

> **'My thoughts . . . are not like yours,**
> **and my ways are different from yours.**
> **As high as the heavens are above the earth,**
> **so high are my ways and thoughts above yours.'**
>
> (*part of verse 18*)

At the time when these words were spoken, the people were in exile in Babylon, refugees away from home. So there is sadness and regret but yet 'Look and see!' says the prophet, and he points forward to a time of celebration in which the whole of creation joins.

> **'You will leave Babylon with joy;**
> **and you will be led out of the city in peace . . .**
> **and the trees will shout for joy.'**
>
> (*part of verse 12*)

† *Father God, when I am confused about life and I have big questions to deal with, help me to trust in you. Help me to discern your ways for me and give me confidence to celebrate your love for me.*

John 2:1-11

Vast reserves of the best wine

At the start of the week we read about the sign of the rainbow, and as the week draws to a close we have another sign. The story of Jesus turning water into wine is, in John's gospel, the first miracle to be performed. It is a revelation of Jesus' glory and causes the disciples to believe in him. Jesus enters into the party spirit, as he often did, and he frequently received the censure of religious leaders for the company he kept.

The organiser of the banquet is so impressed with the quality of the wine that he praises the host by saying,

> **'Everyone else serves the best wine first, and after the guests have had plenty to drink, he serves the ordinary wine. But you have kept the best wine until now!'**
>
> (*verse 10*)

The abundant life that Jesus promised is for this life now, and at every stage of life. It is the calling of the Church, as the body of Christ in the world, to work in the power of the Holy Spirit so that miracles of sharing may continue to happen, enabling everyone to enjoy the good things of this life.

† *Lord Jesus, as I remember the way in which you enjoyed the wedding feast, help me to enjoy today. As I walk in your footsteps help me to bring joy and happiness into the lives of others.*

Let all the nations sing

This psalm is one that lifts the spirit. Its theme is thanksgiving, and it may have been written for a harvest festival. There are echoes of the blessing in Numbers 6:24-26, in which God says that he will look on his people with favour, and give peace. It recalls God's promise to Abraham and Sarah, in Genesis 12:1-3, that he will bless them, and through them all nations. It is this universal promise that is so important in this psalm.

In a world where there is tension and violence caused by racial and ethnic exclusivity, it is vital that we recognise the message of this psalm that God rules the world, and intends blessings for all of the world's people.

The psalm also reminds us that there are so many things to thank God for, including his kindness and justice.

> **May the nations be glad and sing for joy,**
> **because you judge the peoples with justice,**
> **and guide every nation on earth.**
>
> (*verse 4*)

As we remember the abundance of all God's blessings, the psalm encourages us to respond with gratitude and praise.

† *Thank you, God, for all the wonderful things that you offer to me every day. I am sorry that I often just take it all for granted. Please forgive me. By the help of your Holy Spirit, today I will try to praise you all day long.*

Hebrews

1 Jesus, our great high priest

Notes by Marcel Valentin Măcelaru
based on the New Revised Standard Version

For Marcel's biography see p.39.

Introduction

Probably one of the most enigmatic books in the whole New Testament, the letter to the Hebrews is an exhortation addressing Christians in Rome who were facing the gloomy prospect of persecution and mockery. The author of the letter encourages these believers by reminding them that God is faithful to fulfil all his promises, of which the coming and ministry of Jesus Christ, the Son of God, are the culmination. For those who choose Christ, a new kind of covenant relationship with God is available, superior to the relationship between Israel and Yahweh described in the Old Testament. The response believers are expected to give to such a message is endurance in the face of persecution and faithful perseverance.

Text for the week: Hebrews 1:1-3

Long ago God spoke to our ancestors in many and various ways by the prophets, but in these last days he has spoken to us by a Son, whom he appointed heir of all things, through whom he also created the worlds. He is the reflection of God's glory and the exact imprint of God's very being, and he sustains all things by his powerful word.

For group discussion and personal thought

- In what way does the truth that God is with us impact on my life and the decisions I take?
- How do I show concern for fellow believers? Do I exhort them to faithful living?
- Have I paid enough attention to spiritual growth?

Biblical theology in a nutshell

> **Long ago God spoke to our ancestors in many and various ways by the prophets, but in these last days he has spoken to us by a Son, whom he appointed heir of all things, through whom he also created the worlds.**
>
> (*verses 1-2*)

I regard the opening verses of the epistle to the Hebrews as one of the greatest New Testament passages. It is a text pregnant with meaning, so rich that in just a few phrases it presents the heart of the theological message brought to us in the scriptures – a very biblical theology in a nutshell. We are told that the development of history, from its beginning in the Creation event to 'these last days', is marked by God's desire and initiative to communicate with humankind. In the past the relationship between God and humanity was mediated through the prophets. But now we live in a new dimension. A new order has been inaugurated with the coming of Jesus Christ into the world; for in Jesus, God himself has come down to have fellowship with us. What a privilege! What a wondrous vision! Do we really understand the grace that God has bestowed upon us? For if we do, we cannot but exclaim in worship and adoration: Emmanuel, God with us!

† *Lord God, I worship and adore you. Thank you for coming to have fellowship with us. I praise you, Emmanuel, for you are worthy to be praised. I bow down before you and pledge my life to you.*

Hebrews 2:1-18

The manifesto of God's new order

> **It was fitting that God, for whom and through whom all things exist, in bringing many children to glory, should make the pioneer of their salvation perfect through sufferings. For the one who sanctifies and those who are sanctified all have one Father.**
>
> (*verse 10, and part of verse 11*)

We saw yesterday that the coming of Jesus Christ into the world inaugurates God's new order. A new creation takes place, that is, a renewed possibility for an intimate union between God and human beings. This is expressed wonderfully in today's reading through the language of the family. We have become children of God, Jesus' brothers and sisters, adopted into the divine family (see also John 20:17). And what surprises even more is the way God brings about this new creation. For all the power and authority available to him, God chooses the weakness and humility of suffering in order to begin anew. This is the manifesto of God's new order! Through Jesus' death and Resurrection a new family is being formed, one to which we can all belong. For in the new order God is not only the 'Abba' we have come to know in the union between Christ and his Father. 'Abba' has now been given to us. Now we can all know God as Father.

† *Lord God, you are Abba, my Father. Thank you for Jesus' sacrifice through which you made me a new creation, your child, adopted into your family.*

A principle of reciprocity

> **Take care, brothers and sisters, that none of you may have an evil, unbelieving heart that turns away from the living God. But exhort one another every day, as long as it is called 'today', so that none of you may be hardened by the deceitfulness of sin.**
>
> (*chapter 3, verses 12-13*)

The reading for today epitomises the repeated warning that the author of Hebrews gives us, his readers: we had best not trifle with God. The name of the sin endangering our walk is 'unbelief' and its consequences are devastating: loss of the privileged relationship with the Father that we enjoy as his children, followed by unequivocal divine judgement (Hebrews 10:31). What I find interesting, however, is the insistence of this author that the alternative to unbelief is reciprocal exhortation to faithfulness, love and good deeds (e.g. verse 13 cited above and Hebrews 10:24). This clearly implies that no one should forsake the fellowship of their fellow believers. In other words, the continuity of one's fellowship with God, as discussed yesterday, is indirectly, yet unavoidably, connected with a healthy experience of Christian community. Also, there is here a call to each one of us to take an active role within our communities, for exhorting one another means that we are both receiving and giving.

† *Lord God, thank you for giving me brothers and sisters who keep my spiritual well-being in mind. Give me a sensitive heart and an inspired mind so that I may exhort and encourage my fellow believers in the same way.*

Hebrews 4:14 – 5:14

Enjoying today the privileges of tomorrow

> **Let us therefore approach the throne of grace with boldness, so that we may receive mercy and find grace to help in time of need.**
>
> (*chapter 4, verse 16*)

In Old Testament times direct access to God was a privilege enjoyed only by people specifically appointed as intermediaries, such as priests and prophets. In God's new order, however, all believers have the right to approach God directly, to live in his presence. This miracle of divine grace is the blessed destiny that defines our future, as well as a reality which we enjoy here and now. This is what Bible interpreters have called the tension between 'already' and 'not yet' that is characteristic of New Testament theology. Here it means experiencing God today as if we are already living the fullness of tomorrow. Of course, such admission into God's presence has become a possibility not because of our merits but because of Christ's redeeming work. On a practical level, this is a message of encouragement. The work of Christ, our high priest, makes it possible for us to live in hope and pray with boldness, being confident that our needs will be met by our Heavenly Father.

† *Heavenly Father, thank you for Jesus Christ, our high priest. Thank you for the privilege I have of approaching you directly, and I trust that in my time of need I will find help with you.*

If you do not grow you die!

> **Ground that drinks up the rain falling on it repeatedly, and that produces a crop useful for those for whom it is cultivated, receives a blessing from God. But if it produces thorns and thistles, it is worthless and on the verge of being cursed; its end is to be burned over.**
>
> (*verses 7-8*)

Our subject today is something shrouded in mystery, called 'spiritual growth'. On the one hand, it is a mystery because God's work in our lives is for the most part unseen and indiscernible to the eye of reason. As such, we can only come to understand something about it, and its operation and development in our lives, if with our spiritual eyes open we receive the revelation available to us in the Word of God. Consequently, spiritual growth will remain a hidden process to most of us for as long as we fail to seek such revelation. At the same time, in many churches nowadays there seems to be an exclusive focus on activities associated with 'winning' others for Christ, to the detriment of a preoccupation with 'spiritual growth' and 'spiritual maturity'. Witnessing to non-believers is unquestionably a laudable concern, but it should be balanced by systematic learning about 'spiritual growth' accompanied by a fervent look for the 'rain' of the Spirit. For only then shall we produce a useful spiritual crop.

† *Lord God, thank you for your work in my life. Let your rain pour over me so that I may bring forth useful fruits.*

Hebrews 11:1-22

The sixth sense

> **Now faith is the assurance of things hoped for, the conviction of things not seen . . . And without faith it is impossible to please God, for whoever would approach him must believe that he exists and that he rewards those who seek him.**
>
> (*verses 1 and 6*)

In today's reading the author of Hebrews finally comes to the heart of his message, that is, faith. But what and how is this faith? Clearly the text does not talk of just any kind of faith, but of the kind that pleases God. We learn first from the verses above that it is the faith that acknowledges God's existence. It is not enough to allow for the possibility that God is. True faith affirms his existence strongly. Second, it is the faith that knows God intimately. Believing that God rewards shows knowledge of God's work in one's life. This implies a relational knowledge of God. Third, it is the faith that connects us with the spiritual dimension of reality, that gives us access to the divine. What we hope for, what is inaccessible in the physical world, requires faith in order to be reached. In other words, such faith is the 'sixth sense' that enables us to relate to the reality beyond that which can be seen, heard, smelled, tasted and touched.

† *Lord God, I believe that you are and that you reward those who seek you. Help my little faith to grow into the kind of faith that pleases you.*

2 Faith, hope and love

Notes by Anne Roberts
based on the New International Version

Anne's life has been divided between teaching – Geography and Religious Studies – and church administration and teaching. Now almost retired, she works in college administration for part of the year and is a freelance writer and preaches in her local church.

Introduction

The writer of this letter is a realist. He knows the readers face a great assault on their faith and are in need of encouragement. No impression is given that they are third rate because of this need. It was always so for those who seek to follow the Lord. The writer simply sets out to encourage them, from many different angles, to continue in faith, with the examples of those who have faced trials before them; the example of Jesus himself; solid doctrine and right thinking; exhortation to righteous living; and reassurance of God's commitment to them. In today's world we need all of these if we are to keep faith when others are losing it or never even giving it a moment's thought. This difficult book is worth every ounce of effort we can put into understanding it.

Text for the week: Hebrews 12:2

Let us fix our eyes on Jesus, the author and perfecter of our faith.

For group discussion and personal thought

- How does Jesus, as your great high priest seated at the right hand of God, translate into your everyday experience?
- What are the weights and sins you need to throw off in order to run the race of faith?

Hebrews 11:26-39

Sinners yet saints

By faith Moses . . . the people . . . the prostitute Rahab . . . Gideon, Barak, Samson, Jephthah, David, Samuel and the prophets . . . Women . . . others.

(*part of verses 27, 29, 31, 32 and 35*)

Heroes and heroines of the faith, as different from each other as they are from us – men and women, rich and poor, cowardly and brave, prostitutes and princes – but all are our ancestors in faith. Believers are not cloned. Each one is an individual, precious to God, chosen by him to bear witness in their own time and geographical location. What these had in common was faith – at times hesitant, weak; sometimes misplaced. They believed God's promises. He hadn't promised to save them from trouble or even death, but he had promised to save them in it.

And they were all sinners. Moses was a murderer; the people grumbled; Rahab was a prostitute; Gideon was dragged trembling out of the wine press; Barak bargained with Deborah; Samson did his own thing – once too often; Jephthah made a rash promise and his daughter died a horrible death; David was an adulterer and a murderer. Yet none was disqualified. God delights to take failures and make them trophies of grace. We know, as these did not, that God has made this possible through Christ. Whatever you or I have done that we regard as failure in faith, God covers with love and forgiveness. He sets us back on our feet and our names remain on the list.

† *Thank you, Lord, that you receive sinners and count them saints through Christ.*

Christ – there for us

We do have such a high priest, who sat down at the right hand of the throne of the Majesty in heaven, and who serves in the sanctuary.

(*part of verses 1-2*)

Christ sat down, his work complete. He was seated at the right of his Father because his work was acceptable to God. The right hand of the throne is the place of authority over all other authorities and powers. It is unassailable, now and eternally, and Christ is there on our behalf. The old covenant through Moses offered hope, but that hope was only fulfilled in the new covenant through Christ – and it was gloriously fulfilled.

It's easy to get used to all this, so we must read it and reread it; sing it; visualise it; celebrate it. This is what made possible the fulfilment of Jeremiah's prophecy quoted here: God's law in our minds and on our hearts; him as our God and us as his people; knowing him, our wickedness forgiven and our sins forgotten! Here is the antidote to all anxiety and despair about the present life and the one to come. Christ serves as our constant intercessor in the sanctuary of God's presence. There is nothing about us that escapes his view, but the eyes through which we are seen from the throne of heaven are the eyes of the one who laid down his life for us.

† *Lord, give us grace to be true children of the new covenant – with your law in our minds and on our hearts, knowing you, loving you daily.*

Hebrews 9:1-22

Free to serve

Conviction of sin is a work of the Holy Spirit. Sin is the opposite of his will for our lives and a contradiction of our standing in Christ. But the fact is that our wayward natures are prone to sin, even after we have come to Christ. If we do not accept this truth we shall end up very disillusioned when we let ourselves down, or others do.

> **How much more, then, will the blood of Christ, who through the eternal Spirit offered himself unblemished to God, cleanse our consciences from acts that lead to death, so that we may serve the living God!**
>
> (*verse 14*)

The good news is that the blood of Christ cleanses our consciences, even from deliberate sins. They are washed clean of all the filth that sin lays on them. This is where the new covenant is superior to the old. Our consciences are clear – God has said so. If our hearts are repentant God will continually cleanse our consciences. Christ's sacrifice holds good time and time again.

With sin on our consciences we could not serve a holy God. Cleansed from it, we are free to give him our all as an acceptable sacrifice, a continuous act of worship – and we are expected to do so. Our clear consciences cost Christ his life. The only fitting response is to give him ours.

† *Lord, I offer up my life to your service. I am amazed that you want it but your word says so, so I give it to you. Thank you!*

Hebrews 10:19-39

Know your heart

> **You need to persevere so that . . . you will receive what he has promised . . . But we are not of those who shrink back and are destroyed, but of those who believe and are saved.**
>
> (*part of verse 36, and verse 39*)

Having been cleansed from an evil conscience and placed securely in Christ, and given up ourselves for his service, we are now exhorted to persevere lest we should sit back. The world is full of temptations to abort our mission. We ourselves may become discouraged and spiritually exhausted. Sometimes there seems no reason to go on, when even some of God's people are against us. At such times we need each other. Isolated, we are in extreme danger. Together we can still go forward.

False expectations of the nature of the Christian life can lead to disaster. God does not provide a cushion against temptation and false teaching. He gives us all we need, but we are never told that that is a cushion. We need courage; we need our heads as well as our hearts and the whole armour of God, alert to any attack on our confidence in Christ's sacrifice for our sins. To refuse these and go back to the flesh is to insult God's Spirit. To insure against this we must know our hearts. We must seek assurance that they have been well and truly changed, that God is in his rightful place on the throne of our lives.

† *Lord, please grant me that blessed assurance that Jesus is mine – and that I am his.*

Hebrews 12:1-17

Only Jesus

> **[L]et us throw off everything that hinders and the sin that so easily entangles, and let us run with perseverance the race marked out for us. Let us fix our eyes on Jesus, the author and Perfecter of our faith.**
>
> (*part of verses 1-2*)

Other translations have us throwing off 'every weight', rather than NIV's 'everything that hinders'. The weights we must lay aside will be different for each of us and at different times in life. They may include unhelpful aspirations or relationships, regrets, bitterness, anger, addictions, guilt, false accusations. These weights are like a huge pack on our backs. They slow us down and we cannot free ourselves from them. Even looking at the examples of those listed in chapter 11 can add another few kilos to our burden! And then, of course, there's sin. This is much more than a burden. It's like trying to run with our ankles bound. It's a restriction to growth; a poor substitute for all that is good, pure and holy. It's eating the wrong kind of food for our spirits.

Only looking to Jesus gives us what it takes to lay these weights and sins aside. Taking time to consider his cross and what our sins cost him is part of that. Then the constant receiving of the Spirit of Jesus within us, as he offers us all that is necessary to overcome temptation, is our only empowerment. Finally, in him alone is faith, the gift of God, complete.

† *Jesus, I look to you as the author and finisher of our faith. I receive from you all it takes to follow you in that faith.*

He can do it!

Some readers of this letter had turned back to the ways of the old covenant, or were seriously tempted to do so. Was it possible for them to be restored to fellowship with God and to his service?

> **May the God of peace, who through the blood of the eternal covenant brought back from the dead our Lord Jesus, that great Shepherd of the sheep, equip you with everything good for doing his will, and may he work in us what is pleasing to him, through Jesus Christ.**
>
> (*verse 20, and part of verse 21*)

These verses offer solid reassurance that restoration was possible – and always is. Nothing is impossible with the God who brought back from the dead the Lord Jesus. The one brought back is the great Shepherd promised to God's people, and his role is always to seek out the straying sheep and bring them back to the fold.

The word 'equip' is the word used for 'mend' or 'repair', as when the disciples were mending their nets. God can repair the gifts we have misused or neglected. No matter how many times we have stumbled in our Christian walk, no matter how ill-equipped we feel to serve him once again, God can do the necessary repair work. Once again he can begin to do in us those things which please him . . .

> **to whom be glory for ever and ever. Amen.**
>
> (*part of verse 21*)

† *Thank you, heavenly Father, that you brought peace through the Lord Jesus and that peace is secure in him.*

Christian Love

1 The greatest commandment

Notes by Peter Ibison
based on the New International Version

Married and with two children, Peter is a member of the Anglican church in Buckinghamshire where he serves on the PCC and as a churchwarden. He is studying with the Open Theological College and works in the telecommunications industry.

Introduction

Many songs have been written about love through poems, literature, film and theatre. This week we reflect on the teaching of Jesus on the subject. We shall look not only at love's reach (whom we are to love), but also at love's expression (how we show that love). For some, the challenge this week will be to extend our love to wider circles (which may include our enemies); for others, it will be to express our Christian Love more deeply.

Text for the week: Matthew 22:37-38

'"Love the Lord your God with all your heart and with all your soul and with all your mind." This is the first and greatest commandment.'

For group discussion and personal thought

- God loves the outsider. Who are the outsiders in your church and how best can you show them the love of Christ?
- 'Jesus gives the command to love others, not only because it is good for us to do so but because people need to be continually reminded of the love that God has for them.' How much do you agree with this statement? What implications does your answer have for how we live?

Matthew 22:34-40

Love: the greatest commandment

An expert in the law was sent to Jesus with a question about which was the greatest commandment. Some might have said the Sabbath laws, others circumcision, still others ritual sacrifices. Jesus points to two commandments in the Old Testament, both of which speak of love:

> **'Love the Lord your God with all your heart and with all your soul and with all your mind . . . Love your neighbour as yourself.'**
>
> (*part of verses 37 and 39*)

In the answer Jesus gave, we see that love for God comes first. It comes first because it involves our *whole* being: heart, soul and mind. We might think today of these three being individual and separate, but the original Jewish concept was that they are integrated. We love God with our emotions, our bodies, our will, and with all our mental capabilities. This is how we express true worship: by engaging not part but *all* of our being in worship to God.

Love for God also comes first in another way: even though our love for God and love for human beings are inextricably linked, love for God comes *before* our love for others. At times, life will present a difficult choice: to live to please God, or to please human beings. On these occasions we need to be clear about which comes first; in fact, if we choose to please God first, we can be confident that the result will also bless our fellow human beings.

† *Father, as I reflect this week about what love is, place in my heart a deeper love for you. May you have first place in my heart. Amen*

John 15:9-17

Jesus: the example of love

Jesus is about to endure great suffering in Jerusalem and comforts himself by remembering that he is loved by the Father. The Father loves the Son who alone is worthy of that love. Jesus in turn loves us as his disciples:

> **'As the Father has loved me, so have I loved you.'**
>
> (*part of verse 9*)

Jesus offered four evidences of his love:

- Firstly and supremely, Jesus gave his life for us – of his own accord, and for his enemies as well as for those who loved him. If Christ loved us when we were at enmity with him, we can do nothing to make him love us less or love us more.
- Secondly, Jesus shows his love by calling us his friends: partners and co-workers with him.
- Thirdly, he shows his love by confiding in us, through his Word and Holy Spirit, all that he had learned from the Father.
- Finally, Jesus shows his love by choosing us (for discipleship) and appointing us (for ministry and fruitfulness).

All these evidences of Christ's love are rooted in historic fact. Whenever we are tempted to question the love of Christ, we can remember the words of Jesus : 'As the Father has loved me, so have I loved you.'

† *Lord Jesus, forgive me for the times when I doubt or question your love. Help me to remember and call to mind that life-changing love. Help me to share that love with others, for your name's sake, Amen.*

Matthew 5:38-48

Love for enemies

Jesus' teaching in today's passage is unique in the Bible. The Old Testament gave the principle of 'Eye for eye, and tooth for tooth' as a guideline for justice and punishment *within the judicial system*. The principle was never meant to provide a basis for personal retribution; instead, it was intended to ensure that any punishment was proportionate to the crime. The command, therefore, was more concerned with restraint than with permission. Clearly, personal revenge is not sanctioned.

If the first part of Jesus' teaching concerned not applying revenge, the second part concerned charity and grace:

> **'Love your enemies and pray for those who persecute you.'**

(*part of verse 44*)

Where the Jewish people lacked compassion, Jesus offered instead the 'law' of grace, forbearance and forgiveness (where insults are overlooked, work is offered willingly and where loans are given with a generous spirit). Jesus was not so much giving a new law to replace the old as showing how mercy can have the final word.

How does this apply today? Firstly, we must learn to forgive those who have wronged us. This is never easy, but with God, it is possible. Secondly, we must avoid the temptation to punish others (however subtly) for the wrongs they have committed. Finally, we need to grow in grace towards others, being slow to anger and quick to forgive.

† *Father, thank you for the forgiveness you have given me. Help me to extend that same forgiveness to others. Amen.*

Colossians 3:12-17

Love: the great arbiter

Today's passage talks of our confidence and our character. Let us consider, first, our confidence. The apostle Paul reminds us that we are

> **God's chosen people, holy and dearly loved.**
>
> (*part of verse 12*)

Prior to the first century AD, this remarkable statement would have been attributed solely to the Jewish race, but now we see something of God's plan in choosing the Gentiles as his people in whom he dwells by his Spirit. The more we grasp the reality of this love, the less our efforts to change will be focused on seeking divine approval and the more they will flow from gratitude to God for his grace to us. An appreciation of our 'chosenness' is the starting point for becoming changed characters, showing compassion, kindness, humility, gentleness and patience. These are like garments 'to be put on', and love is the greatest. They are each concerned not so much with what we do, but with who we are.

Finally, love finds expression in the call to be at peace with one another. When a dispute breaks out in a sports match, the referee blows his whistle. The peace of Christ is like that: it is to govern in our hearts and arbitrate on all matters of difference. We are to 'do what leads to peace and leads to mutual edification' (Romans 14:19). May this principle govern all our relationships, especially in our churches.

† *Lord, help me this day to show kindness to my neighbour, compassion to those are suffering, humility towards all, gentleness to the weak and patience with those who are working to different timescales! Amen.*

Love in action

An expert in the law came to Jesus with a question about eternal life – but he came to *justify* himself rather than *inform* himself. The response of Jesus was to point him to the law. When we seek to understand matters of faith we cannot do better than to start with what has been written – and to come with an open heart, to be instructed. Both Jesus and the expert were in complete agreement about the law and its requirements for eternal life. However, the expert was wrong in his understanding of scripture because he did not count the Gentiles as his brothers; true religion teaches us to regard everyone as our neighbour.

Finally, consider the contrast between the Levite and Priest on the one hand and the Samaritan, on the other. The Priest passed by and the Levite looked on. The Levite and Priest serve as a reminder of the Old Testament law which 'looks upon' us, but in itself gives little relief. The Samaritan, however,

> **'went to him and bandaged his wounds, pouring on oil and wine. Then he put the man on his own donkey, brought him to an inn and took care of him.'**
>
> (*verse 34*)

The Samaritan reminds us of Christ, who in compassion comes to bring wholeness and healing.

† *Thank you Lord for this parable that speaks of love in action. May I remember that true love is never indifferent to suffering. Help me to be like the Good Samaritan in my response to the needs I see and in my preparedness to cross boundaries in order to meet those needs. Amen.*

Romans 13:8-14

The debt to love one another

The apostle Paul says:

> **Let no debt remain outstanding, except the continuing debt to love one another, for he who loves his fellow man has fulfilled the law.**
>
> (*verse 8*)

This curious expression, 'the debt to love', does not mean that Christians should not have other kinds of debt. Jesus tells us elsewhere not to turn away from those who want to borrow from us, but we are encouraged to bear good witness by managing our finances carefully and avoiding serious debt. Here, the debt is to our fellow human beings, the debt of love. Yesterday we saw how Jesus rebuked a narrow, nationalistic understanding of the word 'neighbour', and here Paul makes it clear that the debt of love is not confined to a small circle of friends (although it certainly includes these). The debt of love we owe is to all human beings. The usual emphasis in scripture is for us to love our fellow believers, but this wider application runs deep in the New Testament.

The passage cites three commandments, concerning adultery, murder and stealing – representative of a respect for family, life and property. Whilst these are normally associated with matters of justice, here love is shown to be the overriding principle. If we love our neighbour as ourselves, then we will cherish the marriage institution, hold life sacred, and respect the property of others.

† *Thank you, Lord, for the passages of scripture I have read this week that speak of love. Grant me a deeper love for others. Open my eyes to see needs around me. Give me discernment to learn how to love well. Amen.*

2 What love means

Notes by Aileen Khoo
based on the New International Version (NIV) and Today's English Version (TEV)

Aileen Khoo has worked in the Methodist Church in Malaysia for 34 years. Currently she is Director of Christian Education at Trinity Methodist Church, Petaling Jaya. She particularly enjoys leading Bible studies, especially experimenting with participatory Bible study methods.

Introduction

This truly is a very difficult topic to write about, even more so to practise. I thought it would be easy, with so many sermons preached, so many Bible commentaries. I was wrong. This is an over-used and greatly misunderstood word: 'I love you', 'I love ice-cream'! What is love really? 'Love is a many splendoured thing', so goes the song. It means many things to different people in different situations. So often love is given conditionally, depending on what we get in return or the mood we are in. To understand love is to know God's love, to appreciate what it means to be loved by God, and how God wants us to love.

Text for the week: 1 John 4:7-8

Dear friends, let us love one another, for love comes from God. Everyone who loves has been born of God and knows God. Whoever does not love does not know God, because God is love.

For group discussion and personal thought

- How can we show love to God?
- Do you have a broken relationship with anyone? If so, what prompt and concrete action can you take to clear the air and pave the way for reconciliation?

Luke 6:27-36

Exceptional love

Love your enemies, do good to those who hate you.

(*part of verse 27, NIV*)

Love is loving those who hate you, loving when you don't feel like it, because love is not a feeling. Love as a feeling often depends on what is done for me: 'If you really cared, you would do this for me.' True love understands what it is to be loved by God and how God wants us to love. It is a love not of power, manipulation or arrangement, but of service and meekness to those who hate you. Such love is vulnerable, but more interested in giving something constructive than in retrieving what has been taken away. It is not the kind of love that we offer in order to get something in return; it is loving action regardless of how the other responds.

The first step to loving those who hate us is to forgive them. The second is to take active steps towards reconciliation. The third is to show our love in concrete service. God loved us when we were God's enemies (Romans 5:8) and Jesus personified this love when he died for us praying for forgiveness for his enemies.

Why should we love those who hate us? Because we are God's children, we reflect who God is in the world. This is not an option, but a command.

† *Remind me each morning of your constant love,*
For I put my trust in you.
My prayers go up to you;
Show me the way I should go.

(Psalm 143:8, TEV)

Sacrificial love

This is how we know what love is: Jesus Christ laid down his life for us. And we ought to lay down our lives for our brothers.

(*verse 16, NIV*)

Love is laying down our lives for another. Love of neighbour and love of God are the two sides of the same coin. Disciples are marked by a genuine readiness to meet needs. Resources are not to be hoarded but shared. When we give, it should not be with strings attached. When we serve, it should be to meet need, not count the cost, not 'If I scratch your back, will you scratch mine?'

Self-denial is the essence of love. Love is not love unless expressed concretely in service; love is expounded through living it out, as God sent Jesus to show us that he loves us, and as Jesus laid down his life for us so that we may live in the presence of God's love. The essence of the child of God is to love and serve. On the cross Jesus gave his life willingly. Eliza Doolittle in *My Fair Lady* sang, 'Don't talk of stars shining above, if you're in love – show me!' God did! He gave his life as a ransom for many. Love for each other shows that we have experienced the love of God and know the character of God. Those who love God more will be able to love others more.

† *Turn to me and have mercy on me*
as you do on all those who love you.

(Psalm 119:132, TEV)

1 John 4:7-21

God is love

This is love: not that we loved God, but that he loved us and sent his Son as an atoning sacrifice for our sins.

(*verse 10, NIV*)

While the New Testament brings the concept of God's love to full expression, it does not begin there. The quality of love is present throughout the Old Testament, for love originates with God. If God is known by what he does, then truly God's name is 'love', for God reveals himself as love. If we don't love, we don't know God, for God is love. So if we are children of God we will radiate with God's love. In Deuteronomy, Moses explained to the Israelites that God set his heart on them, not because they were great but because the Lord loved them (Deuteronomy 7:7-8). In Hosea the same thought is expressed: 'When Israel was a child, I loved him' (Hosea 11:1). Like a mother, God tenderly taught Israel to walk, healing him, leading him with cords of human kindness, ties of love, lifting the yoke from his neck and bending down to feed him (Hosea 11:1-4). 'Love so amazing, so divine, demands my soul, my life, my all', wrote Isaac Watts.

† *I will sing about your strength;*
Every morning I will sing aloud of your constant love.
You have been a refuge for me,
A shelter in my time of trouble.
I will praise you, my defender.
My refuge is God,
The God who loves me.

(Psalm 59:16-17, TEV)

The depth of love

Above all, love each other deeply, because love covers over a multitude of sins.

(*verse 8, NIV*)

To love is to love deeply. Whatever else you fail to do, do not fail to love deeply, for in loving deeply we forgive as the Father has forgiven us. In loving deeply, we love generously. Love keeps no record. We use the gifts we have received in order to serve. To love deeply is not giving hospitality only when it is convenient to us. Practising hospitality is not just inviting someone to your home for tea, but it is laying aside what we are doing to give ourselves, our time, our space to attend to another's needs. It is like being awakened in the middle of the night by a neighbour asking for a loaf of bread. This is going out of the way to show love. We can do it because God provides us with the strength and the ability. The community Jesus brought into being is to exhibit God's love, the humble, self-sacrificing love.

† *May your constant love be with us, Lord,*
As we put our hope in you.

(Psalm 33:22, TEV)

John 13:3-15

Love that serves

> **Now that I, your Lord and Teacher, have washed your feet, you also should wash one another's feet.**
>
> (*verse 14, NIV*)

Do we understand what love is? It is the God who stooped to wash feet! Look at the extent of what Jesus did. Count the number of active verbs – he got up, took off his robe, put on a towel, poured water, washed his disciples' feet, and dried them.

Some of us demonstrate love superficially, just a token expression of our love. We serve only after others have done the difficult part, like pouring water. It is not an easy job pouring water. It's also easy to stop with just this. But not Jesus, he dried their feet. He followed through with his love.

To love the way Jesus loved, is to do so voluntarily. It is doing something that refreshes others with no ulterior motive. It is giving to those that have no means of giving back. It means loving all the way without stopping until the end of one's life. The hands that created the universe take our feet into his. Love is serving one another.

† *Examine me and test me, Lord;*
Judge my desire and thoughts,
Your constant love is my guide;
Your faithfulness always leads me.

(Psalm 26:2-3, TEV)

Heartfelt love

I am sending him – who is my very heart – back to you.

(*verse 12, NIV*)

To love is loving from the centre of our hearts. Paul loved Philemon and he had also grown to love Onesimus, Philemon's runaway slave. He must now help Philemon to love Onesimus, not as a slave but as a brother.

The Chinese character for love (*Ai*) is made up of two radicals – heart (*Xin*) and friend (*Yu*). To love is to give your heart to your friend. Loving means to love from the centre of our hearts. The heart, the centre of our being from which we have life. It's like loving another more than one's own life.

I was at my sister's home looking through her wardrobe as I frequently do, to see what I could borrow for a trip. I picked up a beautiful cardigan which she said I could have. Her son was in the room and he said, 'But Mum, that's your favourite!' To which my sister replied, 'This is what love is, giving up what you cherish most.' The name Onesimus means to be useful. Paul is giving up someone who is useful to him

† *O Lord, I will always sing of your constant love;*
I will proclaim your faithfulness forever.
I know that your love will last for all time,
That your faithfulness is as permanent as the sky

(Psalm 89:1-2, TEV)

3 What love does

Notes by Deborah Dunn
based on the New King James Version

Deborah Dunn is a licensed marital and family therapist near Raleigh, North Carolina, USA. She has a new series of books about romance being released in early 2009. She also teaches disaster education via World Harvest Radio over Asia, Africa and South America. Visit her website at www.deborahdunn.com.

Introduction

Love seems so *disposable* these days. Human emotions are fickle and change all too quickly. Unfortunately, we tend to project these same human frailties onto God. But God is not a human being, and his love for us is very different. He does not change based on our behaviour or how much we do for him. But when we look at the world, we question how a loving God can allow such pain and suffering. When people are cruel to each other, God's love has not failed. It is we who have failed God, because we have not allowed his love to flow through us to others. As followers of Christ, we are commanded to love even our enemies, so that the world will see the God of love in all of his fullness, grace and glory.

Text for the week: Ephesians 5:1

Walk in love, as Christ also has loved us and given himself for us.

For group discussion and personal thought

- Has there been a time when you seriously questioned God's love?
- What actions do you take in your daily life to show others that God loves them, other than just telling them about his love?

Love leads to fellowship

Then those who gladly received his word were baptised . . . and they continued steadfastly in the . . . fellowship, in the breaking of bread, and in prayers . . . And the Lord added to the church daily those who were being saved.

(*part of verses 41, 42 and 47*)

I've been going to church for over thirty years, but right now it is hard for me to find a church that I feel builds my faith. I'll have to admit I'm not that regular in my attendance. But I should not judge a church for what it can do for me; I am supposed to honour God by my faithful attendance and focus on what I can do to help the body of Christ. I'm to give my tithes, minister to those who are hurting, and praise God for how he has sustained me and my family through the week. Even when I do not really *feel* anything of great import, my presence allows God to work through me. God promises to bless my obedience. He cannot pour out his love on the lost unless we show that love to them and help lead them into fellowship with others.

† *Father, please forgive us when we make excuses not to join with the fellowship in our community. Help us find a body of believers who share your passion and vision for bringing the lost to salvation. Father, we pray for the churches that do not set an example of Christian Love, and for those churches attacked by the enemy because they do. In the name of Jesus, Amen.*

2 Corinthians 8:1-15

Trusting God proves our love

As it is written, 'He who gathered much had nothing left over, and he who gathered little had no lack.'

(*verse 15*)

I happen to live in a wealthy part of the United States where most people spend a good part of their lives working long hours to acquire unnecessary things. They are obsessed with how much money they earn. It is sad; for most of them are going deeper into debt no matter how hard they work. They use this as an excuse not to give money to the poor or to share their wealth with others. On the other hand, I see many faithful Americans who are being blessed with great peace, joy, happiness – in spite of persecution, attacks from the enemy, and poverty. Isn't this what we all long for in our hearts? But many of us are too afraid to trust that God will provide for us. God promises us spiritual wealth beyond our imagination, and divine provision for all our earthly needs, as he provided for the Israelites in the desert in this quotation from Exodus. We may not get everything we want, but we will have all that we need. We do not have to hoard, drive ourselves into ill health, or fear that we will not have enough in our old age. In his unfailing love and provision, God will take care of us.

† *Father, please forgive us when we do not love you more than we love our own lives. Help us to focus on building your kingdom rather than our own. In the precious name of Jesus, Amen.*

Ephesians 5:1-2, 25-33

Walk in love

> **[W]alk in love, as Christ also has loved us and given Himself for us . . . For we are members of his body, of his flesh and his bones.**
>
> (*part of verse 2, and verse 30*)

Our scripture reading for today admonishes us to 'walk in love' towards our brothers and sisters in Christ, and most particularly within our own homes. As a marriage and family therapist, I've learned that even though we love our families, they are often the people who annoy, anger and hurt us most. It is easy to love those who require nothing of us – but our families can really try our patience. But I am sure that, as his children, we also try our Father to the extreme. Yet, Christ gave himself for the very children who condemned him to death. He is even now in heaven interceding for us, so that we can one day be worthy to rule and reign with him.

We cannot be acceptable to him if we do not love our wives, husbands, children, parents, and neighbours as he loves us. It is in the practice of that love, even when we are tested beyond endurance, that we are washed clean of our own failures and sins. By treating our families well, we are preparing ourselves for the return of Christ.

† *Father, please forgive us when we are not kind, patient, loving and compassionate, especially to our families. We confess that we are not the Christ-like examples that we should be in our own homes. We ask for strength to overcome our frustrations, anger and selfishness. In the name of Jesus, Amen.*

Hebrews 13:1-6

Brotherly love

Let brotherly love continue. Do not forget to entertain strangers, for by so doing some have unwittingly entertained angels. . . . Let your conduct be without covetousness; be content with such things as you have. For He Himself has said, 'I will never leave you nor forsake you.' So we may boldly say: The Lord is my helper; I will not fear. What can man do to me?'

(*verses 1-2, part of verse 3, and verses 5-6*)

Isn't this the essence of God's message of love to us – that no matter what other human beings do to us, inevitably God will prevail, and it will all work out for our good in the end. It is such a comfort to be able to rest fully in that knowledge. But what about what we do to others, even without knowing it? How often we 'unwittingly' snub someone who smells bad, looks strange, or offends us. Or we speak nastily to someone because we are jealous of their possessions or accomplishments. Remember, God is on the side of those people, too. They are our brothers and sisters in the Lord who need our kindness, whether they are prisoners, beggars, or the wealthiest people in town. After all, they could be angels in disguise!

† *Father God, please forgive us when we fail to be kind to strangers – to those who we feel are somehow beneath us, or above us. Help us remember that we are all equal in your sight. They are your children and our brothers and sisters in Christ, and you love us all without measure. Amen.*

Holding on to love

> **Love suffers long and is kind . . . bears all things, believes all things, hopes all things, endures all things. Love never fails . . . And now abide faith, hope, love, these three, but the greatest of these is love.**
>
> (*part of verse 4, verse 7, part of verse 8, and verse 13*)

These words are a wonderful prescription for a good marriage, if the married couple truly take them to heart. But unfortunately, at least here in America, as soon as the 'honeymoon is over', the love is often over as well. When love becomes difficult, we give up and go looking for the new person, job or activity that we think will make us happy. Often our search just trades one set of relational problems for another. I see people like this in my practice every day.

Whether in a marriage, with an ageing parent, a prodigal child, or a boring job, we often give up too easily. We do not realise the great emotional and spiritual reward there is in endurance and long-suffering. How can we understand the depth of God's love for us if we do not plumb the depths of our love for each other? God wants us to persevere in our relationships because only then can we fully experience his love for us.

† *Father, help us to seek a deeper, fuller relationship with you by holding steadfast to your commandment to love others as you love us. Help us to bear all things, believe all things, hope all things, and endure all things – always striving to love others because you have first loved us. Amen.*

Matthew 25:31-40

The gift of a child

'Assuredly, I say to you, inasmuch as you did it to one of the least of these My brethren, you did it to Me.'

(*part of verse 40*)

In Advent we look towards the coming of the Christ Child – God's love made manifest here on earth in a baby destined to die a cruel death for the salvation of humankind.

November 29 is our only son's birthday. He was a beautiful, healthy baby, and is now almost the same age as Jesus when he died on the cross. Our son loves God with all his heart and soul, but unfortunately he is no longer so healthy because he has Type I diabetes. Managing this illness has become very difficult. We are thankful for every year he is with us, and try hard not to think about the future. I lack Mary's courage. As a mother, I would have done everything in my power to prevent the Crucifixion, and been too selfish to watch my son die. Did she see his future even as she held her baby? Can you imagine her suffering as she watched him die?

This is love – that our Father in heaven and this young woman on earth gave us the gift of a child, in spite of the pain they knew it would bring them. Let us never forget this sacrifice, especially as we celebrate Christmas.

† *Father in heaven, in the midst of the coming celebration, let us not forget the suffering – nor that you are a God of such immense love that you gave your son as sacrifice for the sins of the world, that you felt all he felt, being one with him. Amen.*

Readings in Revelation

1 Letters to the churches

Notes by David Huggett
based on the New Revised Standard Version

David Huggett is a Baptist minister. After pastoral experience in the north of England and London, he worked with the Bible Society, the Leprosy Mission and in adult Christian education. Now retired, he lives with his wife in Somerset and continues to be involved in preaching, writing and local church life.

Introduction

Advent simply means 'coming' and is used in three different ways. Christians have traditionally associated it with the coming of Jesus at Bethlehem that first Christmas. Also it refers to Jesus' promise to return at the end of human history. Thirdly, it reminds us of the many ways in which he seeks to come into our daily lives. In each case the challenge to us today is that we should be well prepared. The first coming of course has already happened and our preparations are so that we may celebrate it in a suitable fashion. For the others Advent gives us the time and space to prepare ourselves for his coming, however and whenever that may be.

Text for the week: Revelation 1:5

From Jesus Christ, the faithful witness, the firstborn of the dead, and the ruler of the kings of the earth.

For group discussion and personal thought

- What steps can we take to recapture a sense of wonder?
- How can we ensure that our 'first love' for Jesus Christ does not cool?
- What particular messages for the church today have you found in the first three chapters of Revelation?

Revelation 1:1-20

A letter with illustrations

Revelation is a letter rather than a book. John, the exiled pastor, wrote to people he knew, who would have listened as the letter was read aloud, maybe in the context of worship. Verse 3 makes that clear. Almost like the Christmas cards we may be planning to send to our friends, John sets out to make his letter as vivid and memorable as possible. He gives them and us a detailed and colourful picture of the one who is going to figure throughout the letter – Jesus:

> **I saw one like the Son of Man, clothed with a long robe and with a golden sash across his chest . . . When I saw him, I fell at his feet as though dead. But he placed his right hand on me, saying, 'Do not be afraid.'**
>
> (*part of verses 13 and 17*)

Rather than trying to interpret each of the symbols he uses, we should aim to gain an overall sense of the wonder of Christ. Attempting to analyse the details is like picking apart a great symphony, trying to grasp the magnificence of the whole piece of music by an intimate study of each note. Keep reminding yourself that this was a letter of encouragement; it was to be read out loud; its vivid poetry was designed to move its hearers to a response in worship.

† *Lord, encourage in me a sense of wonder in all that you are and can be to me. Kindle afresh my imagination that I may catch glimpses of your glory.*

Revelation 2:1-11

It's not fair!

Our world is a very unfair place. For example (on this World Aids Day), more than 5 million people live with HIV/AIDS but have no access to the drugs they need. Many of these are children who have inherited the deadly disease from their parents through no fault of their own. The suffering about to be inflicted on the early Christians by their enemies (verse 10) was not fair either. Although at this time the Romans were tolerant of many religions, significantly both Ephesus and Smyrna had temples dedicated to the worship of the Roman emperor. All citizens had to acknowledge the emperor as a god, using the same word for him – 'Lord' – as Christians would use for Jesus (1 Corinthians 12:3). John of course knew all about suffering, banished as he was to the prison camp on Patmos. In the face of such persecution he knew the value of encouragement and so is quick to commend the Ephesian Christians:

> **I know your works, your toil, ... I also know that you are enduring patiently and bearing up for the sake of my name, and that you have not grown weary.**
>
> (*verse 4*)

Again and again John urges patience and endurance in the face of difficulty. The theme provides a golden thread that is woven through the colourful patterns of the whole tapestry of Revelation.

† *Lord, I pray today for those who feel crushed by the unfairness of life. Give them your strength to persevere.*

Revelation 2:12-29

The promise of better things to come

The seven churches to which John wrote were probably intended to represent the whole of the church in Asia Minor. Like all churches they were imperfect. Their failures seem to have been largely because of their very natural wish to avoid suffering. That, however, can easily lead to adjusting behaviour, or even beliefs, so as to reduce the possibility of opposition. John's criticism of both church and society has led some to think of Revelation as harsh and unloving. But we must not overlook the indications of God's grace and love. At the end of each of these seven letters there is a promise.

> **To everyone who conquers I will give some of the hidden manna, and I will give a white stone, and on the white stone is written a new name that no one knows except the one who receives it.**
>
> (*part of verse 17*)

This is the beautiful but enigmatic promise given to those who remain true to the faith in Pergamum. White stones were sometimes used in the ancient world as tickets of admission to some public event or entertainment. John uses the picture to assure the faithful of their guaranteed place at the heavenly banquet of which Jesus had spoken (Matthew 22:2). But the promise is conditional. The Christians must remain faithful.

† *Thank you, Lord, for your invitation to your heavenly banquet. I look forward to it and ask you for help that I may be ready for it.*

Keeping going

Outwardly prosperous and important, both Sardis and Philadelphia had a hidden weakness. They were situated on or near a fault in the earth's crust which made them liable to earthquakes. Some of their citizens probably remembered a severe quake some years before, when both cities had been devastated. John knows too that there can be similar spiritual fault lines that can devastate the life of a Christian or a church. At Sardis the church appears to have had a tendency to live in the past. A busy, active church, the members relied on past spiritual experience to keep them going. Philadelphia, on the other hand, seems to have been a small, fragile fellowship, easily discouraged by the opposition and slander they faced. So while the challenge to Sardis was to 'wake up' (verse 3), for Philadelphia it was a word of encouragement:

> **I am coming soon; hold fast to what you have, so that no one may seize your crown.**
>
> (*verse 11*)

† *Lord, on this International Day of Disability in particular, we pray for those who are disabled in any way – physically, mentally, emotionally or spiritually. At the same time I confess that I too am disabled because there are faults in my life, although I often try to hide them even from myself. May each one of us discover your healing touch.*

Revelation 3:14-22

Self-satisfied

I reprove and discipline those whom I love. Be earnest, therefore, and repent.

(*verse 19*)

Five out of the seven churches are told to repent. Maybe the Laodicean Christians were surprised to be included. Surely repentance means being sorry for past sins and is something you do once for all in order to become a Christian? Certainly that is part of its meaning, but at its root the word simply means 'changing' – our minds, our attitudes, our whole way of life. Mark suggested it as a summary of Jesus' ministry (Mark 1:15). His miracles and teaching made it clear that he was interested in giving new direction to the whole person. Laodicea was a wealthy banking and textile centre, and maybe the Christians had allowed some of the local culture to rub off on them. They had become so self-satisfied that the Lord says in effect, 'You make me sick' (verse 16). But God is always ready to forgive, however sick we make him, and the result of truly changing – which will include sorrow for the past and also a changed direction to life – will be the joyful anticipation of his warm hospitality (verse 20).

† *Forgive me, Lord, when my life becomes tepid. As I listen again to what the Spirit says to the churches, may my life be renewed, so that I may be a changed person every day.*

A dramatic change

The prison camp on Patmos has now given way to amazing and dramatic scenes in the presence of God himself. Paul had a similar experience (2 Corinthians 12:4), but he was very reticent about it. There is of course no human language capable of describing such deep spiritual experiences. By their very nature they are personal to us. The moment we try to talk about them or express them in pictures or music we seem to lose something. John, who was clearly steeped in the Old Testament, glories in what he has experienced. He uses words and pictures that would have been much more familiar to his hearers, who were brought up on prophetic visions like those of Ezekiel. Once again we need to remember that it is not necessary for us to find a meaning in each symbol. Rather, as we glimpse the overall picture we realise that when we come into the presence of God, words like 'mystery', 'the sublime' and 'wonder' are appropriate. Like the early Christians we need to hear the words,

> **There in heaven stood a throne, with one seated on the throne!**
> **. . . 'Holy, holy, holy,**
> **the Lord God the Almighty,**
> **who was and is and is to come.'**
>
> (*part of verses 2 and 8*)

They were suffering severe pressure from the state and the pagan society around them, and so they are being taken behind the scenes to be shown who is really in control.

† *Whatever I face, whatever my church faces, keep before us the vision of the throne and the One who is there.*

Readings in Revelation

2 Seals, trumpets and woes

Notes by David Huggett
based on the New Revised Standard Version

Introduction

We expect different things from different kinds of literature. We do not, for example, approach a scientific textbook in the same way as a novel, nor do we read a letter in the same way as a magazine article. Revelation is a very particular kind of literature called 'Apocalyptic', which literally means 'unveiling', which was very popular among the first-century Jews. It aims to look into the future using a wide range of striking pictures. These symbols may seem bizarre to us, but with a little patience we can unravel the underlying lessons, which are as valid for us as they were for the Christians in first-century Asia Minor.

Text for the week: Revelation 7:10

They cried out in a loud voice, saying, 'Salvation belongs to our God who is seated on the throne, and to the Lamb!'

For group discussion and personal thought

- 'Opposition is the normal lot of the Christian.' In what ways is this true in your own experience and that of your church?
- How can Revelation encourage and inspire the prayer life of the modern church?
- How could you become better informed about the needs of the persecuted church today?

Where the real power lies

The Roman Empire was based on military power and the authority of state and emperor. It was this power that led to the Christians being at best tolerated, and sometimes persecuted. We can therefore understand that the early believers would find comfort in the Jewish picture of the Messiah as the 'Lion' (verse 5), the king of the beasts. But John has a surprise for them. The Lion turns out to be

> **a Lamb standing as if it had been slaughtered.**
>
> (*part of verse 6*)

Vulnerability, not violence, was the key to real conquest. Even the special word that John uses, which literally means 'little lamb', underlines this vulnerability. Advent of course is the time when we celebrate the coming of 'a child wrapped in bands of cloth and lying in a manger' (Luke 2:12), the unique and truly remarkable example of how vulnerable God became for us. Here John reminds us that it was by his death that Jesus conquered – the ultimate vulnerability (verse 9). When the church relies on human power, or even violence, as it did for example during the Crusades, it is bound to fail. As Sheila Cassidy put it, 'It is OK to be frail and wounded because that is the way the transcendent God made people.'

† *Thank you, Lord, for reminding me that when I am weak you are strong. Forgive me when I try to sort out problems using my own wisdom and to face challenges in my own strength.*

Revelation 6:1-17

No promise of an easy ride

I saw a poster outside a church the other day that implied that becoming a Christian is the guarantee of a happy and successful life. The Christians described in verses 9-11 would not have agreed. Nor would the many followers of Christ who, throughout the church's history and still today, have suffered for their faith. Opposition, often but not always expressed in persecution, is the normal lot of the Christian. Anguish and even anger are natural reactions to it (verse 10), but John's message is clear:

> **They were each given a white robe and told to rest a little longer.**
>
> (*part of verse 11*)

They are to take strength from two facts. Firstly God is aware of what they are going through. He does not rebuke them for their bitter cries, but encourages them to be patient. Secondly, they can be certain that the days of their oppression are numbered. As the seals are opened he assures us and them that evil will be dealt with in a firm and unequivocal fashion. Those of us who live in relative comfort and peace may find the pictures of punishment deeply disturbing. How can a God who is love allow such harshness? But God is both merciful *and* just, and requires us to be the same (Micah 6:8).

† *Merciful God, give courage and patience to all those today who risk their lives for the sake of Christ.*

A great crowd

'Numbers aren't everything,' we are sometimes told. Although true, sometimes Christians do feel threatened when they find themselves a small minority. Jesus' warning that 'few' would find and follow his narrow way (Matthew 7:14) may tempt us to think that we shall always be just a tiny minority – 'A remnant weak and small!' as one old hymn puts it. In particular, opposition, however that comes, can make us feel small and alone. John's answer to this problem is to remind us that in fact the church is vast and inclusive.

> **After this I looked, and there was a great multitude that no one could count, from every nation, from all tribes and peoples and languages, standing before the throne and before the Lamb, robed in white, with palm branches in their hands.**
>
> (*verse 9*)

We are part of a great worldwide church. We are part of a church that spans the ages. Too readily we confine our thinking to our own local fellowship, or our own denomination. The result is that we become isolationist, forgetting our responsibility towards our fellow Christians and denying ourselves the support of that great multitude of believers of every race, colour, denomination, both past and present (Hebrews 12:22-24). It is this great Church that in the end is invincible (Matthew 16:18).

† *Lord, forgive me for my shortness of sight. Touch my eyes that they may catch the vision of your Church.*

Revelation 8:1-13

Pause for prayer

Before John continues with his warnings to opponents of the Church, there is an interlude (verse 1). One of four interludes in his letter, each is like an interval in the theatre; but instead of being merely a break in the action, each has important things to say. We all need interludes in life, and the Church is no exception. When we are deeply committed, we can become over-busy. We then need to pull back and allow a little space, a little silence, to affect our lives, and to give us the freedom to explore more of the experience of prayer.

> **Another angel . . . was given a great quantity of incense to offer with the prayers of all the saints on the golden altar that is before the throne.**
>
> (*part of verse 3*)

Prayer opens up points of contact with that other dimension where God is. It provides us with what has sometimes been described as 'thin places' where earth and heaven touch. Some of the Christians in Asia Minor to whom John was writing may have questioned the value of prayer. They had prayed hard and long, and no deliverance had come. Even John only seems able to promise that there is worse to come. So here, during the interlude, he assures them in dramatic language (verse 5) that prayer will have amazing results as God's spiritual realm collides with this world's earthly power.

† *Father, we thank you for those interludes in our lives when we become especially aware of your loving presence.*

Revelation 9:1-7a, 11-21

God is just

The horrific judgements heralded in this chapter by the blowing of the fifth and sixth trumpets remind us of the story of the plagues Moses brought on the Egyptians (Exodus 7-12). To us they read almost like a modern science-fiction novel, perhaps reminding us that judgement is not confined to some remote future at the end of history. It is an ongoing outcome of the struggle between good and evil. For the early church, that struggle particularly focused on the persecutions they suffered or anticipated. For us it may be the experience of pollution, war, terrorism, disease, poverty – to name but a few. The important thing to remember is that for the Egyptian Pharaoh, the Roman Empire, or our world today, that judgement is not the response of a vindictive God but rather the result of our own human folly. The Pharaoh, we are told, 'hardened his heart'. It's a sorry picture, because the plagues he brought upon himself and his people gave him plenty of warning and every opportunity to repent. And so it has ever been.

The rest of humankind . . . did not repent

(part of verse 20)

† *Thank you, Lord, for your great love and patience. I am part of that world that is so marred by war, pollution, and injustice in all its forms. Forgive us that we bring judgement upon ourselves, and give us grace to repent and receive your mercy.*

Revelation 11:1-14

The importance of faithfulness

The church to which John wrote, although hated and despised by many, was not being subjected to constant or systematic persecution. One emperor actually wrote to a provincial governor in Asia Minor, 'Christians should not be sought out. But if they are accused and handed over, they are to be punished, but only if they do not deny being Christians.' Once in court, it was possible to find a form of careful words that would be legally acceptable and allow the authorities to acquit the accused believer. No doubt some Christians did accept this way out, but to John it was tantamount to betraying Christ. It is against this legal background that we can understand the description of the two figures in this vision who are 'witnesses' (verse 3). The word John uses can be translated as both 'witness' and 'martyr', and he was well aware of the price that many would pay for their refusal to compromise. But even when faced with paying the ultimate price, endurance will in the end be rewarded with a gracious invitation from God himself.

> **Then they heard a loud voice from heaven saying to them, 'Come up here!' And they went up to heaven in a cloud while their enemies watched them.**
>
> (*verse 12*)

Today Christians are still on trial. It may or may not be in a court of law. Some who question them are merely curious, while others are deeply critical. Either way, the witness needs to be trustworthy.

† Lord, I pray for those who today are in prison for their faith. Help them to stand firm as good witnesses to your truth.

Readings in Revelation

3 The triumph of the Lamb

Notes by David Huggett
based on the New Revised Standard Version

Introduction

Although separated by 2,000 years there are remarkable similarities between the Church today and the churches to which John wrote in first-century Asia Minor. They were minority communities who lived in a society with many other religions. To be a Christian meant to stand out from the crowd and brave witness was the order of the day. Even the West today, which once could be called 'Christian', is increasingly becoming a secular and pluralist society. So we can relate easily to the challenges that faced these early Christians. Although John wrote this letter to the churches in a specific situation, we find his writing particularly appropriate for us.

Text for the week: Revelation 11:17

We give you thanks, Lord God Almighty, who are and who were, for you have taken your great power and begun to reign.

For group discussion and personal thought

- What things do you see in your own society that make you angry? What can you do about them?
- What major difficulties do you encounter when you try to make real changes in your community?
- What forms does slavery take today? How can we be involved in setting people free?

Revelation 11:15-19

Anger and the Christian

Anger has traditionally been classified in Christian teaching as one of the 'seven deadly sins'. So it may come as something of a surprise to read about God that

your wrath has come

(*part of verse 18*)

Of course much of our human anger is rightly condemned as sinful: it is frequently petty, a selfish indulgence of bad temper when we feel that someone has got the better of us in some way. God's anger, or wrath, is quite different. Throughout the Bible it is shown to be his right and just reaction to all that is evil. It is best illustrated in Jesus' ministry. He was filled with anger when he saw how commercialism had invaded the sanctity of the temple (John 2:13-19). He also showed deep anger when faced with the crippling results of disease. One of the best-attested translations of Mark 1:41, for instance, is that he was 'moved to anger' by the plight of the leprosy sufferer. Alan Boesak, who could speak from the experience of apartheid in South Africa, suggests that too often 'we lack a holy rage . . . the ability to rage when justice lies prostrate . . . a holy anger about things that are wrong in the world'.

† *Lord, fill me with your spirit of holy anger when I am confronted with the things that are wrong in my own life and the things that are wrong in your world, and may that anger turn to action.*

Revelation 12:1-12

Experience of the wilderness

The woman (verse 5) probably stands for Mary, the mother of Jesus. But perhaps she also refers to all God's people, since Jesus was born out of a community, and it is against him and his community that the forces of evil are arrayed. The wilderness is often used in Christian writings to describe an experience that is common to us all, including even the greatest saints. We all know what it is like to have times when for various reasons our spiritual life seems dull and unrewarding; when worship becomes routine; when prayer goes unanswered; when enthusiasm vanishes. But John also sees this as a place of hope:.

> **and the woman fled into the wilderness, where she has a place prepared by God, so that there she can be nourished.**

(*part of verse 20*)

For John the wilderness was the place to which the Israelites fled for refuge from the conflict with Egypt. For them, but also for us, it can be a place of security, of spiritual nourishment, of learning and deepening faith, of the guiding presence of God himself.

† *Lord Jesus, thank you that you understand exactly how your people feel, because you too went into the wilderness. May such experiences strengthen our faith in you, and equip us to support others who go through it too.*

Revelation 13:1-10

The power of the Christian

There never seems to be a shortage of power-hungry dictators. Hitler and Stalin are names that readily come to mind, but there are those who are alive and well today who are much more interested in power for themselves than in the well-being of those they govern and who are determined to exert their power at whatever cost. Evil is not simply a theoretical principle. It may be located in people, organisations, or states. John pictures evil as a beast and a dragon, but adds that

> **the whole earth followed the beast. They worshipped the dragon, for he had given his authority to the beast, and they worshipped the beast, saying, 'Who is like the beast and who can fight against it?'**
>
> (*part of verse 3, and verse 4*)

Sadly, Christians have not always avoided the power trap. The Crusades and the Inquisition are not episodes in our history of which we can be proud. Not that we can restrict such attitudes to leaders or to history. We are not immune to the seduction of power today. Even well-meaning Christians may be so eager to see other people adopt Christianity that they try to impose their beliefs and attitudes upon them. The Christian does have power, but it is the power of God. And that is the power of love.

† *God of love and power, give me the wisdom to know when I am being foolish enough to impose my views on others, and the grace to resist when they try to impose their views on me.*

The wideness of God's mercy

One poll suggests that more than 70 per cent of the UK's population believe in God, while another tells us that less than 5 per cent go to church on a Sunday. On their own, such figures don't tell us much, for we can misinterpret or manipulate statistics to say more or less what we want. So we need to be careful about interpreting the numbers in the Bible – especially in books like Revelation with its rich imagery and poetry. Some have suggested that the number in verse 1 is to be taken literally, but that is clearly not so. Last Tuesday we were reminded that God's people are a vast multitude (Revelation 7:9). Numbers are not for us to know. What we do need to know is that it is not God's will that any should 'perish' (2 Peter 3:9). His love is far broader and deeper than we can begin to imagine or understand. As F W Faber wrote in his hymn, 'There's a wideness in God's mercy like the wideness of the sea'. That is a comfort, but it is also a challenge – God has given us the task of offering that wide mercy to as many people as we can.

> **Then I saw another angel flying in mid-heaven, with an eternal gospel to proclaim to those who live on earth – to every nation and tribe and language and people.**
>
> (*verse 6*)

† Lord, thank you for your gospel of mercy. Help me to share it.

Revelation 14:14-20

God's appraisals

If you have ever been involved in a self-appraisal exercise, you will know how difficult it can be to get the balance right between acknowledging our strengths and our weaknesses. Yet appraisals – self-appraisal and appraisal by others – seem to be in fashion. Students, clergy, business people – almost every job demands them. They are valuable as long as the person doing the appraising is fair, honest and thorough. Yet there are things that even the most skilful appraiser cannot know, and things which we consciously or unconsciously hide even from ourselves. John's dramatic and awesome pictures of God's judgement, which take up much of the second half of his letter, remind us that all are subject to God's appraisal.

> **Another angel came out of the temple, calling with a loud voice to the one who sat on the cloud: 'Use your sickle and reap, for the hour to reap has come, because the harvest of the earth is fully ripe.'**
>
> (*verse 15*)

Part of being human is taking responsibility for what we are and what we do. In the end the only appraisal that really matters is God's. He alone has complete and accurate knowledge of each of us. He alone will carry out that appraisal with perfect love and mercy.

† *Father, give me daily strength and wisdom to live the kind of life that so pleases you that I may have no fear of your appraisal.*

Revelation 15:1-8

The song of freedom

The theme of judgement continues, but it is set in the context of worship, and uses much of the imagery of the Israelite deliverance from the slavery of Egypt. Notice the reference to the sea (verse 2), reminding us of the crossing of the Sea of Reeds, the song of Moses (verse 3), the tent (verse 5), the fire and smoke (verses 2 and 8), and the plagues. In Exodus the people worship God after their deliverance; but here God's people are challenged to worship him in anticipation of it.

> **Lord, who will not fear**
> **and glorify your name?**
> **For you alone are holy.**
> **All nations will come**
> **and worship before you,**
> **for your judgements have been revealed.**
>
> (*verse 4*)

Freedom has always been at the heart of the Christian gospel (John 8:36); Jesus himself is the ultimate example of what it is like to be truly free. He was not free from suffering, but he was free from personal ambition when tempted in the desert; he was free from the desire to save his life at any cost, for he laid it down voluntarily; he was free from resentment even when crucified, for he forgave the perpetrators. Viktor Frankl, a concentration camp survivor, comments on the generosity of some of his fellow prisoners who had lost everything except 'the freedom to choose one's attitude in any given set of circumstances'.

† *Set me free, Lord, from those habits, attitudes, resentments, fears – whatever holds me captive.*

4 God's wrath and God's salvation

Notes by David Huggett
based on the New Revised Standard Version

Introduction

Michelangelo's great painting on the ceiling of the Sistine Chapel in Rome is a riot of colour and action. It is full of wonderful illustrations of a wide variety of biblical people and events. But it is not intended to be read in a logical kind of way, starting with Creation in one corner and working your way round chronologically until you come to the end of the biblical story. Each scene is complete in itself and yet at the same time is part of the whole. It seems to me that that is how Revelation needs to be read. To try to build up a firm chronology of the future is doomed to failure. John keeps giving us glimpses. He keeps repeating lessons but with different images. The picture overall is designed to encourage and to inspire worship.

Text for the week: Revelation 21:5

And the one who was seated on the throne said, 'See, I am making all things new.' Also he said, 'Write this, for these words are trustworthy and true.'

For group discussion and personal thought

- In what ways does modern culture help or hinder the spread of the gospel?
- What steps can you take to help your church prepare for the 'marriage of the Lamb'?
- 'God is with us.' What differences should that fact make to the way we celebrate Christmas?

Revelation 16:1-12, 17

The web of responsibility

'Networking' is common in the modern workplace as a means of helping everyone to play a full part in supporting one another. So-called internet 'chat rooms' are designed to encourage the development of social relationships. We recognise that, as the priest and poet John Donne put it, 'No man is an island, entire of itself; every man is a piece of the Continent.' There is also a kind of networking where evil is concerned, for sin is never a private thing. What we do affects other people. A multi-national organisation, for example, needed a great deal of water for its manufacturing process but did not consider the devastating effect its new factory would have on the nearby subsistence farmers and their families. The threat to our planet of global warming and climate change reminds us that our sins of greed and carelessness affect not only people, but nature itself. So maybe it is no surprise to read in this chapter of how different aspects of our world suffer and are destroyed.

> **You are just, O Holy One, who are and were,**
> **for you have judged these things; . . .**
> **'Yes, O Lord God, the Almighty,**
> **your judgements are true and just!'**

(*part of verses 5 and 7*)

Along with humankind the whole of creation is to be redeemed (Romans 8:19-23), after first being purged of all evil.

† *Creator God, who loved the world so much that you gave your only Son for it, give us a deep concern for its well-being and the ultimate redemption of all women and men and all creation.*

Revelation 17:1-14

The need for discernment

Evil can be very seductive, as King David discovered when he watched the beautiful Bathsheba from his palace rooftop (2 Samuel 11). Her beauty and his desire eclipsed the wrong of what he did and the subsequent feelings of guilt. John's readers would have easily equated Rome with Babylon, the great city on the river Euphrates which had long stood as a symbol of all that opposed God. There was so much going for the Roman Empire. It was a great culture that had civilised the ancient world. Politically it had brought peace and commercial prosperity. Its art, literature, sculpture, architecture and engineering genius were to provide the basis of Western civilisation. John warns, however, that there is also much that is evil about this great empire and the Christians need to discern it.

> **This calls for a mind that has wisdom.**
>
> (*part of verse 9*)

The need for wisdom is as urgent today for the people of God. There is much in our culture that is good and to be celebrated. But because evil is like a kind of web, it infects and spoils even that which in itself is good. It is not enough for us to resist the obvious evils of our age; we must be alert to those seductive evils that may appear in the guise of the good.

† *Thank you, Lord, that through your death and resurrection evil is already vanquished. Forgive me that sometimes I foolishly join the side of the defeated.*

Revelation 18:1-20

Small is beautiful

How small and insignificant the early Christians must have felt as they saw all around them the signs of the Roman Empire's political, commercial and military power. Most of these Christians were just ordinary people – few were wealthy or influential, many of them were slaves (1 Corinthians 1:26-29). But the Bible constantly emphasises the fact that God is deeply concerned for the 'small people' and largely fulfils his purposes through them – like the shepherds at Christmas. This chapter dramatically reminds them and us that Rome, not the Church, is doomed. History has proved John to be right. Two thousand years later the Church is a vast body which spans the world, while the mighty Roman Empire, and every other great empire since, has been consigned to the history books.

> **Rejoice over her, O heaven,**
> **you saints and apostles and prophets!**
> **For God has given judgement for you against her.**

(*verse 20*)

It is still a lesson to encourage us. Many problems face us – climate change, terrorism, dictatorships, the influence of multi-national organisations, famine, disease. The list seems endless and we sometimes feel helpless. But the powers of evil, however they express themselves, have already been judged, and the 'meek will inherit the earth' (Matthew 5:5).

† *Lord, help me to be aware of those values in my society that are governed by greed and selfishness, and give me the strength to avoid them.*

Revelation 19:1-10

Preparing for the wedding

A Jewish wedding in the first century was a great event, not only for the couple concerned, but also for their extended families. The long ceremony was followed by celebrations which could last up to seven days (John 2). Rather different maybe for us today. Statistics tell us that in the UK divorces continue to rise alarmingly, that more and more people choose to co-habit rather than marry, and that church weddings are declining rapidly. Yet for many people marriage still provides a great social occasion for the family, and thousands of pounds may be spent on it. So we can still relate to the picture John gives us here of the excitement in heaven as the marriage of the Lamb arrives.

> **Let us rejoice and exult**
> **and give him the glory,**
> **for the marriage of the Lamb has come,**
> **and his bride has made herself ready.**

(*verse 7*)

For any wedding to go smoothly there must be detailed preparations, maybe months ahead. John too urges us to be ready for this great heavenly event. Advent reminds us that the Christian Church, the bride, is at present in that period of preparation. We look back to Christ's first coming, but as we look forward to his coming again we have the opportunity to prepare ourselves.

† *Thank you, Lord, that you come to us again and again. Thank you, too, that you will come and we shall at long last meet you face to face. Help us so to live now that we shall be ready then.*

God is with us

The angel announced to Joseph that the baby to be born to Mary was to be called 'Emmanuel' – 'God is with us'. He was a very special little boy. That is at the very heart of the Christmas message, and has sustained God's people throughout history. Now John reminds his readers that in spite of every experience through which they are going, God's purposes for them are to be summed up in his promise to remove all suffering and even death so that he might be with them in eternal fellowship.

> **I heard a loud voice from the throne saying,**
> **'See, the home of God is among mortals.**
> **He will dwell with them;**
> **they will be his peoples,**
> **and God himself will be with them;**
> **he will wipe every tear from their eyes.**
> **Death will be no more;**
> **mourning and crying and pain will be no more,**
> **for the first things have passed away.'**

(*verses 3 and 4*)

Our modern world has pushed God far away. Science has shown us a vast universe, and so God seems to have been consigned to beyond outer space. Secularist society doesn't need him, so has banished him altogether. How good then to remember the message of Christmas that anticipates God's ultimate intention – that he is *with* us. Or as the poet Tennyson put it, 'Closer is he than breathing, and nearer than hands and feet'.

† *Lord, we join with all the hosts of heaven to worship you, the Christ of Bethlehem, and the Christ of glory.*

Revelation 20:1-15

The book that really matters

Perspective was first introduced into art in the fifteenth century. It revolutionised painting. Prior to its discovery, pictures were flat and looked artificial. Perspective enabled the artist to make his work look realistic and alive. Perspective is even more important in real life. John wanted the early Christians who were about to suffer harsh persecution to know that that was only part of the story. The power of evil, which seemed to hold the upper hand, was temporary and ultimately doomed. True, many books would be written about the Romans – their military prowess, their feats of engineering, their cultural achievements. But there is another, a much more important, book.

> **And I saw the dead, great and small, standing before the throne, and books were opened. Also another book was opened, the book of life.**

(*verse 7*)

We have already been introduced to this book (Revelation 3:5, 13:8, 17:8) which records the names of all the faithful. Writers spend time and effort to get their writing published. Politicians and celebrities record even the most sensitive information in their diaries to make sure that one day they will satisfy a curious public. Others risk personal safety to get themselves into *The Guinness Book of Records*. But most books have a short shelf life. Only one book will last for ever. So it is worth making sure that we are in it.

† Lord, thank you for your written word and your living Word. Help me to know both of them intimately and to share them with others.

Readings in Revelation

5 The new heaven and the new earth

Notes by David Huggett
based on the New Revised Standard Version

Introduction

So we approach the climax of this great book. You may well have found it hard going at times, for it is not an easy book for us in the twenty-first century to understand. That in itself is a kind of parable of our lives. For some of us the coming year will include persecution. For all of us it will include opposition and difficulty of one sort or another. But these last chapters of the Bible remind us that there is also glory and blessing to look forward to, and the message remains the same as it was for John's listeners: prepare and persevere.

Text for the week: Revelation 22:12-13

'See, I am coming soon; my reward is with me, to repay according to everyone's work. I am the Alpha and the Omega, the first and the last, the beginning and the end.'

For group discussion and personal thought

- Why do you think that in John's description of the glorious holy city there is no need for a temple?
- What do you think are some of the implications of the prayer 'Come, Lord Jesus'?
- What new insights into the significance of Advent have you gained from your reading of Revelation?

Revelation 19:11-16

Meeting with Jesus

The first time I travelled on a long-haul flight I was of course eagerly anticipating visiting a new country. But I was travelling alone and although I had the usual concerns about reclaiming baggage, getting quickly through customs, finding my way to the nearby city, my biggest concern was that someone would meet me. What a difference it made when I was met by someone who not only welcomed me, but also took over much of the responsibility of settling me into my new environment. I suspect that it will be like that when at last we meet Jesus Christ face to face. Of course we know that he is present with us here and now. We also know how he comes to us in our experiences, especially through the Eucharist. But in this chapter John is talking about that exciting event when the Christ of faith becomes the Christ of vivid personal experience. John uses a similar description of Jesus in chapter 1. But then it was a vision. Now it is reality. He will be immediately recognisable, for,

> **He is clothed in a robe dipped in blood, and his name is called The Word of God . . . On his robe and on his thigh he has a name inscribed, 'King of kings and Lord of lords.'**

(*verses 13 and 16*)

† *Lord, however my life ends, and however our world ends, I thank you that you will be there to meet us.*

Revelation 21:9-27

The holy city

Surprisingly, John compares the glorious life beyond to a city. Surprising, because cities often have problems: traffic jams, pollution, crime, homelessness, squalor. Even people who love the excitement of the city often plan to 'escape' to the country. Wouldn't a better picture be that of some idyllic rural scene – a new Eden perhaps? However, Jerusalem always had special significance as God's holy city and the symbol of his presence with his people. Sadly it was also the place of tragedy, for just a few years before John wrote it had been brutally destroyed by the Romans. Now it is to be the symbol of renewal.

> **The city has no need of sun or moon to shine on it, for the glory of God is its light, and its lamp is the Lamb.**
>
> (*verse 23*)

Walled cities offered security when attacks threatened. Yet Jerusalem had fallen; and even the mighty Rome would be destroyed. The heavenly city is different. It has great wealth with its streets paved with gold (verse 21); it is a place of security with its high walls (verse 12); its vast size (verse 16) makes it possible for immense numbers to be accommodated (verse 26); it is pollution free (verse 27); it has ever-open gates (verse 25). Above everything else, God is at its centre.

† *Mighty God, there are no human minds adequate to grasp, no words adequate to describe, what you have prepared for those who love you. We simply worship you.*

Revelation 22:1-7

The river of life

In the relatively dry Middle East, rivers are of particular importance. From their first appearance (Genesis 2:10), through to Jesus' words (John 8:38), the biblical writers use them as a symbol of life itself, both in a literal and a spiritual sense.

> **Then the angel showed me the river of the water of life . . . flowing from the throne of God . . . On either side of the river is the tree of life with its twelve kinds of fruit, producing its fruit each month; and the leaves of the tree are for the healing of the nations.**
>
> (*part of verses 1 and 2*)

Water, however, not only brings blessing for which to thank God, but responsibility. A site near my home was being cleared for building and someone negligently released a drum of chemicals into a nearby stream. It killed all the fish and in spite of the amazing recuperative powers of rivers it was months before the damage could be undone. There are still 1.1 billion people in our world who lack access to safe water. The leaders of the most powerful nations set as one of their Millennium goals the eradication of world poverty. But that will only be achieved when we can provide clean water for all.

† *Creator God, renew our determination to ensure that each person in our world can have access to safe water without having to walk miles to get it. Saviour God, increase our determination to ensure that each person in our world is offered the eternal water of life through your Son.*

Revelation 22:12-21

And in conclusion

All the visions are ended. The glimpses behind the scenes that John has been given are over. The letter concludes on the high note of worship. Now it is back to the nitty-gritty of living out the Christian life in a hostile world. If these early Christians had expected to be released immediately from their difficulties, they were disappointed. There is work to be done against the background of his promise,

> **The one who testifies to these things says, 'Surely I am coming soon.' Amen. Come, Lord Jesus!'**
>
> (*verse 20*)

All through Revelation it is clear that John and his listeners expected the imminent return of Jesus. But it didn't happen. Others since have thought the same way, and still the years and the centuries roll by. We have to balance against this the other teaching of the New Testament, and in particular the words of Jesus himself, who admitted that even he did not know God's timetable (Mark 13:32; Acts 1:7). We also have to remind ourselves that Revelation was a particular kind of literature (Apocalyptic). It was not concerned with human chronology but with trying to express truths about the future. Its purpose was to encourage faithfulness in God's people and to give them a sense of urgency in their living for him.

† *Lord, come to us each day throughout the coming year. As you do so, give us a sense of urgency as we invite others to come to you with us.*

INTERNATIONAL BIBLE READING ASSOCIATION

A worldwide service of Christian Education
at work in five continents

HEADQUARTERS
1020 Bristol Road
Selly Oak
Birmingham
B29 6LB
United Kingdom

www.christianeducation.org.uk
ibra@christianeducation.org.uk

and the following agencies:

AUSTRALIA
UniChurch Books
130 Little Collins Street
Melbourne
VIC 3001

GHANA
IBRA Secretary
Box GP 919
Accra

asempa@ghana.com

INDIA
All India Sunday School Association
Plot No 8, 6th Cross,
Threemurthy Colony
Mahendra Hills
Secunderabad – 500 026
Andhra Pradesh

sundayschoolindia@yahoo.co.in

Fellowship of Professional Workers
Samanvay
Deepthi Chambers
Vijayapuri
Hyderabad – 500 017
Andhra Pradesh

hyd1_cipiardi@sancharnet.in

NEW ZEALAND
Epworth Bookshop
157B Karori Road
Marsden Village
Karori
Wellington 6012

Mailing address:
PO Box 17255
Karori
Wellington 6147

sales@epworthbooks.org.nz

NIGERIA
IBRA Representative
Hinder House
The Cathedral Church of St David
Kudeti
Ibadan
PMB 5298
Ibadan
Oyo State

SOUTH AND CENTRAL AFRICA
IBRA South Africa
6 Roosmaryn Street
Durbanville 7550

biblereading@evmot.com

Scheme of readings for 2010

READINGS IN LUKE
The coming of the Messiah

THE ECONOMY OF GOD
The economy of grace
The economy of fools

READINGS IN LUKE
Beginnings

CLOTHING
Clothing our nakedness
Robed in honour and glory

READINGS IN GENESIS 1– 35
In the beginning
The great flood
God's covenant with Abraham
Abraham, Lot and Isaac, Jacob

READINGS IN LUKE
Confrontation in Jerusalem
The way of the Cross
The risen Lord

RESTING PLACES AND SACRED SPACES
The divine imperative to rest
Resting places in the Old Testament
Resting places in the New Testament

THE JESUS WAY
Seeing, touching and tasting/eating
Showing, walking and praying
Living and loving

ROMANS 1– 8
Good news for sinners
All have sinned and are now justified
We have peace with God
Life in the Spirit

PETER THE APOSTLE
Peter and Jesus
Peter, a leader

MOODS AND EMOTIONS
From sorrow to joy
From despondency to hope
From anger to creative action
From jealousy to contentment

READINGS IN LUKE
Forerunner and followers
Making people whole

SILENCE
Old Testament silences
New Testament silences

RIVERS OF THE BIBLE

WRITING
Stones, letters and graffiti
Keeping what is important

OLD AGE
Reflections on old age – God is there
Old age – lived with God

MICAH
What angers God?
What does God require and promise?

RECONCILIATION
Be reconciled to your brother
Called to be reconcilers

WOMEN OF THE NEW TESTAMENT
Women disciples
Women in the early church

READINGS IN LUKE
Living in the kingdom
Stories of the kingdom

TREASURES OF DARKNESS
Are your wonders known in the darkness?
God leads the Israelites in darkness
Darkness in Jesus' life, death and resurrection
Riches hidden in secret places

READINGS IN MATTHEW 1– 2
Emmanuel, God is with us

IBRA

International Bible Reading Association

Help us to continue our work of providing Bible study notes for use by Christians in the UK and throughout the world. The need is as great as it was when IBRA was founded in 1882 by Charles Waters as part of the work of the Sunday School Union.

Please leave a legacy to the International Bible Reading Association.

An easy-to-use leaflet has been prepared to help you provide a legacy. Please write to us at the address below and we will send you this leaflet – and answer any questions you might have about a legacy or other donations. Please help us to strengthen this and the next generation of Christians.

Thank you very much.

International Bible Reading Association
Dept 298, 1020 Bristol Road
Selly Oak
Birmingham
B29 6LB
Great Britain

Tel. 0121 472 7272

Fax 0121 472 7575